Mentor Courses

CAMBRIDGE TEACHER TRAINING AND DEVELOPMENT

Series Editors: Marion Williams and Tony Wright

This series is designed for all those involved in language teacher training and development: teachers in training, trainers, directors of studies, advisers, teachers of in-service courses and seminars. Its aim is to provide a comprehensive, organised and authoritative resource for language teacher training and development.

Teach English – A training course for teachers
by Adrian Doff

Training Foreign Language Teachers – A reflective approach
by Michael J. Wallace

Literature and Language Teaching – A guide for teachers and trainers*
by Gillian Lazar

Classroom Observation Tasks – A resource book for language teachers and trainers*
by Ruth Wajnryb

Tasks for Language Teachers – A resource book for training and development*
by Martin Parrott

English for the Teacher – A language development course*
by Mary Spratt

Teaching Children English – A training course for teachers of English to children*
by David Vale with Anne Feunteun

A Course in Language Teaching – Practice and theory
by Penny Ur

Looking at Language Classrooms – A teacher development video package

About Language – Tasks for teachers of English
by Scott Thornbury

Action Research for Language Teachers
by Michael J. Wallace

Mentor Courses – A resource book for trainer-trainers
by Angi Malderez and Caroline Bodóczky

Alive to Language – Perspectives on language awareness for English language teachers
by Valerie Arndt, Paul Harvey and John Nuttall

Teachers in Action – Tasks for in-service language teacher education and development
by Peter James

Advising and Supporting Teachers
by Mick Randall and Barbara Thornton

* Original Series Editors: Ruth Gairns and Marion Williams

Mentor Courses

A resource book for trainer-trainers

Angi Malderez and
Caroline Bodóczky

CAMBRIDGE
UNIVERSITY PRESS

PUBLISHED BY THE PRESS SYNDICATE OF THE UNIVERSITY OF CAMBRIDGE
The Pitt Building, Trumpington Street, Cambridge CB2 1RP, United Kingdom

CAMBRIDGE UNIVERSITY PRESS
The Edinburgh Building, Cambridge CB2 2RU, United Kingdom
40 West 20th Street, New York, NY 10011–4211, USA
10 Stamford Road, Oakleigh, Melbourne, 3166, Australia

First published 1999

Typeset in 10.5pt/12.5pt Sabon

A catalogue record for this book is available from the British Library

Library of Congress Cataloguing in Publication data

Malderez, Angi, 1950–
Mentor courses: a resource book for trainer-trainers / Angi Malderez
and Caroline Bodóczky.
    p.   cm. – (Cambridge teacher training and development)
Includes bibliographical references (p.   ) and index.
ISBN 0–521–56204–X (hardback). – ISBN 0–521–56690–8 (paperback)
1. Mentoring in education. 2. Observation (Educational method)
3. English teachers – Training of.
4. English language – Study and teaching – Activity programs.
I. Bodóczky, Caroline, 1942–   .
II. Title. III. Series.
LB1731.4.M25   1998
371.102–dc21   98–44352   CIP

ISBN 0 521 56204 X hardback
ISBN 0 521 56690 8 paperback

Transferred to digital printing 2004

For all the staff and students of CETT, past and present,
especially the COTs with our love and thanks

Contents

Thanks and acknowledgements

Many people have, in one way or another, supported us in the development of the ideas and activities in this book and in its writing. For providing the initial conditions and opportunities which allowed us to begin the development of this work, our first debt of gratitude is to the Centre for English Teacher Training, Eötvös Lórand University, under the directorship of Péter Medgyes, the Hungarian Ministry of Education, and the British Council, Hungary and its English Language Officer of the time, Helen Thomas. We continue to be grateful to the British Council in Hungary, and Gabriella Guylas and Ian Marvin in particular, for their ongoing support of the work of mentors in English language teacher education and of their development, and the consequent opportunities for us also to develop our work. We also thank other British Councils in the region, those in Romania and Poland for example, for extending invitations to us to participate in their mentor training work. Our present employers, The School of Education of The University of Leeds, and The International Business School, Budapest, have also supported our need for continued involvement in mentor development work, as well as for time and opportunities to complete the writing of this book. For this too we are very grateful.

Individual colleagues from various phases of our professional lives have made many invaluable contributions to our ideas, the activities themselves, or to the writing process. In attempting to list and thank them here, we will not be able to mention everybody. Can we simply say a big thank you, then, to everybody who has taken the time to talk about teaching, mentoring and mentor training with us, whatever the context of those conversations. Amongst these conversation partners we would like to thank specifically Péter Radai, Christopher Ryan, Hazel Fullerton, Donald Freeman, Tony Wright, Rod Bolitho and Peter Tomlinson.

For help in the process of publishing this book we are indebted to both series editors, to Tony Wright for his faith in us and help in developing the proposal, and to Marion Williams for her patience and careful, supportive editing. We thank too the team at Cambridge University Press, in particular Alison Sharpe and Jane Clifford, for their efficient support. Thanks too to those colleagues who have read drafts and made helpful comments (amongst whom were Tamas Kiss, Jayne Moon, Peter Tomlinson and Christopher Ryan), and those who have piloted activities (amongst whom were Sue Mace, Monica Màràsescu and Adrianna Vuscan).

We owe our greatest thanks to the COTs and to all the course participants who have worked with us, for allowing us to use in this book their comments on the activities as they experienced them, but mainly for their input into the jointly constructed understanding of mentoring and mentor training that this book represents.

Finally, our love and thanks to our families and friends who have supported us personally throughout this adventure.

The authors and publishers are grateful to the authors, publishers and others who have given their permission for the use of copyright information identified in the text. While every endeavour has been made, it has not been possible to identify the sources of all material used and in such cases the publishers would welcome information from copyright sources.

Faber and Faber Ltd for the extract on p. 159 from *Zorba the Greek* by N. Kazantzakis (1952); reprinted with permission of Simon & Schuster, Inc. from *Zorba the Greek* by Nikos Kazantzakis, translated by Carl Wildman. English translation copyright © 1952, and renewed © 1981, by Simon and Schuster, Inc.; Jack C. Richards, David Nunan and Cambridge University Press for the extracts on pp. 166 and 167 from 'Models of supervision: choices' by J. G. Gebhard (1990) and from 'Intervening in practice teaching' by D. Freeman (1990) both in *Second Language Teacher Education* by J. C. Richards and D. Nunan (Eds.); Penny Ur and Cambridge University Press for the extracts on pp. 187–191 from *A Course in Language Teaching* by P. Ur (1996); Ruth Wajnryb and Cambridge University Press for the extracts on pp. 198–200 from *Classroom Observation Tasks* by R. Wajnryb (1992); the extract on p. 168 is reprinted with permission from *Mathematics Teacher*, copyright 1983 by the National Council of Teachers of Mathematics.

Introduction

This book is a resource book for trainers, and is not a coursebook as such. It is essentially a collection of activities for use on mentor courses. It begins with a description of the context in which these activities were developed, and goes on to consider who we think might find them useful. This will involve defining and exploring the roles and duties of mentors. The introduction will end with an overview of the organisation of the rest of the book.

Why we wrote this book

In 1990, the Centre for English Teacher Training (CETT) was opened at Eötvös Lórand University in Budapest, Hungary, with the task of developing a new and innovative initial English language teacher training programme. This new intensive three-year teacher training programme focuses not only on the subject (English, in our case), but also on the skills and knowledge needed by novice professional teachers (for a fuller description of the scheme, see Medgyes and Malderez 1996). The teaching practice component was enormously increased from the usual Hungarian six-week block placement to an integrated scheme where student-teachers would have responsibility for teaching a class for the whole school year. The responsibility for the teaching practice component of this new programme was given to us.

As had been the tradition in Hungary for over a century, CETT student-teachers on their practicum would also be under the supervision of a designated teacher in each of the various schools where the teaching practice would take place. The extended teaching practice together with the extended goals of the teacher training programme itself meant that these school-based supervisors, or mentors as we came to call them, would have considerable and different responsibilities, collaborating closely with university based tutors in helping student-teachers achieve the aims and objectives of the programme. In the words of the CETT Curriculum Document (Griffiths and Ryan 1994), they would be helping students to demonstrate the following:

(i)   ability in planning, implementing and evaluating appropriate learning experiences for their pupils

(iv)   ability in using and where necessary adapting ELT textbooks commonly in use in schools

(v)   ability in evaluating and reflecting on their own teaching

(vi)   ability in modifying their teaching strategies in the light of self-evaluation and peer evaluation

(xii) ability in dealing with the most common role relationships, conflicts, negotiations, counselling, needs etc. encountered in the world of school
(1994:5–6)

The overall programme aims relevant to the work of mentors were:

(iii) to make it possible for trainees to practise the teaching of English in a sheltered way so that they would emerge as confident and competent classroom teachers

(ix) to facilitate and develop in trainees the self awareness and interpersonal skills that would enable them to function better in the world of school

(x) to develop in trainees the kind of professional perspective which enables them to locate their teaching in the wider context of the school and community

(xi) to develop in the trainees powers of self-evaluation and a capacity for autonomous learning which together would enable them to complete their training as efficiently as possible, as well as go on to develop themselves professionally after graduation
(1994:4–5)

In order to help the mentors with this new role, we decided to run mentor training and development courses. In keeping with the Hungarian Ministry of Education's requirements for in-service teacher training courses, they were designed for 120 hours, of which 90 are contact hours and the remaining 30 used for between-session tasks and assignments. The courses were run for selected teachers working in primary and secondary schools, who met once a week for four months and then for an intensive week at the end.

Faced with the responsibility for the school-based mentor training, we were unable to find any practical publications on mentor training, and were therefore forced to create our own activities. Initially our work was informed by the theoretical literature on mentoring available at the time, and, inevitably, by our own personal histories, which include, perhaps most notably, experiences in motherhood, psychiatric nursing, counselling training and drama teaching as well as EFL teaching and teacher education. The versions of the activities in this book have, however, evolved into their present form through the invaluable responses and suggestions of participants on courses and our own evaluation of their effectiveness in use. This, then, is the book we would have liked to have found when we first started our work as mentor trainers.

Who this book is for

Although these activities were developed to prepare mentors to work with student-teachers for a specific pre-service purpose and in a specific context, we have used many of them in other in-service and broader trainer-training contexts. In this book we have included only activities that relate to mentoring skills rather than English language teaching skills or broader trainer-training skills, although many activities are useful in a variety of contexts. In many pre-service contexts, mentor courses would also include what we have called 'ELT methodology update', in order to ensure that the mentors and their mentees share a common methodological background. Trainer-training courses would be extended still further to include such things as workshop design, the design of tasks for teacher education and so on.

In pre-service situations, the length of school experience varies enormously, and there may not be time for mentors to do more than start student-teachers off on the road to continuous professional development. Many of the contexts in which mentors work are not as privileged as the one in which these activities were developed: student-teachers may not have had long, in-depth, language teaching methodology courses, nor will their practicum be anything like as long as ours. We nonetheless believe that the activities in this book and the underlying approach (see below) are relevant in any situation. A worst case scenario, for example, might be where student-teachers arrive for a one-week practicum, having had almost no training in language teaching methodology. In our understanding of mentoring as support for professional development, we would argue, in such cases, that it is even more crucial that mentors have expert mentoring skills. They need to be able to establish rapport with the student-teachers rapidly in order to discover what their understanding of teaching is (which all student-teachers will have from their years of sitting in classrooms as pupils), and train them to question assumptions, and to observe and interpret teaching and learning events so that the developmental processes can, at least, begin.

We can also envisage the relevance of this book for other forms of mentor training (see *Mentors and their roles* below). So, those involved in training people to help the professional development of others, whether in the field of education (MA/MEd programmes, trainer-training courses, etc.) or business, may find something of use in this book.

What a mentor is

A number of contextual factors led to a concern with what we would call the teachers in schools who would have responsibility for our student-teachers during their school experience. The learning objectives for student-teachers in this component at CETT were not simply about performing prescribed 'correct' classroom behaviours, such as effective classroom management, or the presentation of a new structure. They were also about achieving deeper teaching competencies, for example, the ability to notice and interpret classroom events appropriately, as well as developing the ability and willingness to continue their own professional development after graduation. For this reason, we rejected the traditional word 'supervisor', which also suggested notions of hierarchy and directiveness inappropriate for most of the processes that would be necessary to achieve these learning objectives. Because of the strong educator role that would be required, as well as the length of time spent working with student-teachers – a complete school year – the word 'trainer' seemed more appropriate. This was further adapted to 'co-trainer', or COT, both to differentiate this role from the university-based trainers and to suggest the close collaborative role between university and school-based trainers. The metaphor in the acronym, COT, was perhaps unfortunate as although it conveyed a notion of security and support, it denied the student-teacher's considerable previous experience – of life, of schools and of teaching and learning – implying, perhaps, that these were not essential starting points in their professional development. This, together with the increasing use of the word 'mentor' in the professional literature about teaching practice, and the realisation that our term was too localised, led us to adopt the name 'mentor'.

However, the literature now fast accumulating under the heading of 'mentoring' reveals a bewildering range of interpretations of the term. Most assume a one-to-one relationship between mentor and mentee, the 'student'-professional in the relationship, but even these often describe differing roles and functions for the mentor. The majority of these can be classified as in Figure 1:

ROLE	FUNCTIONS
1 Model	– to inspire – to demonstrate
2 'Acculturator'	– to show mentee the ropes – to help mentee get used to the particular professional culture
3 Sponsor	– to 'open doors' – to introduce mentee to the 'right people' – to use their power (ability to make things happen) in the service of the mentee
4 Support	– to be there – to provide safe opportunities for the mentee to let off steam / release emotions – to act as a sounding board – for cathartic reasons
5 Educator	– to act as a sounding board – for articulation of ideas – to consciously create appropriate opportunities for the mentee – to achieve professional learning objectives

Figure 1 Roles of mentors
(Fullerton and Malderez 1998)

While any, or any combination, of the roles above would seem to us to justify the term 'mentor', most mentors will be involved to a greater or lesser degree in all five roles. This is particularly true of those mentors who are part of formal professional development schemes. Because this book appears in a *teacher* training series and because of our own background, we shall be exploring the place of mentoring in the development of the professionalism of *teachers*. However, many of the broader arguments that follow, on learning, reflective practice and so on, will be relevant to any profession. We see most of the activities in this book as particularly relevant to those mentors with significant Support and/or Educator roles to perform.

The organisation of the chapters

It is important to stress that this book is not intended as a coursebook, but rather as a selection of activities for mentor course leaders to select as appropriate within their own context. It is divided into three main parts, *Mentor course principles and practice* (Chapters 1 and 2), *In-session activities* (Chapters 3 to 7) and *Projects and assignments* (Chapters 8 to 10), and finishes with a *Conclusion*.

The first part, *Mentor course principles and practice*, begins at Chapter 1, *Basic concepts*, which looks at the principles underlying the development of the activities and the training approach. Chapter 2, *Course procedures*, contains a number of procedures that we have used throughout courses, as opposed to individual session activities.

The activities in the next part, *In-session activities,* Chapters 3 to 7, are activities for use during sessions only. They have been sequenced with a certain sense of chronology. Chapter 3, *Lead-ins*, has a selection of activities for establishing relationships, and for beginning sessions and topics. Chapter 4, *Seeing clearly* comes next, as work on observation needs to start early in a course so that there is enough time to practise this difficult skill. Chapter 5, *Challenging appropriately*, starts with practice activities for the discrete interpersonal skills necessary for all aspects of mentoring work which also require extensive practice. It also contains activities for elaborating the knowledge base necessary for conscious selection of appropriate acts of intervention with a particular mentee – for developing the ability to challenge sensitively.

The next chapter, Chapter 6, *Role-plays*, differs from the previous chapters in that it contains ideas for role plays/simulations only. These elaborate activities are designed to simulate a mentoring event in order to practise the complex open skill of mentoring. This not only involves the use of a combination of the sub-skills that have been worked on individually through activities earlier in the book, but requires the appropriate selection of these skills as well.

Chapter 7, *Assessing teaching*, contains activities that are intended to help mentors turn evaluation into a positive experience for the professional development of their mentee. Imposed external judging of another's teaching seems to us to carry a high potential for unhelpful interference in that person's professional growth unless handled extremely sensitively. We have deliberately 'relegated' this topic to the last of the chapters that contain only in-session activities, partly because we want to get away from the constant judgemental role of traditional supervision, and also because formal evaluation is likely to occur only at the end of work with student-teachers.

The final part, *Projects and assignments,* includes Chapters 8 to 10. Each of these chapters contains tasks to be completed *between* sessions. The activities involve participants working either on their own or in pairs between the sessions and completing a writing, reading or observation task. Insights from the process are then shared when the group is together. Chapter 8, *Observation tasks*, contains two major types of observation activity to be carried out in schools, with preparation and follow-up tasks to be done in session. Chapter 9, *Reading tasks*, contains a rationale and an example of a type of guided reading task to be carried out at home and followed up in the next session through which many of the knowledge-based objectives of the course can be met. Chapter 10, *Writing tasks*, contains the specifications, preparatory procedures and follow-up tasks for two kinds of written assignment which we have found particularly useful. One is a report on a piece of exploratory teaching or classroom research, and the other a reflective Development Report.

The *Conclusion* includes two activities for disbanding the group, and then looks at some ideas for evaluating mentoring, mentor courses and mentor course activities. It finishes by considering some ways of ensuring the continuous professional development of qualified mentors.

The final pages of this volume include photocopiable materials for activities described in the book, references and appendices.

The organisation of the activities

With the exception of Chapter 3, *Lead-ins,* which is in alphabetical order, the activities are arranged according to what we have found is a natural progression from those that focus on one particular element/skill of mentoring to those that combine such skills in a more complex way.

Most of the names of the activities have been created on past courses by participants during the work on reflection grids (see Chapter 2, *Course procedures*: *Reflection grids*). Using the names participants give is a way of helping group 'ownership' of the experience which increases group identity. There is a brief introduction at the beginning of each activity giving the rationale for its use on the mentor course.

Each activity is presented with the following layout:

Aims

These are given in a list, representing a summary of the rationale which is described in more detail in the activity introduction. They correspond to one or more of the macro course objectives (that is, what the participants will have done), but we have chosen to express them as aims (what the course leader hopes to achieve) since as course leaders we find it is easier to search for activities that correspond to what we are aiming to do in a particular session.

Suggested position in course

This heading will only appear when certain sub-skills are prerequisites for other more complex skill practice.

Suggested position in session

This heading will only appear when the activity is part of a natural sequence of activities.

Materials

All materials needed for each activity are listed here. Role-cards and specific task cards are also included for each activity, either under this heading, or in the case of larger task-sheets, in the *Photocopiable resources* section at the back of the book. *NB* In some places, for reasons of space, we have only included the text and an indication of the layout for a task sheet. We would normally copy this at the top of a blank A4 sheet, extending the columns, or other layout features as appropriate.

Leaders will need to provide their own context-specific materials such as videoed lessons and accompanying materials – lesson plans, coursebook extracts, etc. – or make decisions about which of the published material available is relevant for their own context.

Timing

The approximate timing we have given here is based on our experience with several groups, but obviously this will vary from group to group. Discussions very often need to last longer than might be expected, because it is the discussion itself – the struggle *towards* the completion of the task – rather than the outcome, which is so important to learning.

Assumptions

This is another heading that will appear only when appropriate. There is a basic assumption that all participants are teachers, and that they all have a near-native or native-speaker competence in English.

Classroom organisation

This describes the various different organisations that will occur during the activity, so that the course leader can plan in advance how to get participants into the formations required (see Chapter 2, *Course procedures: Random pairing and grouping activities*). We hope most of the terms we use for the various formats are clear, but perhaps we need to define 'melee' and 'cross-group' here. Melee has been called 'market place', 'mingle', 'moving pairs' and so on, and describes the kind of activity where participants move at will around the room forming and re-forming pairs or groups to complete the given task. Cross-grouping occurs after an initial small group work activity where each small group will have worked on a different task. Participants are then re-grouped, forming new small groups with a representative from each of the original small groups, so that outcomes from each of the tasks can be shared.

Procedure

The stages in the procedure of the activity are numbered. Each stage describes what happens during the activity. We have chosen to describe what happens rather than give instructions as we prefer to leave those decisions as to how to give instructions to the individual course leader. However, the language of these descriptions can easily be turned into instructions, if necessary.

Variations

This section will appear only when there are variations that we have either used ourselves or know of from others. Most activities can and, indeed, should be adapted, and *Variations* may give some additional ideas about how this could be done.

Comments

This section is more personal. It contains some of the issues that have come out of our own round-up discussions. These are by way of example only, and should not be taken as necessary or even desired outcomes. We are constantly surprised at how the same activity can produce very different insights for different groups. We have also included some anecdotes of successes and failures, especially where potential pitfalls are not obvious from the procedure.

Participant reaction

This section includes extracts from feedback on sessions provided by participants (see Chapter 2, *Course procedures*) and from Development Reports (see Chapter 10, *Writing tasks*) to give some indication, through authentic examples, of possible participant reaction to the activity.

Acknowledgements

This section will only appear when we know we owe a debt of gratitude to a specific source. If any reader knows the original source of an activity that we have not acknowledged, we would be happy to learn about it and acknowledge it in any future editions of this book.

Language note

We have used 'student-teacher' and 'mentee' somewhat interchangeably. However, we have tended to choose 'student-teacher' to refer to teachers in both pre-service and in-service situations who are, if you like, in their general 'learner-of-the-profession' role. We have chosen 'mentee' when referring to their specific role and relationship with the mentor. Others, in quotations used in the book, have used 'trainee' to refer to people in both the general 'student-teacher' and the more specific 'mentee' roles.

Having looked at who this book is for and what a mentor is, as well as describing the layout of the book, we can now turn to the basic concepts that serve as the rationale for our mentor training and mentor course activities.

1 Basic concepts

In this chapter, we will start by describing our understanding of learning, then go on to consider teaching before looking at how teaching is learnt, that is, at teacher education. We will then look at the concepts that underlie our approach to mentor training and development.

1.1 Learning

A traditional view of the teaching/learning process is one in which the learner is expected to receive external knowledge, transmitted by teachers or books, and this received knowledge is considered to be sufficient to last a lifetime. Such a view is generally known as a *transmission approach* to the teaching/learning process. Current views of this process see it more as interaction, or dialogue – a *dialogic approach* – with information flowing from teacher to learner and back, as well as between learners. In addition, this view of the learning/teaching process sees learning the skills of finding and using knowledge as more important than knowledge itself. It is, therefore, appropriate for the age we live in as it allows us to keep abreast of the increasingly rapid changes, where what is learnt today may well be redundant or invalid tomorrow.

With earlier *behaviourist theories* of learning came a view which has been very influential in language teaching methodology, in which language, for example, is considered a habit to be learnt, and therefore drilled practice makes perfect, although it carries the danger that practised mistakes will perfect imperfection! More recent *cognitive theories* see learning as being less about behaviour and more about what goes on in individual minds. *Constructivism,* for example, sees learning as a two-way process, with the learners linking input to their own personal experiences and perceptions of the world. Input from books, people, personal experience or practice is not seen as information to be added to a store of knowledge, but rather as new perspectives to be considered and possibly used to reconstruct the learner's existing internal knowledge. In this view of learning, the objective is neither a store of transmitted information, nor a set of habits, but rather something that is personally created: schemata or constructs of understandings, that can be added to or taken apart and reassembled in ways meaningful exclusively to the learner. Learning is seen as an assembly and reassembly of knowledge, which may or may not include new input, a process that can last a lifetime. *Social constructivism* (Williams and Burden 1997) acknowledges the important contribution of the context of learning and the other individuals within that context, whether in the particular classroom culture or in the broader educational system and society in which the classroom is found, and views knowledge as jointly and socially created through interaction with others.

When we have asked learners to identify the features of 'good' teaching, that is behaviour which promotes learning, they have invariably cited teachers who, regardless of their methods, seem to have started from their learners' existing knowledge, experience and beliefs, and helped them to link these with the new subject matter. These same teachers would probably say they were 'making things interesting', 'personalising' or 'motivating their students'. From a constructivist point of view, we would explain this by saying they were 'setting up appropriate challenges'. Since we will be using this notion of challenge in a very specific way in this book, we will discuss it in some detail here.

A challenge is a potential opportunity for learning and is anything that makes learners consider or reconsider and possibly reassemble or expand their existing constructs. From this constructivist viewpoint, the setting up of challenges is one of the fundamental acts of teaching. It involves, if you like, putting down stepping stones to help the learner's journey, to speed the changes in the learner's constructs necessary to meet the learning objectives. For example, if the learning objectives of a class are to do with mammals, and the teacher establishes that the children see that 'milk comes from bottles', she might start attempting to expand this construct by showing pictures of milk in plastic bags (as in Hungary) or cartons (as in many countries) before moving to exploring how it got there, through to cows, goats and other mammals including humans. The children's constructs now include not only a range of ideas about how milk is packaged but concepts of its possible origins and milk production as a characteristic of all mammals. The important point is that the children now have a range of equally correct answers to the question 'Where does milk come from?', and which one they use will depend on the context.

The activities in this book are based on a constructivist view of learning in the sense of setting up challenges or being 'concerned with how learners self-organise their own behaviour and experience to produce changes which they themselves value' (Thomas and Hari-Augstein 1985). Fundamental too to the training approach presented here is a social constructivist approach to course processes. It has been our experience that learners, having once experienced the power and excitement of this kind of learning, are, as it were, kick-started on the road to autonomous continual learning.

Having considered the learning/teaching process from the perspective of learning, we will now look at ways of conceptualising teaching.

1.2 Teaching

Tomlinson defines teaching as, basically, 'activity designed to promote learning' (1995:9). This definition of teaching points to the goal-oriented nature of the activity. As for the nature of the activity itself, it involves knowing how to do things, based on knowing about things, and has been described as 'a complex, open skill' (Tomlinson 1995:14). It is 'complex' because the teacher will be doing a lot at once with a lot of people, and it is 'open' because there are many possible ways of responding to similar sets of circumstances. Much of what a skilful teacher does appears effortless, and indeed the teacher will not be consciously focusing on these apparently effortless actions: they have become automatic, intuitive or 'proceduralised'. For example, a skilled teacher, while involved with one group of pupils, will intuitively know what is happening in another group and even raise a controlling hand or give an aside, without losing concentration. These techniques for classroom control would almost certainly have once been at the forefront of their conscious attention, as studies of beginner teachers show (Kagan 1992), but they have now become second nature.

Learning is the goal of teaching, and learning, in terms of the development of constructs, is essentially a different process for every individual. In other words, each individual learner must be considered not simply under a label (a 10-year-old or teenager, intermediate or advanced) but as an individual with their own different experience-base, cultural background, style, feelings and so on. Teaching will therefore begin with getting to know individual learners, and discovering 'where they are' as regards their existing constructs. To know someone, you need to enter into a relationship, so in this sense, although teaching is 'in part about putting together clear, interesting, well-judged lessons . . . above all it is about relationships' (Claxton 1990:17). Teaching is about building relationships between the teacher and each individual learner but it is also, in most contexts, especially where there are very large classes, about managing relationships between learners in any learning group. This is not only because there happens to be more than one learner present, or because teachers may want learners to practise, say, interactional language skills, but because social constructivist teachers will want to use the challenge that each group member's perspective can provide for other learners. 'Success depends less on materials, techniques and linguistic analyses, and more on what goes on inside and between people in the classroom' (Stevick 1980:4).

Perhaps all this explains why, when you ask *any* group of people to brainstorm the qualities of a 'good teacher' there will be categories relating to 'knowledge' and 'skills', but invariably the biggest group of factors can be found under a category one can label 'personal qualities'. Concepts of good teaching, then, have expanded from excellence in *what* is being taught, to skills in *how it is taught* and to considerations of *who* is learning and teaching.

In the next sections, we will be considering how teaching is learnt before going on to consider the mentor's role in the process of learning to teach.

1.3 Teacher education

In considering what is involved in learning to teach, we will need to clarify the possible goals of the learning process as well as what might be involved in the process itself.

1.3.1 *Goals of learning to teach*

The goal of teacher training programmes has often been described as either
'good teaching' or 'being a good teacher'. The latter is really an extension of
the first as it embraces the role of the teacher as both a promoter of learning
and as a member of a professional society. The problem, however, is how to
define 'good' and whether it is a realistic goal at all in a time-bound teacher
education programme. In a constructivist view, it is impossible to define a static
notion of good teaching or being a good teacher, as the process of extending
constructs about their work, themselves and their learners will continue
throughout the teacher's lifetime. It becomes necessary therefore to look at
what is minimally acceptable as a goal, not only in terms of teaching (perhaps,
what is just above the level of being 'dangerous' in the classroom. See Chapter
7, *Assessing teaching*), but also whether the qualifying teachers are able to fulfil
their professional roles in the school and the wider professional community, as
well as whether they have the skill of managing and maintaining their own
continuous professional development. If these three elements are to be the
goals, we need to look at how they can be achieved.

1.3.2 *The dynamic interplay of practice and theory*

Learning teaching has always had a theoretical side and a practical side. Theory
can be considered from two perspectives: it can mean the collective theoretical
knowledge of the profession, which we will call Theory, with a capital *T*. It can
also mean the personal constructed theories of the individual which we will call
theory, with a small *t*. In many teacher education programmes, Theory is learnt
at the university or training institute. In English language teacher education,
this Theory is mainly knowledge of and about the subject, English, as well as
perhaps some Theoretical pedagogy. It is assumed that this capital *T* Theory
can then be transferred into practice which will be learnt on the job, often only
after graduation. The problem is that this transfer very often fails to occur, as
the connections between the Theory and the realities of classroom practice are
unclear.
  However, the business of learning the skill of teaching not only involves
student-teachers constructing their own knowledge about the subject, but also
about a range of classroom activities and processes. It also involves them
developing the skills for the effective selection and use of those activities,
drawing on further Theories (from those of learning to group dynamics, and
classroom management to psychology). It takes considerable and varied
amounts of time to develop expertise in the complex skill of teaching. This is
further complicated by the fact that the information base, the capital *T* Theory,
is constantly and ever more rapidly changing. Therefore, our graduates also
need the skills, tools and processes for continuing their own learning of
teaching throughout their professional lives. They need to become, in Schön's
well-used term, 'reflective practitioners' (Schön 1983).

One way of conceptualising a teacher's expertise lies in viewing 'theory' (with a small *t*) and 'practice' as integral parts of the same skill in a continuous dynamic inter-relationship. Classroom events will inform personal theories, and theories and Theory will inform classroom practice. The central link in this process is the reviewing of actual classroom experience, and the consequent planning for future action in the classroom. At both the reviewing and planning phases, Theory (of linguistics, second language acquisition, psychology, methodology, etc.) can usefully inform understandings and decisions. However, capital *T* Theory is most usefully seen, we have found, as other or outsiders' theories, with a small *t*, and carefully considered against existing constructs, rather than taken as indisputable fact.

In this view of initial teacher education, where the central link is classroom practice, the carefully designed practicum has a vital part to play and can no longer be viewed as a luxury add-on. Without it, teachers are either knowledgeable *about* teaching but cannot apply that knowledge, or can display teacher-like behaviour in one context but cannot learn from the experience nor use professional analytical skills to make sense of new teaching situations and act appropriately. Subject knowledge then becomes, as it were, the 'tip of the iceberg', and you ignore the great mass below the surface at your peril! (See Figure 2.)

The visible tip of the iceberg is the teacher's subject knowledge and professional behaviour. These will be influenced by the 'air', the culture of the whole school and more specifically the classroom in which the teacher works. Similarly, the mass below the surface will be influenced by the surrounding 'sea' of the culture and society in which the teacher lives. Immediately below the surface are the processes the teacher goes through before going into the classroom, those involved with decision-making, lesson planning and so on. In turn, these decisions draw on constructs of the subject, the pupils themselves and a body of knowledge that covers a range of possible courses of action for the classroom and the wider professional world. These knowledge constructs are embedded in deeper understandings about people, learning and teaching, which themselves have been influenced by even more fundamental beliefs, attitudes, feelings and experiences. The two-way arrows in Figure 2 indicate that this is not, of course, a one-way process: the influences flow in both directions. These may be set in motion by something that happens in the visible part of the iceberg. As the teacher reviews what happened there (see *Notions of reflection* below) they will begin drawing from the layers below, considering possible interpretations, other choices that could have been made, and the influences from the deeper levels on what happened. This process may reveal a need to discover more: more evidence, more perspectives from others' knowledge-bases and so on; in other words, to learn from others' icebergs. In the planning, these new understandings, are, as it were, brought back to the surface and emerge as another visible bit of teacher behaviour.

In mentoring work, the reflective process usually starts from a description of something from the visible tip, then goes down below the surface, around a reviewing, selecting, learning and planning cycle. We will now consider the implications of this for teacher education programmes.

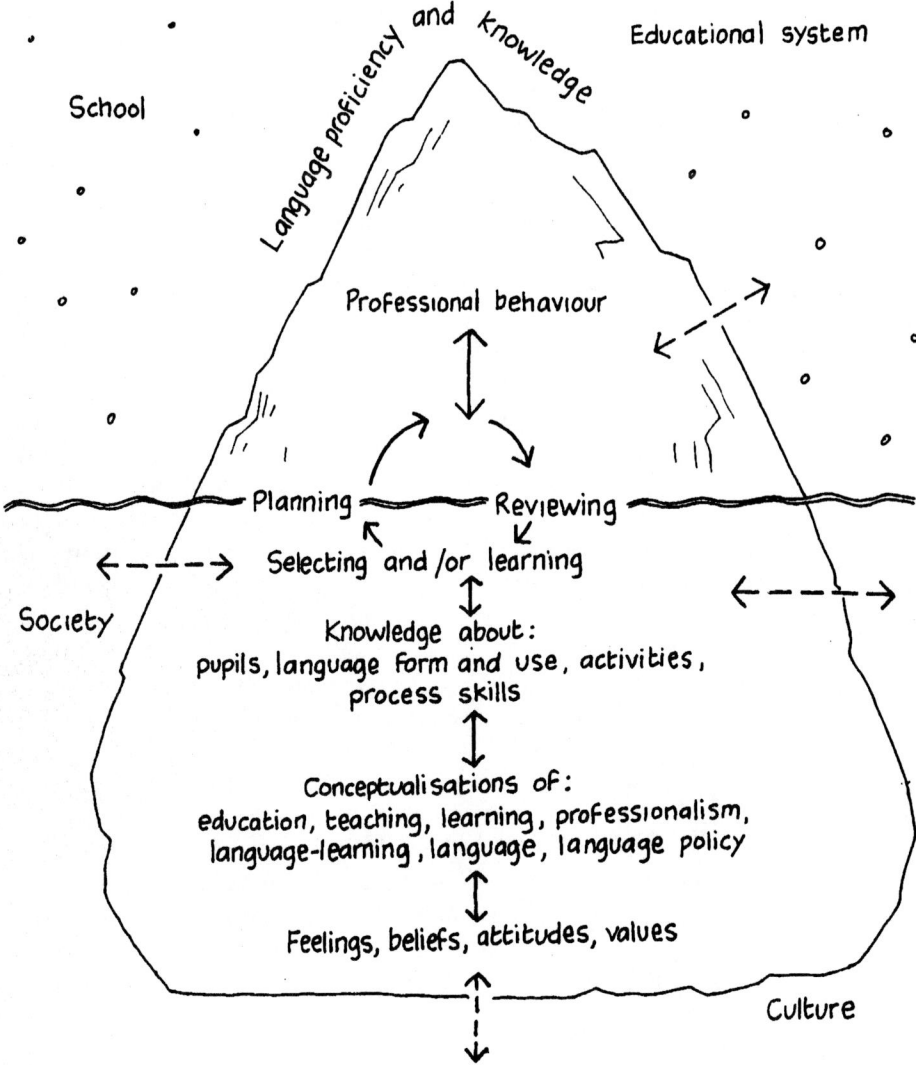

Figure 2 The Teacher Iceberg
(Malderez 1996)

1.3.3 Teacher education programmes

We have found that, initially, many student-teachers are not equipped with the ability to draw on all levels of the iceberg in order to construct a personal understanding of teaching. This may be personality-related, or a result of previous educational training and experience, or because of the strength of the internalised models we all have of 'what being a teacher is'. These models have come from what Lortie (1975) calls the 'apprenticeship of observation': the many years of sitting in classrooms as pupils. Because these models are based only on the visible tip of the teacher's iceberg, it is often difficult for student-teachers to understand that there is a mass below the surface. Beginner teachers therefore, tend to focus on knowledge of their subject and classroom activities. The task of teacher education is to help student-teachers discover and explore the lower layers of the iceberg.

In the teacher education institutions, trainers tend to teach Theory and explore theories, linking them with their students' own experiences and beliefs. The focus is on knowing *about* teaching. In the schools, on the other hand, mentors start from the student-teacher's own work in the classroom and link it to increasingly explicit understandings of elements from the lower layers of the iceberg. These can then be constantly developed. It is during the practicum period that student-teachers need to establish a reflective habit. Establishing reflection as a habit means learning the skills of reviewing which include noticing, interpreting and evaluating, as well as developing the subsequent skills of planning and selecting. All these skills depend on consciously linking interpretations of classroom events with personally constructed theories. To develop these skills and establish this habit of reflective linking requires sufficient time in schools to work from and towards the student-teacher's own experiences of teaching. This reflective habit will help the student-teacher to meet the varied and unpredictable demands of the future. The mentor's main responsibility, then, is to train mentees in this process, this linking of theories and practice in personally significant ways, rather than to train specific teaching behaviour.

Such a view of a school-based mentor's role is significantly different from the more traditional one, where the student-teacher would watch and imitate prescribed methods and be evaluated and judged according to the supervisor's view of what constituted 'good' teaching. The traditional approach is based on a deficit model of learning teaching (what is 'wrong', and what needs to be put 'right'). Mentoring, as we define it, is based on a growth model of learning teaching (how to help each individual mentee become the best teacher they can possibly be). As one of our mentors put it 'my trainee mustn't become a second "me", but an enriched herself'.

1.3.4 Interteaching

Freeman (1992) has proposed a model of the learning-to-teach process that we have found insightful. It has not only helped us to conceptualise the process but has also given us insights into the role of teacher educators at particular moments in a student-teacher's development. Freeman derived his concept of interteaching from Selinker's (1972) interlanguage model of second language acquisition. The parallels seem striking as both teaching and language use are open, complex skills (see Johnson 1996, Tomlinson 1995).

What follows is our analysis of these parallels. We will begin by looking at the starting points, go on to consider the goals, before describing the processes, the continua, and how movement along those continua is encouraged through the mediation of the teacher or teacher educator.

In interlanguage and interteaching theories, the entry points for both processes (learning a second language and learning teaching) are similar. The second language learner begins the process having learnt his or her native language and hence a set of rules for language use through socialisation in a language community. The learner teacher also arrives with an understanding of teaching, acquired through the process of socialisation within an educational community (classroom, school, educational system, etc.).

The goals of both processes are also extremely similar. The goal for language learners could be described as effective communicator ability through the target language. A problem with this goal is that it has yet to be fully described, and is extremely context dependent. Furthermore, even native speakers of the target language have yet to achieve this goal in all contexts (we, for example, would not be effective communicators with Harlem rappers). Similarly, the goal of learning teaching could be described as effective teacher ability. This too has yet to be fully described and is extremely context dependent (we may be fairly effective teachers in Hungarian higher education, but how effective would we be with a primary class in an Icelandic fishing village?).

Selinker's interlanguage theory describes the learning continuum as starting from the rules/theories of the learner's own language, and proceeding through a series of rule-governed stages to approximate as nearly as possible the system of the target language. The rule-governed stages are idiosyncratic, and lead the learner away from working from the L1 rules/theories to building up L2 rules/ theories (L1 being the mother tongue, and L2 the target language). In the same way, student-teachers enter the learning teaching process with preconceived theories of teaching derived from their experience as pupils, and proceed through a series of stages based on their current hypotheses.

Movement along these continua happens as a result of the student constantly testing their hypotheses, receiving feedback as to their effectiveness, and modifying them to form a new hypothesis to be tested. In language learning, learners need to notice the language they are using, consider its effectiveness, then look at others' use of language in similar situations (others' theories) as well as Theory from grammar books and so on, before reformulating a new working hypothesis. In the classroom, these processes can be speeded up by the teacher, through what have come to be known as language awareness activities.

Student-teachers, in the same way, may be helped to move more rapidly along the interteaching continuum through what we may call teaching awareness tasks. The teacher educator, particularly the mentor, in teaching awareness tasks, will help student-teachers to notice what happens when they teach, in terms of their action and its effectiveness, and consider the hypothesis underlying this action. The teacher educator will then challenge this hypothesis with examples from their own experience (theory), others' theories and Theory, and will then give them a task to do, even if it is only to consider the question 'So what else could you have done?'

So far we have looked at some basic concepts and models to explore learning, teaching and learning teaching which have important implications for the work of mentors. We have also begun to explore the role of mentors in helping teachers move along the interteaching continuum. In the following section we will build on these discussions as we consider how mentoring is learnt.

1.4 Learning mentoring

If the goal of the learning teaching process is one of creating skilled professional teachers, then the goal of the learning mentoring process is similarly one of creating skilled professional mentors. Just as having a good subject knowledge is not enough to be a good teacher, so being a good teacher is not enough to be a good mentor. It requires additional skills and knowledge. The Mentor Iceberg might look like this:

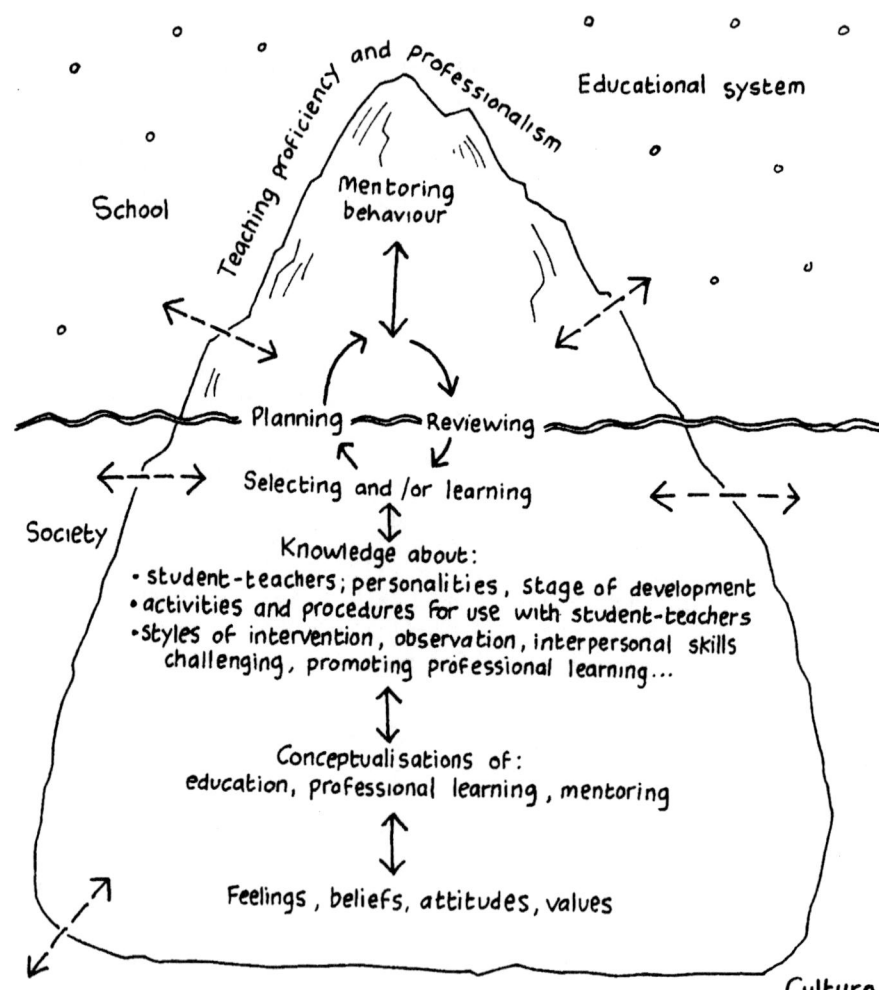

Figure 3 The Mentor Iceberg
(Malderez 1996)

Many of the things in the Mentor Iceberg above and especially below the surface will have to be learnt, as they are not necessarily part of the make-up of a competent classroom teacher. The need for mentor courses therefore becomes clear. Time is needed to acquire the additional knowledge and skills, as well as possibly challenge existing models of the role stemming from the would-be mentor's own beginning-teaching experiences with their own supervisor. What skills and knowledge precisely does a mentor need to have in order to help mentees become reflective practitioners?

In the rest of this section, we will look more closely at some of the concepts already discussed, as this exploration will provide the rationale for the content, processes and resultant training approach of mentor courses.

1.4.1 Towards a course design

In order to get closer to mentor course design, we will explore more deeply some notions contained in the term 'reflective practice' before returning to the importance of relationships in social constructivist learning.

Notions of reflection

The following three facets of 'reflection' have been fundamental to the design of our mentor courses, their activities and processes.

a) Holding up the mirror

The word 'reflection' is naturally connected with the word 'mirror', and at times a mentor may need to act as a mirror to provide a clear image from a different perspective. Lesson observation is a traditional supervisory act after which evaluation and/or advice is given. The purpose in mentoring, though, is often qualitatively different. In this case, it involves the mentor's ability to see, record, and subsequently 'hold up the mirror'. The mentee can then see again, or see differently, the events of the lesson and reconstruct their own understandings, so moving along the interteaching continuum. The practical mentoring sub-skills of non-evaluative observation, and the recording and giving of data are, we find, among the hardest to acquire.

b) Thinking over

Reflection can also mean thoughtful deliberation ('let me reflect on that'). All descriptions of reflective cycles (see, for example, Chapter 9, *Reading tasks*) include this phase of thinking over classroom events, and reflecting on them in order to plan future action. Freeman (1992), for example, describes a cycle of professional development during which we 'name', that is, talk about teaching (revealing existing constructs), then 'apply', that is, teach, based on outcomes of discussion, then 'reconceive' (building on or reassembling those constructs), through looking back over what actually happened, naming again, and so on.

This habit of 'thinking over' can be encouraged through regular discussion, during which the language for 'naming' can be developed, and the vague or the implicit made explicit through the necessity of communicating with another. Mentor courses, therefore, include practice in ways of conducting or participating in discussions concerned with 'thinking over', so that the mentee can make useful decisions regarding 'application'. This will also mean working on the development of a shared language, a bridge between the discourses of training institute and school which are often very different. The importance of this was highlighted when one mentor commented at the end of a course, 'Now I have a language with which to think and talk about teaching'.

c) Modelling

Finally, reflection also carries the meaning of a copied model. The modelling, in this case, is no longer simply a question of the mentor's demonstrating to a student-teacher what to do in a classroom (but see below). It is, rather, the demonstration of their commitment to their own professionalism and professional development. This is shown through a myriad of daily acts, such as the way they seek their pupils' and mentees' opinions; turn to the professional literature and colleagues for ideas; interact with parents; contribute to staff meetings; attend in-service events and so on. Mentee and mentor will, ideally, be working in parallel, alternately modelling and imitating enthusiasm and commitment for their work and their own professional development (the Model role described in Figure 1). One mentor has described mentoring as 'a permanent refresher course'. This kind of modelling needs to be explicitly discussed on mentor courses and demonstrated, in turn, by the course leader's own behaviour. In fact, all elements of such courses have a powerful modelling potential and we will indicate these opportunities as the discussion develops *(see particularly Teaching mentoring below)*.

When learning teaching is thought of as skill learning, see *Teaching* above, then the trainer of a skill can be called a coach. (Schön uses this word, too, to describe the role of the trainer in developing reflective practitioners.) Coaches do demonstrate sub-skills at the beginning of the coaching process. The aim here, however, is not to demonstrate a particular method, activity or technique to be added to the mentee's repertoire, but rather to demonstrate the *teaching/ learning principle in action*. The mentor will be modelling not 'the best' way of behaving, but a (contextually appropriate) way of putting a principle (the below the surface of the iceberg) into practice (see 4.9 *Helping the mentees see*). Many practicum programmes start with a period of observation for the student-teacher who needs to be helped to see behind the surface-level of activities.

These three elements of reflection will be present in post-lesson discussions, which can be likened to an exploratory classroom research process. The starting point for thinking over the lesson will be the classroom events seen as raw data. These data will come not only from the mentee's recollections, but also from the mentor when they 'hold up the mirror', as well as any formalised pupil feedback, and occasional audio or visual recordings. This ensures the use of different perspectives, a form of triangulation.

The next, interpretation phase ('What could it mean?'), will automatically involve bringing in other data from previous experience, the existing theories of mentee and mentor, as well as consciously turning to Theory, with a capital *T*, to draw on outsiders' theories. Interpretation will almost inevitably lead to some degree of evaluation of what occurred in order to make informed decisions about what to do next. External evaluation either by the mentor or institution, when it occurs, would not, however, come here, but after the final action planning stage (see Chapter 7, *Assessing teaching*, for more on this).

The final action planning ('What now?') stage will examine the implications of this analysis and lead to the planning of future action. It may include decisions to check out interpretations, decisions about what to do next in the classroom, as well as decisions on how to further the mentee's own professional learning.

This whole process is what a student-teacher needs to be able and willing to undertake alone in order to manage their own professional development. In post-lesson discussions, mentors will need not only to encourage work towards standard levels of classroom teaching competence, but also towards their mentee's mastery of reflective practice.

1.4.2 Helpful relationships

Given the importance of relationships in learning, none of the mentor's roles can be effective if the mentor lacks the ability to form appropriate helpful relationships.

'Help' in the educator role in mentoring has a very different meaning from the normal social sense of the word. This type of help, as in helping someone to learn, has been variously described by others as, for example, Williams and Burden (1997) who call it 'mediating', or Tomlinson who refers to it as 'influencing' (1997, personal communication). We prefer Freeman's term 'intervention' (1990) to describe what it is mentors do, as it highlights the idea that everything a mentor says, does, or even arguably is, will make a difference to a mentee's development. In order for the interventions to be helpful, they need to be carefully considered. Giving advice or doing something for someone will not necessarily assist a student-teacher to construct their own view, link their practice to their own theoretical understandings of teaching. In the educator role, helpful behaviour might be, for example, encouraging explicit talk about the mentee's beliefs (hypotheses), and providing selected data either from observations, 'Theory' or the mentor's own experience. All this is designed to challenge gently those hypotheses and lead the mentee to a more complete conceptualisation of the particular teaching focus in question, in other words, a teaching awareness task. The word 'gently' above is highly significant as, in our view of the sensitive management of constructivist learning, challenge does not mean aggressive accusation! The further away the new perspective is from the learner's existing constructs, the stronger the challenge will be, and therefore, the more potentially shocking and disruptive in terms of relationships. But challenge is always necessary for learning to occur (see Vygotsky 1979). Therefore, mentor course leaders and mentors themselves need to consider how strong the challenge is likely to be, in other words, where to put the stepping stones for a particular group or particular mentee. This is a vital skill, not only from the point of view of learning, but from the point of view of maintaining relationships.

This notion of 'help' with its apparently implicit focus on the support role (see Figure 1) will often lead to a self-selected mentor being a nurturing kind of person, who has a natural ability to create the basic trust that enables a fruitful relationship to grow, and years of life experience in such interpersonal skills as conflict resolution. Ironically, however, the 'naturals' may not always be the best at all the roles, for example that of the educator (see Figure 1), if they have not also consciously considered the nature of 'help' in fulfilling the mentoring roles of their specific context. Conversely, people with less naturally nurturing personalities can be made aware of the importance of the underlying relation-ship and be taught ways to create it. Equally, student-teachers who will be aware of the importance of forming relationships with their pupils, will need to be willing to extend this to their mentor.

The quality of mentoring will be influenced both by the mentor's and mentee's personalities and ways of being with people. Mentees differ in their levels of interpersonal skill, as well as in their stages of professional development, in their styles and paces of learning, and they all have different biographies and personalities. The mentor must be able to form, consciously, the kind of relationship which will be helpful, in the above sense, to each particular mentee. They need to be able to draw on a range of interpersonal skills, including counselling skills. Edge (1992:4) maintains that the type of interaction that truly fosters self-development involves 'learning some new rules for speaking, for listening, and for responding in order to cooperate in a disciplined way'. These can (and should) be learnt by prospective mentors and their mentees.

The quality of mentoring will also be affected by what the mentor chooses to do to foster the mentee's professional development. Appropriate choices depend in part on the range of activities that mentors have at their disposal, but also, and crucially for this discussion, on their knowledge of each particular mentee. This kind of knowledge may depend on a high level of interpersonal skill, especially when mentor and mentee do not have much time working together or do not have a natural empathy. It is the mentor's ability to empathise that enables them when making choices to 'stay in touch with the fine line between excitement and anxiety, challenge and threat' (Claxton 1989:190).

While the kind of mentor we envisage will mainly be working in one-to-one relationships, most learning relationships are in fact established in the context of groups, as in the case of mentor courses. These courses will need to pay attention to the dynamics of the group, especially to the fostering and maintaining of relationships between members of the group (see *Teaching mentoring* below).

1.4.3 Course aims and objectives

All mentor courses will aim to help participants to gain the knowledge, skills and confidence necessary for their mentor roles. We have found it useful to divide the objectives into three main groups. However, the order in which these are given does not imply that a course will work towards their achievement sequentially. On the contrary, many objectives will be addressed concurrently and throughout the course.

By the end of the course, participants should:

a) have made explicit and shared
   - their own beliefs, attitudes and feelings about learning, teaching and mentoring
   - their own beliefs, attitudes and feelings about professional development
   - the impact of the course on their own learning
b) have knowledge about
   - concepts of professional learning
   - the role of mentoring in professional learning
   - beginner teacher development
   - the importance of relationships
   - counselling techniques
   - observation, observation tools and recording methods
   - mentoring styles and possible impacts
   - a wide range of activities and procedures for mentoring student-teachers
   - assessment and evaluation: criteria, tools and processes
   - the content of the training-institution-based programme(s) student-teachers have undergone
   - a range of tools and activities for their own further professional development
c) have practised skills in
   - relationship management: forming, maintaining and ending
   - active listening
   - sensitive language use in mentoring discussions
   - the conscious use of body language
   - observation, and recording those observations
   - assessing individual mentee's needs in order to select appropriate intervention style and activity, or provide concrete practical help
   - helping mentees become capable of independent self-evaluation and resultant action planning
   - assessing and evaluating student-teachers' work against the contextually accepted standard
   - some tools and activities for their own professional development

How these objectives can be translated into a course design is elaborated below in 1.5.2 *The leader as course designer.*

1.5 Teaching mentoring

The focus now changes from learning mentoring to teaching mentoring. The training approach we have used for mentor courses has grown out of considerations of reflective practice and the notions of professional learning already discussed, as well as the kind of course objectives presented above. In the sections below we provide a rationale for the training methodology, and then consider the role of the course leader.

1.5.1 Training methodology

In this section we will be revisiting many of the by now familiar concepts, through the perspective of the work of the course leader in designing, selecting, sequencing or implementing activities.

Making the implicit explicit

As we stated above, work to achieve many course objectives will run concurrently (see 1.5.2 *The leader as course designer*). The constant discussion during work to fulfil all of the objectives is, in fact, the fundamental methodology of the course. These discussions provide the opportunities for the construction of new meanings, socially and individually.

However, one fundamental premise on which the approach is based is that it is only when participants have become aware of an issue that it is possible to start exploring existing, often implicit, constructs through explicit talk. Using specifically designed awareness-raising tasks or activities which provide contrived shared experiences is one way of bringing out the issues. Many of the introductory activities in *Lead-ins* (Chapter 3) are designed, often through symbolism or metaphor, to help bring into conscious awareness some aspect of mentoring as well as to provide a powerful shared experience. Other shared experiences such as completing reading tasks (see Chapter 9), observing (see Chapters 4, 6 and 8), or participating in video-based simulations and role-plays (see Chapter 6) form the basis on which to deliberate, in order to reveal and challenge participants' existing constructs. All written assignments (see Chapter 9) will also inevitably encourage participants to explore and clarify, for the sake of communication, their beliefs and understandings. An activity review process (see Chapter 2: Reflection grids) is another useful tool in making the implicit explicit.

Knowledge

We approach the knowledge objectives, including capital *T* Theory objectives, of mentor courses in the same way. A constructivist view of learning requires helping participants first to recognise a 'need to know', for example 'the stages of professional development', to discover and acknowledge what they already know about them – in this case, at the very least, their own stages – and then to consult other sources of knowledge. These may be other participants, through comparing and contrasting their experiences; the course leader, either as a fellow professional or as someone who has synthesised the literature; or through the literature itself, by studying different writers' conceptualisations of professional development. Many of the lead-in activities (Chapter 3) aim to generate a 'need to know'. Some of these, together with many of the discussions, have a 'discover and share what you already know' function. The reading tasks (Chapter 9) as well as mini-lectures (see Chapter 5 *Challenging appropriately*) will provide further knowledge input. This input is not offered as a truth to be learnt, but rather as another viewpoint to add a further dimension to each participant's knowledge base. Follow-up stages of many activities provide opportunities for active reshaping of constructs and the making explicit, often through discussion and sharing of ideas, of these reshaped or new constructs.

Skills

In order to acquire a skill, there has to be an initial desire to achieve proficiency. Skills require practice and this takes time, which will differ from one person to another. This may sound obvious, but it is not enough simply to read about, say, interpersonal skills: they can only become genuine tools in a mentor's repertoire if repeated practice has made them almost second nature. This mastery, however, will not be simple behaviourist imitation, but will be based on new understandings (elaborated constructs) developed during discussions about the skills practice itself as well as during work towards achieving the various knowledge objectives of the course. It is this mastery that is one of the major sources of a mentor's confidence.

The book contains activities to practise skills in isolation (see Chapters 4 and 5), as well as practice in combining the skills during more complex simulations and role-plays (see Chapter 6).

1.5.2 *The role of the course leader: the importance of modelling and congruence*

On a course where modelling is a specific course objective it is essential that leaders practise what they preach, and model the kind of modelling mentors are expected to perform. Broadly speaking, this involves matching what is taught and how it is taught. This is what we mean by congruence of training. More specifically, it will involve the course leader in modelling reflective practice and making explicit the application of theories (small and capital *T*) in their practice and the influence of that practice on their theories. In addition, they need to model attention to relationship management; professionalism and commitment to their own professional development; as well as the ability to fashion the course to the needs of the group. This may sound an impossible profile, but another aspect of this congruence is being able to be patient with all learners including oneself. In other words, it means attempting to live up to what you believe, and genuinely trying to be a mentor of 'student' mentors, and sharing those trials with the group (another case of modelling)!

Activities and the leader's role

We will first examine the course leader's role, starting from the point of view of what they actually do in sessions, when these are seen simply as a series of activities. After the initial organisation and setting up of an activity, a large proportion of the leader's time will be spent observing participants at work. In the later, whole-group, follow-up discussions, part of the leader's role may well be to offer data from these observations, in the sense of 'holding up the mirror', for the group to interpret and draw conclusions for their collective and individual needs. In so doing, course leaders will be modelling both the observer's role in reflective practice, as well as a way of training student-teachers in reflective practice. Furthermore, through this practice, participants can experience the impact that such processes can have on professional development, and as always, each individual's experience can be shared in order to deepen explicit understandings. Finally, if the course leader can share with the group their thinking about the effectiveness of their skills in observation and 'holding up the mirror', picking up comments during the discussion as feedback data, interpreting them and considering their implications, they will be providing a model of professional development at another level: that of the mentor seeking student-teacher comments on their own mentoring.

The course leader's role during activities will not always only be that of observer. Early on, before the participants have built up a real relationship with the leader, or later in the course when the leader is beginning to withdraw from their learning process, there may be occasions when the leader may choose to leave them to get on with the activity on their own, even to the extent of leaving the room. This again is more modelling, this time of the possible benefits of not going in to observe the mentee at the beginning or end of their teaching practice. There will also be occasions when the leader may need to intervene in small group activities in order to help a group of participants get started or keep going, taking care not to be drawn into the discussion or seen as the authority which would probably be unhelpful (though see *The leader as 'expert'* below). On the other hand, many relationship-building activities are occasions when it is helpful for the leader to participate as an equal member of the group.

It goes without saying, that the leader will not only be 'holding up the mirror' during round-up discussions. The leader will also need to elicit and possibly synthesise outcomes, checking that these interpretations are accurate, and clearly owning any new contributions they, in fellow-professional role rather than 'authority', make to the discussion.

The leader as 'expert'

In our view of the teaching-learning process the power that the leader's status automatically confers will not be used to provide answers, or push a party line. This is not to say that leaders should not on occasion give mini-lectures.

Both leaders and mentors need to be aware that their very role gives them status and power. Traditionally, this confers both the right for the leader/mentor to 'tell' and the expectation for the participants/mentees to be 'told'. In our view of learning, 'telling' has its place, but for reasons which are not to do with reinforcing the power and status of the 'teller', nor to do with reinforcing the transmission metaphor of teaching and learning. In our type of 'telling' situation, what is told is viewed as just another source of knowledge, amongst many (texts, other participants/mentees, etc.), to be contrasted against the receivers' own constructs. Authority in the subject is not the same as power over the teaching-learning process or dialogue. Tiberius (1986) argues that what he calls the 'dialogical metaphor' of teaching and learning is '. . . more adaptive . . . because it *includes* the transmission process'. He goes on to explain that 'dialogue involves a process of mutual transmission of information resulting from negotiation between the teacher and students'. This two-way information flow is fundamental to learning.

In addition, it becomes a form of self-exposure on the leader's part, and therefore contributes to personal-professional trust-building which helps to build the kind of relationship conducive to professional development. Course participants are constantly called upon to reveal, to expose or tell what they know or think. The course leader's occasional 'telling' ensures that information goes both ways. If the ideas are offered as one professional sharing their constructs with others, inviting challenge and delighting in the opportunities such challenge offers for their own professional growth, then the experience can model how to use challenge constructively. In these 'telling' situations, then, the mentor/leader will in effect make themselves vulnerable, just as mentees and participants are expected to make themselves vulnerable by first making their constructs explicit, then by accepting and using challenges to those constructs. As with all courses which have a goal of continuing autonomous learning, the leader's job will increasingly be to hand over responsibilities to the group, becoming eventually just another colleague of equal status. In this way, leaders rather than reinforcing their power and status in fact become equals in the sense of professionals pursuing their own development, modelling not only how to use others in professional development processes, but also the letting go of status and power that mentors will aim for with their mentees.

We also know from personal experience how tiring purely experiential workshops/courses can be. Even in contexts where lectures/'straight input' are not the expected norm, they are useful, apart from all the reasons stated above, as a very welcome break from intense experiential work.

Intermember relationships: the leader's role

We will now turn to the leader's role in the area of relationships, looking at issues of group dynamics. Because of the crucial importance of the issue of relationships in mentoring as well as the need for the course leader to 'walk their talk', we will focus on why group dynamics are so important and how issues from this field can inform course processes (see for example Dörnyei and Malderez 1997).

Defining groups

Groups in the socio-psychological sense are by definition pools of resources where the whole is greater than the sum of the parts. Intermember relationships are both an indication of a group's existence in the socio-psychological sense as well as the key to creating a group. In the old 'jug and mug' view of knowledge transmission, the existing knowledge of the individual student – their resources – was neither valued nor drawn upon. It was not relevant to what was to be learnt, nor could it, in this view, contribute to another's learning. There was therefore no need for intermember relationships. In a social constructivist view of learning, as we have suggested above, such relationships are crucial.

This kind of professional learning requires revealing and sharing deep-seated personal beliefs and attitudes which renders participants potentially very vulnerable, as they are, in a sense, putting an aspect of their professionalism on the line, in a way that teachers are rarely called upon to do. For people to take these risks, they need to feel safe within their learning environment. To a large extent, this depends on the trainer's ability to create that environment by unconditionally accepting all contributions (see, e.g. Rogers 1983), paying attention to physical aspects of the environment, as well as consciously seeking to promote trusting relationships between all members of the group.

Group forming

All groups go through recognisable stages. The first is group formation, which involves starting off relationships between all members of the group, including the leader. When we consider that in a course with nineteen participants and one leader, there are 190 potential relationships to be formed, it is clear that traditional beginning-of-course ice-breaking activities go little way to forming these one-to-one relationships. The leader will need to provide many further opportunities for their formation, through, for example, trust building activities and those which require self-disclosure, as well as ensuring the group mixes by paying attention to the pairing and grouping for activities (for some examples of random grouping activities, see 2.3). This formation stage also requires group goal-setting and the establishment of certain group norms.

Group maintaining

The next three phases of group life are described by Tuckman and Jensen (1977) as 'norming' or when a routine is established, 'storming' or when difficulties and tensions emerge, and 'performing' or when the group is finally working fully towards its objectives. These are more unpredictable than the other two phases ('forming' and 'mourning' or ending) from the point of view of when, if, how and how often they occur, and how they are managed. Earlier we mentioned vulnerability when we discussed the exposure of deep-seated beliefs necessary for constructivist learning. This vulnerability comes partly from a fear of loss of face through being judged and found wanting. When this happens, a normal defensive reaction is to attack, which can be one of the causes of storming. Another reason why storming may appear is precisely because people know each other well enough to speak up – people are past the initial polite stages of their relationship. However, in our experience, the storming phase seems also to be a manifestation of another kind of vulnerability, whether as a contributory factor or a major cause of the storming. Work on deeply held beliefs and attitudes can have a destabilising effect, especially when the learning involves significant change, the re-forming of constructs rather than simply their elaboration. As a result of the unpredictability of these phases, the leader's role is also less easily predictable: it could involve using conflict resolution skills, renegotiating the group goals or norms, but above all will certainly necessitate the modelling of sensitivity, unconditional regard, empathy and so on (Rogers 1983) – skills which are also essential for a mentor.

Group disbanding

The final phase of the life of any group, is the disbanding, 'mourning' or ending phase. It is an important phase from the point of view of the affective side of relationships, as well as ensuring that individuals have the resources to continue their own professional development without the support of the group. Both of these factors are particularly important on mentor courses, where relationships will have been especially strong because of the almost intimate nature of the work on professional beliefs, making the disbanding potentially painful. The ability for autonomous professional development is especially vital for mentor course participants not only for the sake of their own learning but also because this will form the model element of their mentoring. The trainer will therefore need to select activities in which participants have a chance to think over the course, in terms of both feelings and learning, and say goodbye personally (see *Conclusion*). In addition, they will need to ensure that participants have each other's addresses and phone numbers, and even possibly set up more formal networks.

Leader-participant relationships: the leader's role

In discussing group dynamics, we have been concentrating mainly on the participants' pedagogical need to build relationships in order to use other people's perspectives to help their own learning. In other words, the major reason for course participants to relate to others is so that they can learn. The course leader, on the other hand, has a principal role of helping others to learn, which similarly needs to be based on knowledge of each participant. Because the leader has a special role within the group, and will not be able to participate in many of the construct-revealing activities (see 1.5.1. *Making the implicit explicit*), they will need to find other ways of getting to know the participants in this sense. All written assignments, whether those in Chapter 10 or others, such as learning journals and so on, can provide valuable information, as can astute monitoring. However, this one-way information flow will not create the general trusting atmosphere necessary. The work on group dynamics above has addressed the development of trust between participants, but we have not yet discussed the issue of the group trusting the trainer. In order to develop two-way relationships with each participant, the trainer can participate on an equal basis in some relationship-building activities, as well as take every opportunity to talk to people, informally, such as chatting during the breaks or at parties, or formally through tutorials and interviews. In addition, the trainer can use certain processes such as the feedback dialogue (see Chapter 2, *Course procedures*) and activity round-up phases, as well as more formalised input sessions to reveal their own professional constructs to the whole group. How this is done, though, is crucial (see *The leader as 'expert'* above).

The leader as course designer

Partly because there is not, to our knowledge, such a thing as a coursebook for mentor courses, but mainly for all of the reasons of appropriate intervention discussed above, course leaders will also need to be course designers.

Each course we have taught has been different, at the very least because of the different individuals in each group, and because of our own learning on the previous course. When other contextual factors have also changed, including perhaps the time available, then the depth, breadth and focus of the learning experience we have been able to provide has also been different. Having said that, it is fair to say that we have developed a consistent approach to all mentor course design, and think of it in terms of 'horizontal strands and vertical phases', with activities and experiences designed to reach and link all levels of the developing Mentor Icebergs of participants (Figure 3).

We conceive of two broad categories for the strands which run the length of any course. These are process strands and skills development strands. From the perspective of a course leader's overall role as 'mentor of novice mentors', as it were, the process strands allow modelling of the support and educator roles and demonstrate what we have called training congruence. (See Figure 1 *Introduction* and 1.4.1 *Notions of reflection: modelling*.) Through the skill development strands, on the other hand, the participants are guided to work directly on their ability to fulfil their own support and educator roles.

There are two main process strands. The first concerns issues of group dynamics and individual affective issues, and allows us to fulfil our support role. The second allows us to fulfil our educator role through the selection of activities within skills strands which attempt to create an awareness-raising, articulation, challenge and re-articulation sequence of experiences for participants, as well as our own explicit revealing of those sequencing decisions. This is largely achieved through procedures described in Chapter 2.

There are also two broad skill development strands. The first is concerned with interpersonal skill development and is designed to help participants focus on their support role without which they are unlikely to be effective educators. The second is on observation and complex mentoring skill development and is designed to enable participants to achieve their educator role objectives effectively.

The phases roughly correspond to times when new strands are introduced and woven into the increasingly detailed picture, as well as to phases in group dynamics terms. Phase 1 starts, if you like, with the focus on the course leaders' support role for participants through particular attention to group dynamics and the forming of the group, in order to prepare a firm affective ground for learning (1.5.2 *Intermember relationships: the leader's role*). The awareness-raising processes which are a necessary foundation for the work of course leaders in their educator role, are also begun, as is work on the skill of observing. This is partly because observation as a skill needs considerable time to develop, and partly because it will meet most participants' expectations of relevant course content. Phase 2 adds considerations of the participants' future support role as mentors with the beginning of interpersonal skill development. The strands already begun also continue, although the amount of time devoted to them in isolation will diminish. Phase 3 sees more intensive work on the participants' educator role, through considering the impact of things a mentor says and does on a mentee's learning – the possible forms and impacts of their interventions. Again the previous strands are kept going and incorporated. Phase 4 extends and combines all these areas in complex whole mentoring skill practice. The final phase returns again to a focus on the participants themselves and their own future learning and support needs.

Below, as an example only, is one of the most elaborate designs we have ever made before a course began (Figure 4). It was designed for a course of 72

PHASE 1 (Three to four 3-hour sessions)

Group-forming activities; trust-building activities; explorations of beliefs about learning, teaching and mentoring; and raising awareness of the difficulties of objective observation. (Procedures and activities from Chapters 2, 3, 4 and 5.)
Between-sessions: Peer-observation + Professional learning cycle set at the end of this phase. (Chapters 8 and 10)

PHASE 2 (Ten 3-hour sessions)

Discrete mentoring skill practice; continuing work on interpersonal skills; observation practice; the development of language appropriate to different styles of mentoring intervention. (Chapters 4, 5 and 6)
Between-sessions: Peer-observation file due mid-phase. First development report due end of phase. Reading tasks. (Chapters 8, 9 and 10)

PHASE 3 (Seven 3-hour sessions)

Intensive practice of various forms of mentoring interventions; action-planning; observation practice; assessing teaching. (Chapters 5, 6 and 7)
Between-sessions: Professional learning cycle report due mid-phase 3. Second development report due end of phase. Reading tasks. (Chapters 8, 9 and 10)

PHASE 4 (Two 3-hour sessions)

The role of mentors in different phases of professional development; formats for staff development in schools. (Chapter 6)
Between-sessions: Reading tasks. (Chapter 9)

PHASE 5 (One 3-hour session)

Reviewing; planning for the future, and disbanding the group. (Chapter 10)
Between-sessions: Final development report due. (Chapter 10)

Figure 4 Sample course design

contact hours, 120 participant hours overall. We never do a more detailed course design than the example above, as the session feedback (Chapter 2, *Course procedures: The feedback dialogue*) will determine the precise sequencing of activities, timing of the introduction of strands, depth of exploration of particular aspects and so on. If we made more detailed decisions beforehand, we feel, we would be tempted to keep to them whatever was actually happening on the particular course. We would then be less responsive to the particular participants, as we would not be guided by them in our planning decisions. (See Chapter 2, *Course procedures: The feedback dialogue*.) Not only would the learning opportunities we offer be likely to be less effective, but we would fail to model the necessity of responding to the particular learner and the particular situation.

This chapter has been an attempt to share our constructs of the work of mentor course leaders. We have approached this through a description of the path our own thinking has taken. We hope it will help to show the rationale for the activities that follow – why we designed them and how they could be used. Mentor courses have undoubtedly been among the most challenging and rewarding experiences in our own professional development. We hope it will be the same for others.

2 Course procedures

Introduction

There are a number of consistent features of our sessions that reflect our training approach and help to give coherence to the course as a whole. Some of them are in a sense repeated activities, others have to do with the physical surroundings and atmosphere.

2.1 Reflection grids

This procedure is based on Bolitho and Wright's Reflection Grids (1993). It is a process of systematic review which we have found extremely helpful for bringing out course, session and activity objectives; promoting the sharing and development of constructs, as well as practising skills of articulation. In this process, time is allowed at the end of every activity for participants to think over the activity they have just experienced and make notes under various headings. The headings we often use on mentor courses are: 'name of activity', 'purpose', 'brief description', 'feelings during activity', 'implications for mentoring', 'implications for teaching'. At the end of the session, participants in small groups refer to their grids and share their perceptions on each activity. Finally there is a round-up discussion of each activity (drawing principally on the 'purpose', 'implications for mentoring' and 'implications for teaching' columns) where useful features are 'unpacked' under three major headings: 'For us as a group', 'For our work with student-teachers' and 'For our work with pupils'.

The example below (Figure 5) is the summary of such a round-up discussion for 3.2 *Blind adventure* (Chapter 3, *Lead-ins)*.

For us as a group	– trust-building, self-disclosure and working on relationships and the group dynamics of the course – making explicit existing constructs about the beginnings of professional learning – ability to empathise, remembering how it feels to be a beginning teacher
For our work with student teachers	– the importance of trust, and developing relationships – the need to find out existing constructs about learning and teaching

For our work with pupils	– trust-building and group dynamics – whole person involvement – use of imagination and visualisation – using students as resources – the language of instructions

Figure 5 Example of a reflection grid summary for 3.2 *Blind adventure*

As course leaders, this process is a source of learning for us both in the sense of seeing new possible purposes for activities and as a means of finding out more about where the participants on a particular course are in their development.

2.2 The feedback dialogue

One of the most important course procedures we use is the feedback dialogue. It not only models a process mentors will want to model for their mentees: that of seeking feedback from learners, but it provides both the course leaders and the participants with valuable insights into the group and its development.

At the beginning of a course, we initiate a brief discussion on what a teacher would find useful to know from their students after each lesson. It usually emerges that this is information on the content, process and atmosphere of the session, as well as an indication of how and what students feel they are learning. Five minutes before the end of each session, participants are given a small 10×10 cm piece of paper (to avoid giving the impression they need to write long and complicated summaries) on which they give us this feedback. (Examples of the kind of comments written are given in *Participant reaction* at the end of each activity presented in this book.) We then process the feedback, categorising the data and writing up extracts grouped under the categories we have assigned on an overhead transparency. These are presented and discussed during the first twenty minutes or so of the next session. Although we have called this stage of the process 'feedback on feedback' (Bodóczky and Malderez 1992), it does not involve any evaluation and it is not a one-way process: the initial interpretation, through selection and categorisation of the feedback slips, will be the leader's, but one of the main purposes of this follow-up is precisely to check on these interpretations. This is why we now prefer the term 'feedback dialogue' to describe the whole process.

We have used two alternative ways of conducting the second ('feedback on feedback') stage as courses progress. One is to give the feedback (once it has been read and 'processed ' by the leader) to a participant, or group of participants, to prepare and present on OHT at the next session. The other is to redistribute the slips at the beginning of the session, asking participants to ensure they do not receive their own feedback, and then in a seated circle, invite one participant to read out the slip they have. Others with slips containing a similar theme or comment are then invited to read theirs explaining the connection they see with the previous piece of feedback, until all the slips have been read and issues discussed. The advantages of these alternatives are that the categories (and implied interpretations) are decided by participants, and, not least, that they are labour-saving for the course leader! Amongst disadvantages are that the rationale for the leader's planning decisions may be less immediately transparent, and that individuals' handwriting may be familiar to others, and the consequent potential lack of anonymity affects the openness of what is written (though in a well-bonded, trusting group this need not be so). In addition, we have found participants need to have experienced the standard procedure often enough to understand the underlying rationale well for these alternative procedures to be effective.

There are many purposes for including the feedback dialogue discussion at the beginning of every session. The first is that it serves as a link, reminding the group of what happened during the last session and what they were thinking and feeling as a result, as well as setting up participants' expectations for the session to come. Gradually, the understanding of how their feedback has contributed to the selection of activities and processes leads to a genuine collaborative course design process. It also encourages everyone to work on the wording of valuable feedback. Seeing this collected feedback can be both reassuring and helpful to participants. Early in courses, many participants find the anonymity of written feedback enables them to reveal their worries more readily, and it is reassuring for them to find that others share them. On the other hand, seeing that sometimes others have different worries and needs may help to increase their tolerance of each other, as well as of activities and processes they personally find less useful. It will be a constant reminder of the different needs, styles, preferences and so on of the different people they work with. In addition, it is a helpful process because it is another example of using different perspectives to think over a shared experience. These will not only be different people's perspectives but they will also reflect the changes that have gone on in the individual participant's perspectives since the previous session, as a result of their own deliberations, conscious or otherwise – the automatic process of digestion that will have happened in the intervening period. The discussions will allow these comparisons to be made explicit and provide a new springboard for the next phase of the work on the course.

For the course leader, the process of the feedback dialogue is also very important. Reading the feedback slips has been a vital component of our session planning. Course leaders can check their intuitive impression of what the next step in the course should be, modifying it as they get a clearer picture of where people are in the development of their understandings. In addition, this feedback will often determine the selection of appropriate methodology for that particular group at any particular time. By categorising the feedback and writing it up, the course leader will be sharing their interpretations and professional constructs partly through the 'labels' they give the categories. They will also be revealing how they are using the feedback to plan the session. Because of this explicit self-disclosure, course leaders will be rendering themselves professionally vulnerable, in other words modelling what they are expecting from the participants. This can help cause a shift in the power relationship towards the participant (and see Chapter 1: *The leader as 'expert'*). If the leaders have written their own end-of-session notes and compared their subjective impression of the effectiveness of the session with the data in the feedback, it can prove an invaluable tool in fine-tuning their own perceptive ability. Sharing this with the participants, possibly on the overhead transparency, will be another type of self-exposure, as well as modelling a process for the management of autonomous professional development.

This regular session feedback is also invaluable for formative and summative evaluation purposes during and after courses. Reviewing the feedback from a whole course, or a number of courses, can often reveal interesting longitudinal patterns. (The comments about storming and destabilisation in Chapter 1: *Group maintaining* were developed as a result of considering several courses in this way.) The feedback dialogue has become such an invaluable part of our mentor sessions and courses that we believe we would be unable to achieve our objectives without it.

2.3 Random pairing and grouping activities

The main aim of pairing and grouping activities is to get participants to interact and therefore form, and deepen, relationships with as many members of the group as possible. They also serve the purpose of getting participants out of their seats and moving about, a useful change after a more sedentary activity.

Language teaching methodology contains many pairing and grouping activities that can be used on mentor courses either as they are or adapted. There is a kind of random grouping activity where the whole group is asked to line up according to some criterion (colour of hair, birthday, size of feet, number of hours slept, etc.) after which members are counted off in groups in the order in which they now stand, ready for the next activity. As well as non-specific, 'self-disclosing' criteria, such as those mentioned above, we have also used more 'mentor' ideas such as 'length of time in the teaching profession' or 'number of hours teaching practice during teacher training'. Another variation is to give each participant part of one long quotation on a key mentoring concept, as a linear jigsaw to be put together.

Small jigsaws which do not end up as line-ups but small groups, involve putting together word-sets based on, for example, styles of intervention, stages of development, elements of reflective cycles, etc., or short quotations relating to mentoring. For example, we gave each participant in a group of 18 a card, in order to form five small groups (see *Photocopiable resource 1* on page 153). Line one contains styles of intervention, line two stages of beginner teacher development, and lines three, four and five, different descriptions of the reflective cycle (Dennison and Kirk 1990, Freeman 1990 and our own).

The choice of word-sets or quotations can be used to recycle, review or preview topics and language of mentoring. In completing these jigsaws, without showing each other their cards, participants will not only mix but also consider the meanings of their word sets or quotations.

Finally, many of the lead-in activities (Chapter 3) which are melee or moving-pairs (stand up and mill about) in organisation and which do not have a natural end can be stopped by asking participants to freeze where they are, and groups can be formed according to where they happen to be standing.

2.4 Peripherals

As the physical surroundings in the training room are so important in creating the general atmosphere of the course, pre-prepared posters can have a valuable role. These are used not simply as decoration but also they can help create a special identity for the course through 'ownership' of the room. Later, the addition of participants' own posters will increase this feeling of ownership. Furthermore, the content of the posters, a selection of relevant, catchy and often metaphorical sayings or quotations related either to mentoring in general or to the objectives of the course or a particular session can serve the purpose of raising awareness or giving a different perspective on a particular issue – a kind of peripheral learning. Where possible, the message is reinforced by illustration to enhance the impact and for the sake of the visual learners. We do our own drawings, using thick coloured felt-pens, as it is a form of self-disclosure. In our case, because of our lack of artistic talent, it presents us with the opportunity to draw on the resources of the group, by asking for more able illustrators!

It might not be possible to leave the posters up from one session to the next, but changing the peripherals regularly not only means being able to select appropriately for each session, but also avoids the phenomenon of not 'seeing' what is always there. In addition, it enhances the observation skills as participants notice that posters are in a different place or that the leader has deliberately done something to the poster, such as turning it upside down, to highlight the tendency to see what you expect to see. Although selecting and putting up the posters takes extra time before the start of the session, participants not only appreciate the effort because *'it's like coming to a tea party'*, but also welcome the opportunity for having informal chats both with the leader and other early-comers.

Some of our posters contain the following:

– We were given two ears and one mouth, that we may listen more and speak less
– You can't teach anybody anything, you can only help them to learn
– You teach yourself
– Years wrinkle the skin, but lack of enthusiasm wrinkles the soul

2.5 Music

Using music can also influence the atmosphere of the course. It can facilitate work at the deeper feelings layer of the participants' Mentor Icebergs. It can set the mood, for instance, by energising the group on a dark day or enhancing concentration during silent individual work, and it can powerfully influence the imagination during visualisations. In addition, it is useful during pair and group work as it can act as a 'screen' both between groups and to cover the potential embarrassment of the first people to start talking. Finally, changing the volume of the music can act as a gentle signal for the beginning and end of activities.

The kind of music we tend to use is either classical, New Age or even jazz. We prefer using lesser-known pieces, as music that is too well-known to the group can be distracting. People stop concentrating on the work and even start singing, or groan when it is turned off in the middle of a movement or melody. Another problem with using music at all, which sometimes emerges from the feedback dialogue, concerns the difficulties that certain types of learner might experience. Pure 'auditory' learners will concentrate only on the music, while pure 'visual' learners may be irritated by the noise. As with most things on these courses it is a question of trial and error, and negotiation.

In this chapter we have discussed some of the procedures we use throughout our mentor courses. The following eight chapters will be devoted to the activities themselves.

3 Lead-ins

Introduction

Man 1: How do I get to Wetherby?
Man 2: Well, I wouldn't start from here, if I were you, mate!

You may not be in an ideal place to start a journey, but you can only start from where you are. Where you start from may not make a difference to whether you get there or not, but it will certainly affect the route you take, and therefore be one of the factors affecting both your enjoyment of the journey and the time you need for travelling. When the journey is a learning journey, both enjoyment and time are important. Enjoyment, in the sense of fun as well as the satisfaction of achievement, is important because it affects successful learning in both the short term and the long term. Time is important because there is rarely enough of it, and it will certainly need to be used efficiently.

The first steps on any journey are often the hardest. We have found the starting phases of any course to be crucial, as people are coming from different places to join the course's 'route to Wetherby'. Getting everybody going in the same direction is about beginning the learning process. One of the starting points will be guiding each participant to a realisation that there is a need to learn mentoring, which leads to a conscious process of thinking, observing, reading and talking about mentoring. On very short courses, generating the 'need to know' is even more crucial, as it may be *all* there is time for. In favourable situations, when participants are autonomous learners, in the sense of being experienced as reflective practitioners, generating this need may be sufficient for the learning eventually to occur.

In course terms, another major starting point will be beginning relationships and group processes (see Chapter 1: 1.5.2 *Intermember relationships: the leader's role*). This chapter, then, contains a collection of short lead-in activities developed for use on mentor courses. (Longer awareness-raising activities relating specifically to certain topics can be found in later chapters.) Some of them may be familiar, as they are adaptations of activities used in ELT or other training contexts. They are all designed to start the group process, a new session or a new mentoring topic. However, they all have multiple objectives, which depend as much on the implementation of the activity as on its design. Some of the activities were designed with an ice-breaking function as their major objective (e.g. 3.14 *Name hooks*). Other activities have a more prominent 'warmer' function (e.g. 3.13 *Musical mentoring*), where warmer is defined as an activity that brings the group together again, thereby supporting

Group dynamics:
    I-B = Ice-breaker/group building
    W = session warmer
    GP = group processes, maintaining intermember relationships

Awareness raising/generating the need to know:
    I   = interpersonal skills, intervening as a mentor
    O = observation
    M = mentoring, being a mentor

ACTIVITY	I-B	W	G P	I	O	M
3.1 Adverbial walking		X	X	X	X	
3.2 Blind adventure	X	X		X		
3.3 Blind visitor		X	X	X	X	
3.4 Compliments		X	X	X		
3.5 Going back to your mentor				X		X
3.6 Group's mime story		X	X	X	X	
3.7 Group poem			X	X		
3.8 Heads and tails				X		X
3.9 I am a person who . . .		X	X	X		
3.10 Mentor mix		X	X		X	X
3.11 Mentoring metaphors			X			X
3.12 Mirrors		X	X	X	X	X
3.13 Musical mentoring		X	X			X
3.14 Name hooks	X			X		
3.15 Prisoners		X		X	X	
3.16 Smelly socks group			X	X		X
3.17 The nature of help			X	X		X
3.18 There's a teddy on the table					X	X
3.19 Tick tock	X			X		
3.20 What have you done?		X			X	
3.21 What's the question?	X		X			

Figure 6 Uses of lead-in activities

group processes, as well as one which creates links between sessions. Some activities have a major objective of generating the need to know about a new topic or theme (e.g. 3.9 *I'm a person who . . .*).

The activities in this section appear alphabetically, as their multiple objectives make it difficult to group them in any other way. The table (Figure 6) above indicates the objectives for which we have used them.

Activities

3.1 Adverbial walking

Interpersonal skills are vital to the mentoring process. Part of the successful mastery of these has to do with accurate interpretation of others' body language. Body language is a large part of communication, and we all interpret others' body language from the perspective of our cultural and personal experience. We are generally accurate within our own culture, but even then we sometimes misread others' body language as these signals vary from person to person. In teaching, for example, a child staring out of the window could indicate that the child is bored or distracted, but it might also mean the child is processing some ideas. Equally a teacher or mentor's physical behaviour may send unintended messages. It is essential, therefore, that we also become aware of the messages we send, as well as check out assumptions about states manifested by certain bodily signals.

Aims:
– to raise awareness of similarities and differences in the physical manifestation of emotional states

Suggested position in course: During work on observation/ interpersonal skills

Materials: None

Timing: 15 minutes

Classroom organisation: Standing randomly spaced, with room to walk about

Procedure:
1. An adverb of emotion is elicited from the group, for example, 'nervously' or 'happily'. They then walk about the room in the manner of that word, for approximately 30 seconds to a minute.
2. At a given signal, everyone freezes. Participants are asked to comment on what they found themselves doing and what they noticed others doing (body movements, expressions, pace, noises, etc.).
3. Steps 1 and 2 are repeated several times with different adverbs each time.
4. A final discussion centres around implications for teaching/mentoring of similarities and differences of individual ways of expressing emotional states.

Comments:
This activity reveals that although one emotion may give rise to typical expressions (e.g. noise often accompanies happiness), a number of emotions may share the same outward effects (e.g. fear and boredom can both produce blank facial expressions) which clearly has implications for observation and the dangers of interpreting what is seen without further exploration.

Participant reaction:

'I was surprised to see how many different expressions people used when we had to act "nervously".'

'I'm going to use it in my own classroom to help my students not only remember adverbs, but to help them understand each other better.'

3.2 Blind adventure

Trust-building is vital on any course where participation and collaboration will be required. In mentor courses this is even more necessary as the work will be personally and professionally very revealing and therefore potentially face-threatening if not carried out in a supportive and trusting environment. Empathy for beginner teachers is a prerequisite in mentoring work. Here, empathy can be developed through participants recalling and sharing their own experiences through the powerful medium of metaphor.

Aims:
– to build trust
– to explore participants' own beginning teaching experiences

Suggested position in course: Early, but not before a certain amount of trust between leader(s) and group has been established

Materials: None

Timing: 15 minutes

Assumptions: There is some degree of trust between participants already

Classroom organisation: Pairs, standing, in a room with some space to move around (tables, chairs and other pairs become obstacles to negotiate during the adventure)

Procedure:
1. Pairs decide which partner is *A* and which is *B*.
2. *A*s become 'blind', i.e. they shut their eyes.
3. *B*s have three minutes to take their partners on an imaginary adventure. They tell their partners where they are taking them (the moon, the seaside, the forest, a special place, etc.), and begin to lead them, describing what is underfoot, ahead, etc. Somewhere in the adventure they encounter some danger which they safely overcome to reach their destination.
4. Roles are reversed and *A*s now lead 'blind' *B*s on a new adventure.
5. Pairs are now asked first to discuss the effectiveness of the guiding; and then to find metaphorical similarities between each adventure and the leader's experiences of beginning teaching (e.g. 'the lion was class 2c that nearly caused me to leave teaching altogether', etc.).
6. Whole-group feedback on interesting metaphors, and discussion of the role of the mentor/guide.

Comments:

This is an extremely powerful activity and one which we frequently refer back to during the course, when participants will even find new significance in their 'adventure'. Not surprisingly, perhaps, participants vary in whether they appreciate the gentle and protective type of guide, the encouraging, liberating but risky guide type, or the firm, directive but rather restraining type. The metaphors from the adventures for stages, events and circumstances in participants' early careers, on the other hand, have surprised us. This is partly because many metaphors seem to relate not simply to the classroom, but to the wider context, too: a mountain was 'my first year', a bear was a headmaster, a welcome cave was 'my friend's kitchen after work', and a rocky stream to cross was a staffroom!

Participant reaction:
'I really loved this activity. I was surprised to find I could associate the adventure with my career.'

Acknowledgement:
This is an adaptation of an 'adventure' variation of 'Blind Trust' which we learnt from Tom Hunter, College of St Mark and St John, Plymouth.

3.3 Blind visitor

Mentors need the skills of careful listening and visualising of events (in the classroom, staffroom, etc.) in order to be able to understand as fully as possible those situations in which they were not present. A mentor's work also involves understanding people, that is, empathising with them and checking out their understandings. This activity works on all of these skills as well as building interpersonal relationships in the group through individuals inviting their partner into their own world.

Aims:
– to raise awareness of the need to develop listening, visualising, empathising skills

Suggested position in course: Before work on e.g. 4.7 *Getting a clear picture*, at the beginning of work on mentor intervention skill development

Materials: Blank paper and pencil (1 per 'guest')

Timing: 30 minutes

Assumptions: Partners are not familiar with each other's schools

Classroom organisation: Seated pairs, *A*s and *B*s

Procedure:
The first part of this activity takes place in the imagination only – it is not acted out. Both partners may talk.
1. *A*s close their eyes, they are 'blind'. *B*s, who have invited *A*s to their school for a week, welcome them, guide them round – pointing out everything they might need to know (bathroom, staffroom, classrooms, where to get coffee, where things are kept, etc.).
2. After 5 minutes, *A*s open their eyes and attempt to draw the layout, etc. of *B*s' school.
3. Roles are reversed and the activity is repeated.

Variations: Guests can be invited to participants' homes, rather than schools, which has a more personal focus

Comments:
This activity invariably appeals to language teachers who see it as a useful exercise to practise giving directions as well as details, like furnishings and so on. It also helps them to see their familiar school in a different way, and they often find that they are 'noticing' things they hadn't thought about before.

Participant reaction:
'It showed me how important it is to give clear instructions. Sometimes I am not clear so students don't know what to do.'

Acknowledgement:
This is an adaptation of 'Blind Guest', in Baudains, R. and M. Baudains (1990). *Alternatives*. Harlow: Longman. Rod Bolitho and Tony Wright, College of St Mark and St John, Plymouth introduced us to the original activity.

3.4 Compliments

In Europe most people feel uncomfortable about receiving compliments or positive feedback. We all tend to see our own and others' weaknesses more readily. Yet it is important to recognise, accept and build on our strengths too. This activity encourages participants to think positively about the other participants and their role in the group, as well as helping them to avoid or overcome inappropriate modesty. Seeing their own strengths through another's eyes leads to deeper relationships within the group.

Aims:
– to raise awareness of the possible difficulty of giving and receiving positive feedback

Materials: None (soft background music)

Timing: 10 minutes

Assumptions: Participants know each other well enough to be able to give compliments which are more than external (clothes, etc.), and rather about personality, working relationships, etc.

Classroom organisation: Melee

Procedure:
1. Participants mingle, paying each other sincere compliments and accepting them without false modesty.
2. Whole class (or small group to whole class) discussion on ease or otherwise of accomplishing task.

Comments:
Because in many cultures people are uncomfortable about accepting compliments and tend to play them down and because of the importance of acknowledging strengths in a mentoring context, it is important to give sufficient time to the post-activity discussion (Step 2). The discussion sometimes

turns to the use and abuse of praise in the teaching (and mentoring) context. Praise, when it is sincere, can encourage further learning and support relationships. On the other hand, it can lose all meaning when it is routinely and insincerely meted out, as well as, more dangerously, encourage dependency on outsider judgement. This discussion, in turn, raises some of the fundamental issues of mentoring (Chapter 1: 1.4 *Learning mentoring* and Chapter 7, *Assessing teaching*).

Participant reaction:
'Positive thinking: the most wonderful experience was giving compliments. You would have been happy to see my mentees and students doing the same in an English lesson and discussing the importance of positive thinking in real life.'

Acknowledgement: There is a similar activity in Moskovitz, G. (1976). *Caring and Sharing in the Language Classroom*. Rowley, Mass.: Newbury House.

3.5 Going back to your mentor

Participants' beliefs, attitudes and feelings about their future role as a mentor will be built on previous experience. It is therefore very important that this experience and its influence on their present concepts is made explicit as it is the starting point of their own development as mentors. It is also important because their future work will involve helping mentees uncover *their* existing constructs of teachers and teaching in order to 'challenge' (see Chapter 1: 1.1 *Learning*).

Aims:
– to reveal and make explicit participants' own experiences of having a mentor

Suggested position in course: Early, but not before trust has been established

Suggested position in session: During or as a lead-in to work on the role of a mentor, observation or on the nature of help. It is a good idea to do this activity immediately before a break, so that participants have more time to release any emotions that may arise

Materials: Music (New Age, Meditation – *not* well-known or recognisable music as participants will make other associations)

Timing: 20 minutes

Assumptions: That somewhere in participants' previous teaching experience they have had a 'supervisor'. (In contexts where this is not so, participants could be asked to think of someone in any area of their life who has acted as a mentor/helper/guide.)

Classroom organisation: Participants sitting (or lying) as comfortably as context permits, followed by self-selected pairs

Procedure:
(Before visualisations, which are potentially very emotionally powerful, we like to remind participants that they are always free to stop taking part in an activity should they wish to.)

1. As the music plays softly, participants are led through an appropriate relaxation exercise. A simple one involves asking participants to tighten every muscle they can – close eyes, screw up face, tighten arms, back, stomach and legs – for a minute, then let go. With eyes still closed, participants are asked to breathe deeply, in and out.

2. The course leader, in warm soft tones, then takes participants back to their time with their own mentor, drawing on all the senses (seeing, hearing, feeling, smelling) to recreate the scene, pausing between each suggestion to allow participants time to visualise. The following is an example: 'You are with your mentor. . . Look around and see the familiar objects . . . Listen, what can you hear? . . . Experience the familiar smells . . . Are you sitting or standing? . . . Where is your mentor in relation to you? . . . What are you feeling? . . . Look at your mentor's face . . . Are they smiling, serious? . . . Look at their eyes . . . what expression can you see? . . . How does this make you feel? . . . You are talking, what are you talking about? . . . Now speed up the film until you reach the end of the conversation . . . You are saying good-bye to your mentor. . . What can you hear? . . . How are you moving? . . . Where are you going now? . . . How are you feeling? . . . Hold that feeling with you as you let the scene fade . . . And come back into this room in your own time . . . When you are ready open your eyes . . . And now turn to your partner and share your experience.'

3. Following the discussion with their partner, participants are offered the opportunity of sharing with the group anything they would like to.

Variations: Visualisations can be used to recall various experiences such as those of beginning teaching, of previous lessons, etc.

Comments:

We have both experienced several occasions when the use of visualisations has provoked tears. We have found that, far from being the disaster it might seem when this happens, participants, if left to 'recover' quietly, will, more often than not, find the experience valuable, if not cathartic. Anyone who has not tried visualisation need not be put off by this as no one has ever held it against us and it seems to be an invaluable way of getting at existing constructs, as feedback has shown.

Participant reaction:

'Seeing my reaction, you'd think I'd had a terrible mentor, but it wasn't the case, I just had very mixed feelings towards her. The activity made me very nervous. It was only later when you asked me why I'd gone on with activity if I didn't like it that I realised I'm too obedient, I do what I'm told even if I don't really agree.'

'I loved the visualisation of my mentor. Now I know more about mentoring, I could see how skilful he was!'

'I didn't like re-visiting my mentor, but at least I know what kind of mentor I don't want to be.'

3.6 Group mime story

Any whole group task will help to give the group an identity and cohesion, especially when it is successfully completed. In this activity participants need to observe non-verbal behaviour, interpret it as best they can, and use that interpretation as a coherent part of the 'story'. This raises the awareness of the importance of both giving clear, unambiguous non-verbal signals, and accepting that these might be interpreted in a way that was not intended. It thus draws attention to the need to check assumptions when interpreting observable data, as well as to accept and respect different perceptions.

Aims:
- to enhance or maintain group cohesion
- to develop observation skills
- to focus on non-verbal communication
- to focus on perception gaps

Materials: None

Timing: Depending on the size of the group, 10–15 minutes

Classroom organisation: Standing circle

Procedure:
1. Leader (or previously primed group member) without any verbal instructions at all, mimes picking up 'something' from the floor. They endeavour to show what 'it' is by the way they hold it, their facial expression, what they do with it, etc. They then 'pass it on' to the person on their right, who having decided what 'it' is, reacts in some way before passing 'it' on. The leader may need to mime the instruction to pass 'it' on.
2. 'It' is passed round the circle having various adventures with each participant until either there is an obvious end to 'its' story (it blows up, flies away, etc.) or it is returned to the leader who ends the story.
3. Whole group discussion on the individual's perceptions of the story, the accuracy of body language, etc.
4. The whole activity is repeated, with someone else starting it. If the first story finished before all participants had had the chance to receive 'it', the next person will begin the new story.

Variations: Could be done seated, though this allows for less movement

Comments:
This works best with a group with some especially creative members, otherwise the mimes may become repetitive, and the story boring. Participants, as language teachers, often notice how, as a group, we adhere to unspoken rules of story structure. The story starts with the introduction of 'it', 'it' undergoes various adventures until the story ends. We have silently obeyed the rules of narrative discourse structure, and yet many of us will have created a different story. When the discussion follows this line, connections are often made between the interactive, co-constructed nature of stories, our own 'meaning-making' of 'it' and its adventures, and the heavy input we are likely to bring, as mentors, to the 'stories' we hear of our student-teacher's teaching.

Participant reaction:

'At first I was afraid to take the "animal" but then I decided it was furry so then it was all right'.

'I loved the warmer, I really felt we were a group as we tried to "take over" the story from each other. Everyone has something else to add.'

3.7 Group poem

The importance of investigating underlying beliefs, feelings and attitudes about teaching has been discussed at length in Chapter 1. This is an easy, non-threatening way of beginning to examine some of them. Like the preceding activity, this can also generate a feeling of group cohesion through the successful completion of a whole-group task.

Aims:
– to enhance group cohesion (successful completion of whole-group task)
– to uncover group feelings about teaching

Suggested position in session: possibly before work on mentoring metaphors

Materials: black- or white-board

Timing: 30 minutes

Classroom organisation: Whole group, seated

Procedure:
1. Group brainstorms adjectives they associate with teaching. Leader writes these on the board.
2. Individuals choose the four adjectives which best describe teaching for them, and write these down.
3. Leader points to each of the adjectives on the board in turn, and finds out (show of hands) how many people have chosen each one. The four 'winners' are kept, and the others rubbed off.
4. Participants are now asked to forget about teaching. The leader points to the first of the four chosen adjectives and elicits new associations by asking: 'What else for you is (adjective 1 – for example, "wonderful")?' These need to be more than one word, e.g. someone offers 'a smile', the leader will ask the group 'Whose smile? When?' and so on, to arrive at a more detailed idea, like 'a child's smile at Christmas'. Three or four phrases for each adjective are elicited and written on the board, such as, in the same example, 'a phone-call from a long-lost friend', 'frosted spider-webs on sunny winter mornings', or 'floating in warm seas'. Again, the participants vote (without writing it down this time) for the one they like best for each adjective, and the 'losers' are rubbed off.
5. Leader then reveals that the group has created a poem about teaching, and 'reads':
    'Teaching is as (adjective 1) as (phrase chosen)
    Teaching is as (adjective 2) as (phrase chosen)

Teaching is as (adjective 3) as (phrase chosen)
Teaching is as (adjective 4) as (phrase chosen)'

Variations: Another theme could be chosen, by the leaders or the group

Comments:

The leader may decide to present the similes in whatever order seems most 'poetic'. We usually put the poem up on the wall, or give copies to all the participants. Sometimes the words become catchphrases for the group, which also increases their sense of group identity. The following is an example that one group produced:

Teaching is as exciting as a date with a special person
Teaching is as challenging as learning to live with someone
Teaching is as rewarding as seeing your garden flower
Teaching is as hard work as carrying sacks of potatoes.

Participant reaction:

'What poets we are!'
'It's amazing how we created such a lovely poem.'

Acknowledgement:

We first learnt a version of this whole-group poem from Carolyn Walker, University of Exeter.

3.8 Heads and tails

Every strength has within it the potential for weakness, and likewise every weakness has within it the potential for strength. Knowing this, for ourselves and others, is invaluable in our work as teachers and mentors.

Aims:
– to explore 'the other side' of our strengths and weaknesses as teachers
– to work towards the kind of acceptance which allows growth towards 'becoming the best teacher/mentor *we* can be'

Suggested position in course: Early in work on interventions

Materials: One coin per group, poster paper and pens

Timing: 30 minutes

Assumptions: Trust has been built between group members

Classroom organisation: Self-selected groups of 4 to 5

Procedure:

1. The group decides on order of 'play', and elects a note-taker.
2. First player tosses the coin. Heads = 'strengths', Tails = 'weaknesses'. According to how the coin lands, the player first tells the group one of their professional strengths or weaknesses, and then describes 'the other side of the coin'. The note-taker records these ideas. For example,
   Strength: 'I'm good at performing, miming etc.'
   Other side: 'There's a danger of wanting to be centre stage all the time'

Weakness: 'I'm very disorganised and messy'
Other side: 'It allows for creativity, lack of pigeon-holing'

3. This continues round the group (twice or three times, as time permits), so that a group list of professional strengths and weaknesses and their 'other sides' is built up.
4. Each group presents these on a poster.
5. After viewing all the posters, participants comment on implications.

Variations: This can be done in pairs as a quicker activity, without making a poster, but possibly with a follow-up round when each pair shares with the whole group one or two surprising findings

Comments:

Participants enjoy this activity as it challenges some of the accepted norms, and puts some of what they see as their weaknesses in a better light.

Participant reaction:

'It made me realise that we can turn so-called negative things into something positive.'

'I was surprised to discover that being untidy has a positive side! I'd still like to be tidier, but I think I'll feel less guilty about being untidy now.'

3.9 'I'm a person who . . .'

Self-disclosure is a fundamental part of forming better relationships, and this activity gives participants the opportunity to share things about themselves without revealing anything they would rather not. The fact that the listener has to recall what was said develops active listening skills. In ELT terms, this activity is a good example of a student-generated, meaningful drill (relative clause, time adverbials, present perfect, simple present, etc.).

Aims:
– to promote active listening
– to get to know each other better (self-disclosure, intermember relationships)
– to practise synthesising, summarising

Suggested position in course: Early on in counselling/interpersonal skills work

Materials: None

Timing: 15 minutes

Classroom organisation: Seated pairs, *A* and *B*

Procedure:

1. In each pair, *A* has exactly one minute to talk about themselves, beginning each sentence with the words 'I'm a person who . . .', *B* listens carefully.
2. *B* has exactly 30 seconds to repeat what *A* has said, beginning with 'You're a person who . . .', and listing what they remember, but without repeating 'You're a person who . . .' each time.
3. Pairs discuss the experience: how far *A* felt understood, both while talking

and when hearing *B*'s summary and how *B* was able to concentrate, listen and recall.

4. *As* and *Bs* swap roles and repeat Steps 1–3 above.
5. General whole-group discussion of experience.

Variations: Time could be extended (but see comment)

Comments:
As can in fact find it surprisingly difficult to keep talking for a full minute. This may be because in many cultures talking about self for any length of time is unacceptable. Furthermore, because there is a freedom to choose what to divulge, a certain amount of censoring goes on which takes time. This very freedom, however makes it a fairly 'safe' activity. Some participants, on the other hand, feel the challenge is more in being able to listen with concentration and full attention – even for a minute!

Participant reaction:
'I'm a person who enjoyed the game "I'm a person who . . .".'
'I discovered I'm more of a talker than a listener.'

Acknowledgements: We first learnt this activity in co-counselling training.

3.10 Mentor mix

Working towards specific goals is an important part of the work of a mentor and mentee, but how these goals are reached, the strategies used, will depend to a certain degree on the mentee's personality. This activity raises these issues in an amusing and energetic way.

Aims:
– to reinforce information about the course components
– to practise observation while also involved in the activity
– to raise awareness of strategies for achieving goals
– to raise awareness of the need to know the goals

Suggested position in course: Near the beginning, but only after some group trust has been built

Suggested position in session: Before a whole-group goal setting discussion (see *Variations* below)

Materials: None

Timing: 15 minutes

Classroom organisation: Seated circle with no spare chairs and one person (initially course leader) standing in the centre

Procedure:
1. Elicitation of 4 to 6 course components (e.g. 'active listening', 'observation', 'post-lesson discussions', 'action-planning', etc.), depending on the size of the group.
2. The chosen course component names are given out round the group, so that

several participants, sitting in different parts of the circle, have the same component name.

3. The course leader calls out the names of one, two or three components and those participants must move to another chair. They may not sit down on the same chair (or on the one on either side of it – if it is a group of more than 12). The course leader also tries to find a chair.

4. The one person left without a chair, then calls out either one, two or three component names, as before, or calls out 'Mentor mix'. If 'Mentor mix' is called, everybody (including the caller) must find a new chair. The aim of the game is, always, to find a chair.

5. The game continues as above until the course leader asks the participants to chose someone to observe closely, without saying who they are. (See also *Variations*.) Participants observe, if they can, *how* that person gets what they want, that is, a chair.

6. The game continues until the course leader decides there has been enough opportunity to observe strategies.

7. Participants share what they have observed, checking assumptions if there is enough trust in the group to name who was being observed, and reveal their own strategies.

8. Conclusions are drawn about e.g. the need to know where you are going and to put in energy to get there, being careful, nonetheless, of others pursuing their goals.

Variations: In step 5 participants can identify a partner for mutual observation. Then in step 7 pairs first discuss what they observed with each other, check out assumptions, etc. before contributing to the whole-group discussion.

In this form the activity is also a useful introduction (raising awareness of the need for explicit goals) to a pyramid discussion leading to the development of explicit group goals. Participants can be asked individually to complete the stem 'By the end of the course, I . . . ' Then in small groups asked to share their goals and agree on, say, four per group. These are then collected, discussed and refined in the whole group. A poster of the goals can be made and subsequent activities and sessions related to them. At the end of the course, these can be referred to in the final feedback.

We have used this game in many other teacher preparation courses renamed 'Staffroom', 'Co-co' (communicative competence), etc.

Comments:

This is a particularly useful activity for times when the energy level of the group is flagging. Strategies for reaching seats vary considerably. There are participants who rush madly to an empty seat, often on the opposite side of the circle, and others who carefully observe the emptying seats and then calmly slip into the nearest one. Some people always manage to find an empty seat, while others repeatedly find themselves left in the centre. This also calls for discussion.

Participant reaction:

'I didn't like the competitive nature of this activity, so I kept getting left without a seat. I'm obviously not "pushy" enough!'

'I enjoyed having to work out the best way to find a seat. I discovered I very often didn't have to run or push, if I kept calm.'

Acknowledgement: We learnt this activity from Joan Agosta in a South West of England Language Teachers' Association (SWELTA) workshop in the '80s under the name 'Fruit Salad'.

3.11 Mentoring metaphors

The power of metaphor is very strong. In this activity it seems to assist participants in articulating their beliefs about mentoring as they try to explain their metaphors. If the activity is done near the beginning of the course, and then again at the end, it provides very clear evidence of the progress that each participant has made in their understanding of the mentor's role. It also serves to illustrate the importance of knowing where a student-teacher is at the beginning of the school experience.

Aims:
– to discover and make explicit participants' concepts about the nature of mentoring
– to share differing perceptions

Suggested position in course: Early and at the end

Materials: OHP, flip chart, or poster paper and pens

Timing: 15–20 minutes

Classroom organisation: Individual, whole group

Procedure:
1. Participants are asked to think of a metaphor for their concept of mentoring.
2. Participants in turn tell the group what their metaphor is and why they have chosen it. A volunteer participant with good drawing skills illustrates each one on the OHP acetate, flipchart or poster.
3. The other participants can comment and ask questions, but not evaluate others' metaphors.
4. The drawings are kept until the end of the course, when the activity is repeated and the results compared.

Variations: The activity could be repeated occasionally at later in-service mentoring meetings

Comments:
We have had a wonderful range of metaphors from the perennial 'gardener', to 'springboard at the deep end of a swimming pool', to the more obscure 'hook for a bucket in a well'!

Participant reaction:
Beginning of course: 'I loved the metaphors – they really got me thinking.'
'It was fascinating how many different metaphors our group had. I don't understand them all, but I look forward to finding out more about them.'

End of course: 'My original metaphor was based on my experience of being mentored. That's why I changed mine completely. It showed how much our own experience influenced our first pictures.'

'My gardener metaphor was too authoritarian. It prescribes and limits the plant's options, choices and rights. And worst of all, the plant can never be a gardener. Thank you for focusing my attention on that.'

Acknowledgements: We first learnt the use of metaphors in training from Rod Bolitho, College of St Mark and St John, Plymouth.

3.12 Mirrors

We have talked extensively about the role of mirroring in Chapter 1 (e.g. 1.4.1 *Notions of reflection*; 1.5.2 *The role of the course leader: the importance of modelling and congruence*). This activity exemplifies the importance of the mentor as 'reflector of action', helping learners to 'see themselves' and raises issues concerning the place of copying – its uses and limitations for learning teaching.

Aims:
- to develop concentration and observation skills
- to work on non-verbal communication
- to develop empathy in order
- to anticipate another's thinking and action
- to initiate work on meanings of mentoring

Suggested position in course: As an introduction to work on styles of intervention

Materials: None

Timing: 10 minutes

Assumptions: A certain level of trust has been established in the group

Classroom organisation: Standing pairs, possibly of similar heights, facing each other

Procedure:
1. Partners decide who is *A* and who is *B*.
2. *A*s begin to move, gesticulating as if looking in a mirror. *B*s attempt to follow as if they were the reflection in a mirror. They try to follow so closely that an observer could not tell who was the 'person' and who the 'mirror'.
3. Roles are reversed.
4. Partners discuss how they felt, their perceived success and the relevance to mentoring (e.g. empathy of thought and feeling versus the dangers of pure, thought-less copying).
5. Pairs report back to the whole group interesting outcomes of their discussion.

Comments:
Having similar heights in partners has the advantage of making the actual

mirroring activity more realistic and achievable. Ensuring similarities in partnerships, in a mentor course context, might give rise to discussions on issues of compatibility between mentor and learner. We sometimes also discuss the Neurolinguistic Programming (NLP) use of subtly mirroring the person you are talking to. One problem we had is mentioned below.

Participant reaction:
'The mirroring was very embarrassing because we were opposite sexes, and I felt as if I was making eyes at him. He also felt uneasy.'
'As we got used to it, we began to make only tiny moves, which was very challenging. We had to look very carefully!'

3.13 Musical mentoring

Encouraging participants to make their constructs explicit is a fundamental aim of a mentor course. Through the affective use of music and movement, as well as small, changing groups of people, participants often find it easier to expand on their feelings, beliefs and attitudes about mentoring. Although it is by no means meant to be a test, the activity will reveal a great deal about the group's and the individual's stage of development.

Aims:
– to share understandings of the many aspects and perceptions of mentoring

Suggested position in course: Towards the end

Materials: Lively music; a prepared set of sentence stems such as:
Mentoring is . . .
Mentoring involves . . .
I think I'll enjoy mentoring because . . .
Without mentoring, student-teachers . . .
I define mentoring as . . .
Mentors are . . .
Mentoring will help me . . .
This course has taught me that mentoring . . .

Timing: 15 minutes

Classroom organisation: Melee

Procedure:
1. When the music starts, participants move about the room. When it stops, they get into groups of three or four with the people nearest them, and all complete the sentence stem given.
2. The above is repeated using a different sentence stem. Participants form different groups each time and must not use the same idea twice.
3. Whole group. Participants have the chance to question or react to things they've heard.

Variations: Other appropriate sentence stems can be used, about elements of mentoring (e.g. observation), or early on, to bring out reasons for attending the course (e.g. I'm here because . . . , I feel . . .) etc.

Comments:
Repeating this activity at different times on the course can help participants to explore their changing constructs, which can be challenging whatever the degree of change.

Participant reaction:
'I got a chance to talk to people I haven't worked with for a while, and it made me think.'

3.14 Name hooks

The use of 'pegs' as a memory aid is well known. This activity uses both sides of the brain (drawing: right side; and analysis: left side) to help participants learn each other's names, by linking a person's name to something that will remind you of it when you next see that person. (For example, John has grey hair: we are reminded of Long John Silver – silver hair – in Treasure Island. We put that thought away carefully for next time we meet John.) It involves self-disclosure (through the choice of hook, and the proficiency of drawing!) as well as the bridging of perception gaps as participants try to guess each other's names from the drawings, beginning the vital process of building trust within the group.

Aims:
– to facilitate the learning of people's names

Suggested position in course: Probably first session, but see *Variations*

Materials: Sticky labels, post-its or paper and pins (1 per person), coloured pens

Timing: 20 minutes, depending on group size

Assumptions: Most participants do not know each other

Classroom organisation: Individual, then melee

Procedure:
1. Course leader elicits examples of memory hooks.
2. Each participant receives a piece of paper and pens.
3. Each participant draws an illustration of their name. It is important that no one discloses their name at this stage.
Our names have looked like this (see Figure 7 opposite):
4. Participants attach their drawings to themselves, and move around the room trying to work out each other's names from the drawings. (Participants keep their name drawings, and wear them at subsequent sessions, until names are known.)

Variations: For smaller groups, and/or when the group knows each other, but you don't know them, participants can give a word metaphor – a mental picture, instead of drawing. (For example, for us it might be 'a lion sitting by a car' and 'an angel'.)

Figure 7 Our name hooks

Comments:

This activity often causes great hilarity as the perception gaps between understanders and illustrators are bridged. Some people are embarrassed as they feel they can't draw, however we find our own simplistic efforts (see above) shown first help to reduce any tension. If you feel uncomfortable because of this, see *Variations*.

Participant reaction:

'I'm not very good at drawing, but the others seemed to be able to guess my name!'

'My name is too difficult – I ended up with pictures illustrating syllables of my name.'

'I loved these hooks – I'm a visual person and I know they will help me remember who people are.'

3.15 Prisoners

We mentioned the importance of congruence in training methodology in Chapter 1 (1.5.2 *The role of the course leader: the importance of modelling and congruence*). Here we focus on congruence in communication, the sense of ensuring that our bodies and our words are sending the same message. Although it is possible to adopt appropriate facial expressions and other accompanying body language consciously for a particular effect, it is often the eyes which reveal a lack of congruence. If body language sends the strongest messages in face to face communication, then it is the eyes, 'the windows of the soul', that betray the most. Raising awareness of the importance of the messages we often involuntarily send with our body language, and how these are interpreted or misinterpreted are important elements of mentor courses.

Aims:
– to work on rapport-building
– to focus on eye-contact

Suggested position in course: During work on counselling skills

Materials: None

Timing: 15 minutes

Classroom organisation: Standing circle (the dungeon); participants stand at arms-length distance from each other, with arms at their sides

Procedure:
1. One volunteer ('the prisoner') leaves the room.
2. The group decides where the 'gate' in the 'dungeon' should be, that is between which two participants, the 'gateposts'. The remaining participants form the 'walls'.
3. The 'prisoner' is called into the middle of the circle and attempts to find the way out of the 'dungeon' through eye-contact only – no sound or other gestures. The two 'gateposts' try to call the prisoner towards them. 'Walls' repel. If the 'prisoner' tries to go out through the 'wall', participants raise their arms to prevent escape. If the 'prisoner' finds the 'gate', he or she walks freely through.
4. Brief discussion of experience – who was easy to read, who not, why; how difficult it was to communicate through eye-contact only, to separate eye-contact from other body language, etc.
5. The game is repeated with a new 'prisoner' and new 'gateposts'.

Variations: A recommended variation of this which can be used as an introductory activity to *Prisoners* is when pairs take turns calling and repelling their partners through eye-contact. We like to start off in two lines, one line of As and one of Bs. In the first practice, the A line will be stationary as the As attempt to attract and send back their partners at will. They then swap roles and the B line will be static. This preliminary activity helps to relieve the tension and raise awareness of the difficulty and challenge of working only with eye-contact and no grimaces, etc. for communication.

Comments:
We have sometimes been challenged that this is an unnatural activity as meaningful eye-contact is accompanied with appropriate facial expression at least. However, it is an activity which is fun to do, and encourages group cohesion, and such discussions actually help achieve the aims of the activity.

Participant reaction:
'I liked the "Prisoner" game. I'll try it with my students, I think it will help them to be nicer to each other.'
'It's very difficult not to use any other gestures or expressions. At first I didn't think it was possible.'

3.16 Smelly socks group

Labelling people is a dangerous game. Labelling yourselves as something unpleasant, and justifying it, has the power to make people stop short and reconsider their prejudices. The question of judgement is one that will come up over and over again in mentor courses. It is essential therefore that participants accept differences of perception and are aware of the importance of context in value judgements.

Aims:
– to promote group cohesion
– to raise awareness of the positive aspects of any situation
– to raise awareness of the need to seek for contextual explanations

Suggested position in course: During initial work on observation

Materials: None

Timing: 10 minutes

Assumptions: Participants are comfortable with each other

Classroom organisation: Small groups (6–8), seated

Procedure:
1. Participants agree on what would socially be an unacceptable trait they have in common, e.g. 'We've all got smelly socks'. (This, obviously, may not necessarily be true.)
2. They give themselves this as a group name: 'The smelly socks group'.
3. They decide together on all the reasons why having this trait is in fact a useful, 'good' thing. For example, 'Our guard dogs need to know where we are. We are a very self-sufficient group, we don't need outsiders, and we want to keep them away.' etc.
4. Each small group proudly reports to the whole group their name, and the reasons why their 'trait in common' is such a useful thing.

Variation: At Step 4 each group in turn reports only their name – with pride. Other participants are then first asked to guess the reasons each group has for being proud of their anti-social trait.

Comments:

We have had some fairly horrible examples of 'unacceptable social traits', but the fun of exaggeration, and subsequent bonding, make it a powerful activity. It has often led to fruitful discussions on the relativity of judgements.

Participant reaction:

'This was great fun – we don't usually have the chance to be outrageous.'

'It made me think: everything is so relative, isn't it?'

'I was so tired I couldn't come up with any disgusting ideas, but I swear there are so many of them in me.'

Acknowledgement: This is a variation of an activity on making group names (Smelly Foot Tribe) from Hadfield, J. (1992). *Classroom Dynamics*. Oxford: Oxford University Press.

3.17 The nature of help

The concept of help has been discussed in some depth in Chapter 1 (1.4.2 *Helpful relationships*). All of us are very willing to give help to others, yet most of us have experienced times when the help we ourselves have been offered did not match what we needed, wanted or expected. Indeed there may have been times when we have even resented being offered help at all.

Aims:

– to explore the nature of help

Suggested position in course: Before work on interventions

Materials: Small slips of paper, poster paper and pens

Timing: 45 minutes

Classroom organisation: An even number of small groups of 4–6 people

Procedure:

1. Each group is given a pile of slips of paper. Working individually to begin with, half of the small groups complete the sentence beginning 'Giving help is . . .', the remaining groups complete the stem 'Receiving help is . . .' Participants work silently, writing as many different endings as possible, each on a new slip of paper, for a timed two minutes.
2. Individuals share and compare their endings in their small groups, categorising them in any way they wish.
3. The small groups' task is to create a free verse poem with the title 'Giving help is . . .' or 'Receiving help is . . .', by putting their sentences in a suitable order. Although no ideas may be left out, exact duplicates can be, and some rewording may be allowed for the sake of the coherence or cohesion of the poem.
4. Poems are written up, possibly illustrated, and displayed in the form of posters.
5. Participants walk round and read the poems.
6. Comments are invited in a whole-group format.

7. Possible follow-up: participants are asked to keep a journal for a week on the help they have given or received, and their reflections on these instances.

Variations: The whole group is divided into *A*s, and *B*s. Each half works on one of the two different stems. Then small groups are formed with, say two *A*s and two *B*s, to create a composite poem on 'Giving and receiving help'. Another variation would be to work on any other topic relevant to mentoring.

Comments:

We have found that some groups are reluctant to keep to the format whereby each sentence of the poem begins with the same stem. Although this need not matter, it does seem to make the poem less powerful, and provide fewer ideas.

Here are two examples:

> **Receiving help**
> Receiving help is a way of creating nice feelings,
> Receiving help is a good feeling if it is given with feeling and respect,
> Receiving help is at times an act of patience and respect,
> Receiving help is a challenge, but it isn't always a pleasant thing.
> Receiving help is difficult sometimes and isn't always helpful,
> Receiving help is understanding and maybe not agreeing,
> Receiving help is not to be ashamed of,
> Receiving help is a compromise every now and then . . .
> Receiving help is a way of cooperation.

> **Giving help**
> Giving help is care,
> Giving help is humility,
> Giving help is good for you,
>   and it is responsibility.
> Giving help is never judging,
> Giving help is not rejecting right away,
> Giving help is not always welcome,
>   and it doesn't mean forcing our way.

Participant reaction:

'It is interesting that we all had the same ideas.'
'It took a bit too long, we should have been in smaller groups. But it's a nice activity.'

3.18   There's a teddy on the table

Mentors need to have keen eyes, and to able to see 'newly' each time. It is sometimes quite difficult to notice new behaviour if it is entirely appropriate to the situation and context, or connected to something so familiar that we have ceased to pay attention to it.

Aims:

– to raise awareness of the fact that we often overlook new things if they are appropriate, or in familiar no longer closely observed contexts

Suggested position in course: During work on observation

Materials: A variety of small objects which are not normally in the room, put in odd places before any of the participants arrive

Timing: 5 minutes

Classroom organisation: Individual/whole group

Procedure:

1. Somewhere towards the end of a session, participants are told that there are 10–15 'strange' objects in the room. Without looking further, they are asked to write down as many as they have noticed.
2. Lists are compared in small groups
3. Participants get up and look for the objects missing from their lists.
4. Discussion leading to such things as it is more difficult to notice new, but appropriate things, etc.

Comments:

We have used a variety of different objects, depending a little on the session room itself. It is important for them not to be too obvious, and that some should be wholly appropriate – but new – while others are inappropriate, but in taken-for-granted areas likely to be no longer really seen. Safety pins in curtains, a well known visual turned upside down, a flower stuck in the top of a picture, the leader's T-shirt inside out are some of the things we have used.

Participant reaction:

'I was surprised how many things I didn't notice, even when you told us to look for them!'

'Once I noticed the pen stuck on the curtain, I began to look for other things, as I suspected you were playing a game with us, though I didn't notice them immediately.'

3.19 Tick tock

Introducing oneself can often be a little embarrassing, especially in cultures where it is not customary. By finding out about their neighbours, participants begin to break the ice and to form the relationships so essential for the work of the group. The use of a ball and changing places also helps the more kinaesthetic participants to memorise the names.

Aims:

– to help form the group, through learning group names
– self-disclosure
– movement (breaking 'territoriality')
– having fun

Suggested position in course: In first or second session

Materials: Soft, largish ball or toy

Timing: 10 minutes

Classroom organisation: Circle, seated or standing, course leader in the middle

Procedure:

1. Group members ask their immediate neighbours their names and for a piece of personal information they would like to share with the group.
2. The course leader throws the ball to a participant and says either 'tick' or 'tock'.
3. If the course leader has said 'tick', the participant introduces the person on their right, and adds the personal information. If the leader has said 'tock', the participant introduces the person on their left adding the personal information.
4. The participant returns the ball to the course leader, who throws it to someone else, saying 'tick' or 'tock' and the above procedure (Steps 2 and 3) is repeated.
5. This continues until the course leader throws the ball saying 'Tick-tock'. Now everyone must change places so that they have new neighbours. The course leader joins the circle, and the person who caught the ball becomes the thrower.
6. After some hurried consultation with new neighbours, if necessary, the game continues.

Variations: Different or specific pieces of information can be elicited, depending on the participants, session objectives or the nature of the course. For example, the aspect of teaching that interests them the most; a personal goal for that day's session; an interesting classroom observation made in the last week.

The activity can be used later in courses, without the names and introducing phase, as a reporting/feedback format.

Comments:

We learnt the hard way to be careful about not requiring participants to disclose things that are *too* personal too early in the group life. At the beginning of one course, we asked the participants to say what they valued most in life. Most participants said things like 'friendship', 'family life', 'love', 'tolerance', etc., but one said 'koala bears'. Clearly this participant did not feel safe enough to reveal anything too personal. This needn't have caused a problem but others felt let down as they had also been feeling a little insecure, yet had taken the risk. In their feedback, they were clearly upset, e.g. 'people shouldn't say silly things when the rest of us are trying to be honest'.

Participant Reaction

'The game meant we met a lot of people right at the beginning.'
'It was a bit embarrassing when I couldn't remember someone's name, even though I had just asked her what it was.'

3.20 What have you done?

This warmer is a useful example of the significance of careful objective observation. Because it does not involve any value judgement, it establishes the idea of simply reporting what has been seen, or in this case, changed.

Aims:
- to reestablish contact with the group
- to introduce the theme of careful observation

Suggested position in course: Before work on observation, but after initial group forming

Materials: None

Timing: 10 minutes

Classroom organisation: Small groups, standing or sitting

Procedure
1. All small group members study each other for a maximum of one timed minute.
2. All turn away from each other, and make one small change to their appearance (e.g. take off one shoe, put watch on other wrist, etc.).
3. At an agreed signal, all turn back and report their observations to each other, '(I see) you've moved your watch', etc.

Variations:
1. Whole-group activity, with one person leaving the room, and all others making changes
2. Whole-group activity, with one person leaving the room and that person making a change
3. Whole-group activity, with one person leaving the room, and one of the remaining people changing something

Comments:
Although many ELT participants know this activity, they enjoy doing it and then making new links, this time with observation and its importance in mentoring.

Participant reaction:
'It was fun!'
'The second time, the changes were much less obvious so it was harder, but good fun.'

3.21 What's the question?

The use of appropriate questions is an essential part of the mentor's skill, both to arrive at an understanding of the mentee's constructs, and in order to challenge those constructs (see also 5.7; 5.8 and 5.9). Although this activity does not really address the subtleties of questioning techniques, it is a useful lead-in to more specific work on the use of questions in mentoring.

Aims:
- to develop interpersonal relationships
- to introduce the topic of question varieties

Suggested position in course: Near the beginning to develop relationships, or when working on question forms in interventions

Materials: Post-its, sticky labels, or small pieces of paper and pins

Timing: 15–20 minutes

Classroom organisation: Individuals to melee

Procedure:
1. Participants write the *answers* to questions they would like to be asked, and stick these on to themselves.
2. Participants move about asking the questions they think are behind the answers until they find the correct question.
3. They continue until everyone has discovered the questions behind most answers.
4. Post-activity discussion to bring out the fact that there are many different ways of getting the same answer, and that the better one knows the person, the easier it is to find the right question.

Variations: If the group is large, the activity can be done in two smaller groups. There can be a specific focus for the answers, e.g. personal information for the beginning of the course, participant's last lesson for a teaching focus, a complex mentoring activity, etc.

Comments:
We like to take part in this activity, not only to get to know the participants better, but because we can demonstrate on our labels answers to a variety of question types (e.g. *yes/no* or *wh* questions, as well as less direct, more open ended ones).

Participant reaction:
'It was interesting how many different questions could be asked to get the same answer.'
'I think it is useful as a way of getting to know each other, but I don't think it helps much with question types.'

4 Seeing clearly

Introduction

This chapter presents activities for developing the skills of observing lessons.

Observation is generally a requirement of a mentor's job. Indeed, one of the most potentially useful things a mentor can do is to watch the mentee teaching, but if it is not handled sensitively it can cause problems or friction, and can even be damaging or dangerous. It is not easy to observe in a way that is useful to a mentee: observing appropriately is a difficult skill to learn, and therefore, like all skills, requires practice.

Making a lesson observation useful for a particular mentee's professional learning depends on what happens as a result of that observation, for example the way in which the mentor uses their observation notes during the post-lesson discussion. This in turn is greatly affected by what has happened in the mentor's mind during the observation. The mentor will inevitably judge and interpret what they see (see *4.5 Humans and aliens* below), yet this may not be of primary use to the mentee if they are to have the opportunity to develop their own constructs. What they will need first and foremost is pure evidence of what the mentor saw, rather than judgements, so that they can decide on their own interpretations of what goes on in their classroom.

In addition, the mentor's interpretations and judgements may well be misguided unless they are very conscious of the effects of the context of what they are seeing, as well as the influences of their own background.

Contextual perspectives

It is important, therefore, that mentors develop an awareness of the context in which the observation takes place. Context here refers as much to *when* each observation takes place as to *where* and *who with*. We will explore each of these in turn.

When each observation takes place is important for a number of different reasons. The nature of the observation will be influenced by both the mentor's and teacher's current understanding of teaching, that is to say, by their present position on their personal interteaching continuum (see Chapter 1: 1.3.4 *Interteaching*). In other words, the observation will be affected by *when* it occurs in the professional lives of both mentor and mentee. Mentors need to be conscious of the possible influences of their own past development and histories on the inevitable interpretations and evaluations they bring to what they are seeing and hearing (see Chapter 1: 1.4.1 *Notions of reflection*). In addition, a mentor observing teaching will inevitably be thinking about what to do with what they are observing. As they do this, they will need to consider the time of each observation, with respect to both the stage in their relationship with the particular student-teacher, and that student-teacher's stage of development. Not only will the observation be influenced by when it takes place in the professional lives of the mentor and mentees and in the mentor–mentee relationship, but also by the time it occurs in the academic year, the week and the teaching day.

Where the observation takes place, in which country, in which educational system, in which school, within which curriculum and in which class, will make a difference to what it is possible to observe, because different classroom cultures will have different norms. This can cause problems for both insider and outsider observers. For the insider, it might prove difficult to notice the normal or expected, while for the outsider appropriate behaviour in the context might seem strange or inexplicable (though this will provide a learning experience for the observer, as there is always a contextually appropriate explanation).

Who with, in terms of the participants in the classroom events, the age, level and kind of pupils as well as the personality and style of the mentee, will also affect what can be observed.

Issues of context, therefore, are relevant in both the actual observation as well as the interpretation of what is observed. Observation, interpretation and consequent judgement or evaluation will probably be happening concurrently, but it is vital that mentors are able to understand the three elements as potentially separate.

This contextual awareness during mentor courses is addressed more through the selection of videos of teaching than through the activities themselves.

Observer's perspectives

The ability to observe lessons clearly will be affected by a number of different factors. Some of these are internal or personal to the mentor, such as beliefs about good teaching, while some of them are external, such as the physical position of the mentor during the observation. Both the internal and external factors are affected by the human tendency to judge. We will look at each of them in turn.

Personal or internal 'blinkers'

One of the main obstructions to clear vision concerns the observer's notion of what 'good' teaching is. This will have been informed by their fundamental beliefs about the teaching-learning process arising from the local educational context; the mentors' own school experience as learners; and their own training, development and experience as teachers, from both the affective and cognitive points of view (see Chapter 1, and e.g. 3.5 *Going back to your mentor*). Arising from this, and of vital importance, is whether the observer is fully aware of this 'blinker' and its origins (see e.g. 3.7 *Group poem*, 3.8 *Heads and tails*). Teachers watching teaching, then, will inevitably compare and measure what they see against their own understanding of the teaching-learning process. This becomes unhelpful behaviour if mentors give in to the ensuing natural temptation to share the outcomes of those comparisons, rather than the more helpful factual observations. Learning to suspend judgement, as far as possible, while observing would seem the wisest course of action.

Further beliefs and understandings which affect a mentor's ability to see clearly come from their previous experiences of observing teaching; their relationship with the mentee (see Chapter 5, *Challenging appropriately*); their previous experiences of observing the mentee; and their understandings and knowledge about (beginner) teacher professional development (see Chapter 5, *Challenging appropriately* and Chapter 9, *Reading tasks*) and so on.

External 'blinkers'

Apart from elements of context, as described above, the most obvious external factor is the observer's physical viewpoint: there will almost always be some areas of the classroom, some pupils and some actions or events that they will inevitably be unable to see or hear. Nor will they be observing all the time: while they are *making notes* on observations, they cannot be *observing*. Less obvious, but equally important, are the limitations imposed by the observation schedule or check-list the observer is using (see 4.2 *Rabbits and snakes*, as well as the video-based observation tasks). In addition, no matter how objectively we record what we have observed or how appropriate the observation schedule, there will almost always be judgement in the *selection* of what is recorded. This is especially true if the mentor, rather than the mentee, decides on the focus of observation.

The tendency to judge

In addition to these 'blinkers' there is a fact of human nature which can hinder the effective use of observation. If an aim in mentoring can be considered as helping mentees develop an ability to make their own informed judgements, then making the judgements for them will not help them to learn. Yet we are judgemental by nature. Whenever we are touched by others' actions or the results of those actions, we tend to measure them against our own beliefs and attitudes. (Another way of viewing this is by considering it as 'constructivism in action' – see Chapter 1: 1.1 *Learning*.) We then often express this, to ourselves at least, as some sort of evaluation or judgement: 'What a wonderful garden!' 'That was really horrible food.' 'How rude!' or 'Poor thing'. Whether or not we actually speak our evaluations is another matter, because as humans, we have learnt to consider the possible effects on the receiver.

Judgement can be valuable when it is understood by both parties to be the expression of the constructs of the evaluator rather than an objective 'truth'. It can be valuable too in helping the 'socialisation' of the student-teacher into the school cultures of the context. ('Record books must be completed every week',

'You've got to finish when the bell goes – you over-ran again', 'This is the school marking policy' and so on.) However, whether 'socialisation', in the sense of perpetuating *all* existing norms, is the desired outcome of the mentoring process will have to be explicitly considered. If the education system is one that requires pure replication of the status quo, then the type of mentoring we are proposing here would probably not be appropriate, as it allows for individual freedom and choice for learners, whether pupils or student-teachers.

As facilitators of another's professional development, then, mentors need to be aware that explicit judgemental feedback may not be very helpful to the mentee. Mentors need to add considerations of the possible impact of expressed judgements on the student-teacher's *learning* to those of the possible impact on the *relationship*.

Becoming aware of the factors which colour every single observer's ability to see clearly, and learning to recognise and deal with them is one of the major objectives of a mentor course. This chapter contains activities which aim to demonstrate the existence of such factors and provide some means for reducing their potentially negative effect. Other chapters contain activities which have the potential to help individual participants to discover many of the 'blinkers' and context specific factors that obstruct clear seeing. Practice in the skill itself will continue in many of the activities in subsequent chapters (Chapters 5, *Challenging appropriately* and 7, *Assessing teaching*, in particular). The work on developing a range of options for action after observations, as well as considerations of the mentees themselves, their stages of development, personality and relationship with their mentor will be found principally in this chapter and the next.

Activities

4.1 Seeing: who, how, what and why?

The following, which can be used as either a presentation or a summary of some of the pitfalls in trying to see clearly, is the only example in the book of an activity which is essentially a lecture. The rationale for including such an activity type follows. (For a fuller development of this argument see Chapter 1: 1.5.2 *The role of the course leader: the importance of modelling and congruence*.)

In many contexts participants expect in-service courses to include lectures from the trainer. Mentees may also expect, and occasionally need, the mentor to 'tell them how it is' – depending on the student-teachers' stage of development. In addition, although the major focus of mentor training is on the novice-mentors' developing beliefs, attitudes and constructs, it is valuable for participants to understand where the course leader is coming from for the sake of their professional and personal relationship. Similarly, there is a parallel need for two-way disclosure in the mentor–mentee relationship.

Aims:
- to present or summarise and reinforce the concept of barriers to effective 'seeing'
- to give a visual experience of the above
- to meet any cultural expectations of leader-given input
- to reveal some of the leader's beliefs, attitudes and constructs
- to demonstrate the role a mentor may need to take with their mentee

Suggested position in course: During introductory work on observation, either before or after other activities in this section

Materials: Overhead projector; prepared transparencies, based on the illustrations: in *Photocopiable resource 2* on page 154 (or enlarged and copied); a sheet of paper, same size as transparencies, with a number of different sized holes cut out

Timing: 10–15 minutes

Classroom organisation: Whole group

Procedure:

1. The course leader presents Transparency 1, inviting comment and if necessary pointing out that the teacher's vision is limited by their physical position in the classroom.
2. Transparency 2 is superimposed. Comments are invited to elicit that:
   a) the observer's vision is limited by their physical position in the classroom.
   b) not everything the teacher sees can be seen by the observer and vice versa.
   c) some things can be seen by both, but from different angles.
   d) some things can be seen by neither teacher nor observer.
   e) if all the pupils were consulted as well, most things would be seen.
3. Transparency 3 is superimposed. Comments are invited to elicit:
   a) that our vision is obstructed by 'mental baggage' (internal factors – see introduction to this section).
   b) details of the contents of the 'baggage' (see introduction to this section)
   c) size and contents of imagined pupils' 'baggage'.
   Pupils' 'baggage' will inevitably be smaller, and therefore less obstructive from one point of view – as it contains their experience of teaching/learning as pupils, but not as teachers. On the other hand, because they cannot have a teacher's perspective, their vision is also more limited. (Lay spectators, for example, can watch skilled ice-dancing and appreciate its beauty, but most people are incapable of seeing the detail of movement that determines the judges' marks. If they are not skaters themselves, spectators can rarely say how the figure was achieved or why it received the marks it did. What they can report, however, is the overall impression it made on them.) Pupils inevitably see the events of the lesson differently and their initial comments will be both impressionistic and based on affective factors. Further probing, however, will reveal perspectives that make their observation equally valuable in giving a clearer picture.
   d) to get as complete a picture of the lesson as possible, it is necessary to consult everybody in the room.

4. Finally, the holed paper is superimposed over the three transparencies, and participants are invited to guess its symbolism (e.g. the various foci of an observation check-list), and comment on how it affects their 'seeing':
   a) some things are highlighted.
   b) some things are obscured.
   c) parts of the highlighted areas will still be obscured by the observer's standpoint both physically (external) and mentally (internal).
5. Whole-group round-up of implications:
   a) as observers we cannot completely eradicate these blocks to clear 'seeing', but we can become as conscious as possible of their existence and inevitable effect.
   b) the more observers, the clearer the picture will be.

Variations:
1. As in Silent Way, using gesture only, without saying a word, the course leader presents each transparency in turn and invites comments from the participants.
2. The illustrations above are copied and captions removed. Small groups are each given a set and asked to order and make sense of them. One group presents and the others add and comment.

Comments:
We have sometimes found participants are rather overwhelmed as they come to appreciate something of the task that lies ahead of them, and have needed reassurance. We have, at these times used the graph of the 'emotions of change' (see 5.15 *Beginner teacher development*) to illustrate the 'normality' of their feelings.

Participant reaction:
'This was an extremely useful demonstration.'
'I had never really thought about these "blocks" before.'

4.2 Rabbits and snakes

This activity serves to highlight the fact that we often fail to notice things until our attention is drawn to them, after which we tend to focus on those things to the exclusion of others. A possible danger, therefore, of having a specific focus or foci of observation is that other, possibly more important, aspects of a lesson may be overlooked, while the object of the focus may loom inappropriately large.

Aims:
– to raise awareness of the need to conceive of something in order to perceive it
– to raise awareness that we notice things our attention is drawn to and miss other things
– to raise awareness of the effects of focusing our observation on specific items

Suggested position in course: Near the beginning, before actual observation practice

Materials: One copy each of one picture + task (*Photocopiable resources 3* on page 155) for half the group and one copy each of the other picture + task (*Photocopiable resources 4* on page 156) for the other half

Timing: 15–20 minutes

Classroom organisation: Individual to pairs to whole group

Procedure:

NB Important: The success of this activity depends on the participants' being unaware that half the group is looking for a different kind of animal in the same picture. For this reason the tasks are deliberately not labelled A and B. Care will therefore need to be taken when distributing the pictures that the group does not become aware that there are two different tasks.

1. Participants are given the picture and task.
2. Participants work individually, for a maximum of one minute, searching their picture for the animal indicated.
3. Group is divided into pairs, one *A*, one *B* (in fact, 'rabbits' and 'snakes', but this must not be stated). They ask each other what they found in their picture, and decide on the implications (see *Comments*).
4. Whole group discussion of similarities and differences in the results of Step 2 above, and lessons to learn with regard to observation (see *Aims* above).

Comments:

It may be that while searching for rabbits, for example, participants found a snake or two, or vice versa, but the likelihood is that both partners will be surprised to be shown just how many of the other animals there actually are in the picture. This activity often produces lively debate on the nature of perception, and how easy it is only to notice what you expect. This has led to discussions on the dangers of 'labelling' learners in general as well as more specific implications for observation in mentoring.

Participant reaction:

'Once I knew there were snakes, I could see a lot.'

4.3 Complex picture

When there is a lot of activity going on in a classroom, as invariably there is, it can depend as much on your 'mental baggage' as on your physical standpoint what it is you see. This activity can help to bring out differences of perception resulting as much from *who* is observing as from the physical position of the observer. In addition, individuals, given no specific focus, will tend to concentrate on what is easy *for them personally* to recall and record.

Aims:

- to raise awareness of the influence of an observer's standpoint on clear observation
- to raise awareness of the possible drawbacks of non-focused observation

– to highlight the value of pooling different perspectives to get a clearer picture
– to highlight the fact that objective recording of evidence is possible (even if differently selected)

Suggested position in session: During the introduction to observation skills training

Materials: A very large detailed picture/poster with plenty going on: full of objects, people, actions, etc. (e.g. at a railway station, or a shopping centre, such as those used for beginner language learners)

Timing: 15–20 minutes

Classroom organisation: Group seated in such a way that most of them can see most of the picture

Procedure:
1. Participants have 30 seconds to look at the picture.
2. The picture is removed and participants have one minute to write down as much as they remember, without consulting anybody else.
3. In pairs or small groups participants compare and contrast their observations, discussing the reasons for these similarities and differences.
4. Whole group discussion of the implications of the above for mentoring, with outcomes of discussion collected on a board, flip-chart or poster.

Comments:
The discussion tends to bring up the following points:
Factors influencing what people observe: previous experiences, interests, personality, memory recall strategies, physical ability (short-sight, seating, etc.).
Recalling techniques: categories (objects, actions, people) detailed part of the whole versus overall impression.
Tendency to interpret: the 'translation' into language will begin to reveal some interpretation through the inevitable use of personal schemata. For example, one of our participants wrote 'man running to catch train', whereas the picture actually showed a man in a running position looking in the general direction of a ticket collector, a platform and a standing train. However, because a picture of this kind does not usually challenge deep-seated beliefs or prejudices, the recording of the 'evidence', although interpretative, will almost never be judgemental. This is a useful reference point when working on evidence-giving. (See e.g. 4.5 *Humans and aliens*.)
Recording techniques: differences in note-making, such as key words, shorthand, whole sentences and so on.

Participant reaction:
'My partner listed quite different things from me. She went for activities, I concentrated on the different shops and things. It was quite a surprise to compare out lists.'
'I can see how we need to be trained to observe! At first I didn't know how to remember all the things in the picture. I thought it was a competition, so I tried to remember as much as possible, which made it very difficult.'

4.4 Your money or . . .

This is another activity which highlights the difficulties of removing one's personal 'blinkers' in order to see clearly. In this case the 'blinker' is the participant's existing syntactical schemata.

Aims:
– to demonstrate how we see what we expect to see, rather than what is actually there

Suggested position in session: During the introduction to observation skills training

Materials: A large copy of the following diagram:

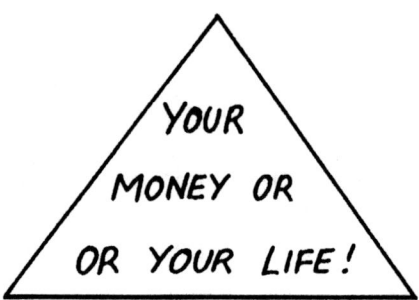

Timing: 5 minutes

Assumptions: Participants are not familiar with this type of diagram

Classroom organisation: Whole group

Procedure:
1. The diagram (enlarged to enable all participants to be able to see it) is flashed up for no longer than 2 to 3 seconds.
2. Participants shout out what they saw (usually most of them will say 'Your money or your life').
3. The diagram is held up again, and the 'truth' revealed.
4. Whole-group discussion of the implications for observation.

Variations: Any other short, culturally appropriate saying/cliché could be used, making sure that the repeated words are on different lines

Comments:
When one knows this trick, it is quite surprising to find so many who do not see it immediately. This highlights the two-fold purpose of the activity: participants see what they expect to see, even though what is actually there seems blindingly obvious to those in the know.

Participant reaction:
'How many of us didn't notice the two "ors"! It's a good demonstration.'
'I knew this activity, but I was very surprised that it wasn't obvious to the others.'

Acknowledgement:
A slightly different version of this appears in Woodward, T. (1991). *Models and Metaphors in Language Teacher Training*. Cambridge: Cambridge University

Press. We are grateful to Christopher Ryan for our particular version of this well-known diagram.

4.5 Humans and aliens

We have gone into great detail about the human's tendency to judge in the introduction to this chapter (see above *The tendency to judge*). This activity allows us to acknowledge and discuss the place of judgement in the mentoring process.

Aims:
– to raise awareness of the fact that we will inevitably 'judge'
– to set the scene for the beginning of work on 'helpful' ways of recording and giving evidence (acknowledging our beliefs and judgements, and making conscious decisions about which of them to share with the mentee)

Suggested position in course: Early, after initial introduction to observation, and possibly after some reading-based tasks on, for example, the nature of help. This will probably be the first video-based activity

Suggested position in session: After appropriate lead-in (see e.g. *The nature of help*, or *Smelly socks group*), and after introductory activities for 'observation' work

Materials: A ten-minute extract from a video of local (possibly student-teacher) teaching; video play-back facilities

Timing: 45 minutes–1 hour

Assumptions: Participants have neither seen the video before, nor know personally the teacher in it

Classroom organisation: Individual – small group – whole group, repeated

Procedure:
1. Participants are asked to watch the video and note down what they see (no specific focus is given, nor are any guidelines given for note-making).
2. Participants share their notes in small groups, and are asked, say, to compare similarities and differences. The course leader monitors for evidence of judgemental recording and talk, and notes down examples from each group.
3. The course leader reads out or writes up a selection of heard or seen judgemental comments under two headings: 'I heard . . . ' and 'I saw . . . ' (see also 4.6). These are selected from all groups but specific sources are not mentioned. Comments are invited and discussed.
4. Having recognised the 'Earthling' characteristic of observing judgementally, participants are now asked to imagine that they are aliens. These aliens have never experienced teaching or learning – they were born fully equipped for their life as aliens. What's more, they have never been to Earth before, but they do understand English!
   Participants watch the video again, this time as aliens.

5. As in Step 2 above. Participants remain in aliens role until Step 6.
6. As in Step 3 above, then leading to whole-group discussion of the whole activity.

Variations: If time is short, it is possible to omit the second video-viewing, in which case participants simply re-write their notes as aliens. However, a second viewing is preferable as participants will often see differently in the alien role.

We have sometimes used a visualisation to help people get into role. This could be included in Step 4 (see 3.5 *Going back to your mentor* for an example). Here, the visualisation would include a relaxation phase, information about a planet and the aliens on it, a voyage by space ship to earth, the landing and the journey to a classroom.

Comments:

Participants have always commented in an almost exclusively judgemental way in the first, human, half of this activity, despite any previous practical experience or reading. In addition these judgements are generally negative ones: 'She should have picked up that mistake', 'The board-work was so messy', 'It would have been better if she had . . . ' This may be in part because near the beginning of a course participants feel the need to prove that they 'know what good teaching should be'. Participants could therefore feel they have fallen into a trap. We have found that pointing out that everyone in the group reacted in the same human way, as well as acknowledging that trainer to trainer talk is different from trainer/mentor to student-teacher talk helps to save face.

With hindsight, we know we have rather over-emphasised in the past the dangers of 'judgemental feedback', as can be seen in some of the participant reactions below. This was partly because of our context where observation for *judgement only* was largely the norm, and we were, perhaps, over-enthusiastic in trying to get participants to 'see the other side'. It was also, of course, partly because our own ideas were less developed. Since then, we have learnt much from and with the mentors and our colleagues at CETT. We fear, however, this may be an example of our own 'dangerous teaching', as we had reports of mentors 'too scared to give any opinion', even when asked by their mentees and assured that it would be considered as just that, an opinion. Luckily ongoing meetings with mentors have allowed us to address this issue.

Participant reaction:

'It was shocking that we immediately began to evaluate. I knew that I shouldn't be, but even so I found I could not avoid it.'

'It's what we are used to: life *is* judgemental. Won't our trainees expect this?'

'When I was doing my teaching practice, my supervisor was always like that, so I thought it was my job, but now I understand there are other ways.'

'That was a powerful activity!'

4.6 'I heard, I saw, I noticed . . . '

This activity and 4.8 *Focused observation* are examples of video-based observation practice and awareness-raising tasks, focusing on the skills of observing and/or recording observations. These activities may also be used during the observation for video-based role-plays (see Chapter 6).

For this practice we like to use videos which are as close as possible to the real-life conditions (in terms of both place and people) in which post-course mentoring observation will be carried out. It is often difficult to perceive things when they are unchallenged elements in the observer's schema of 'lesson', and therefore work with local videos can usefully challenge things that are normally taken for granted, in a way that work with videos from different contexts may not.

One way of recording and/or giving evidence is through the use of 'I-statements'. The use of I-statements – a technique used in counselling – enables the observer to 'hold up the mirror' for the teacher to see again, and possibly differently, some events of the lesson (see Chapter 1: 1.4.1 *Notions of reflection*). This evidence is 'owned' by the observer through the use of '*I heard . . . /saw . . . /noticed . . .* ' thus acknowledging the subjective viewpoint of the observer (physically and in the selection of what is 'noticed'). Used in a non-judgemental way it allows the mentee to interpret this evidence in any way appropriate to their level of development. An experienced mentor will have selected evidence for a reason. If the mentee is unable to make any use of that evidence the mentor will either want to move on to other techniques (see, for example, Chapter 5: 5.10 *Excavating the iceberg*), or wait for the appropriate moment in the mentee's development to raise the issue again.

Aims:
– to develop/practise the skill of recording and/or giving evidence in a non-judgemental, factual, way through the use of I-statements
– to help overcome some of the internal factors that prevent clear 'seeing' and reporting

Materials: A video of a local lesson, preferably with a number of different activities and processes

Timing: Length of viewing + 20 minutes

Classroom organisation: Individual to whole group

Procedure:
1. Participants watch the video and take notes under the three columns.

    I heard   I saw   I noticed

2. In whole-group format, participants offer factual statements about what they observed. The course leader will take the part of the mentee, 'making use' of factual evidence as appropriate. For example, if offered 'I saw three children yawning during the reading activity', the 'mentee' might respond 'Yes, I was wondering if the activity was a bit long, or . . . um . . . actually it *was* rather stuffy in the room too, I could have opened the window'. If, on the other hand, the 'mentee' is offered, 'I saw three children looking bored' (the contributor has interpreted what they saw), the 'mentee' freezes, pretending not to hear, until the contribution is rephrased. The 'mentee' reacts in the same way if there is a judgemental contribution such as, for

example, 'I noticed the reading activity was too long'. This continues until it is clear that the group understands the concept.

3. Participants in small groups compare and discuss the contents of their columns, that is, their different perceptions, as well as 'correct' any remaining interpretative or judgemental statements.

4. Whole-group round-up discussion of the whole activity.

Variations: Step 2 could be replaced by a whole-group discussion of what to look out for

Comments:
We have found that it is harder than it might seem to make truly non-judgemental 'I-statements'. What usually emerges from this activity is that the use of adjectives and qualifiers is already interpretative, and therefore often judgemental. We have found it useful to start an 'Unhelpful Language List' poster, which can be added to as the course progresses. From the examples above, words such as 'too', 'long', and 'bored' would be put on the list. Subsequent additions are likely to include such things as negatives ('I didn't see . . . ', when unsolicited is almost always judgemental), directive modals such as 'should' and 'must' as well as other qualifiers, adjectives of emotion and so on.

Warning: In mentoring interventions (as opposed to observation recording and reporting), the continual use of 'I-statements' sounds very artificial, and consequently becomes extremely irritating to the receiver. This tends to emerge when role-play work begins. Once the principles of 'ownership' and factual evidence-giving have been established, both in practice situations and in actual mentoring, it is natural to leave out the stem ('I saw . . . ' etc.).

Participant reaction:
'Discussion of judgement and I-statements was more useful than reading about them a hundred times.'
'The part where you were the mentee was interesting – it offered "anticipation".'

4.7 Different observers

This activity again highlights the blinkers different observers bring to observation and the recording of those observations, through the comparison of two sets of authentic observation notes made while observing a lesson in a Sri Lankan classroom.

Aims:
– to illustrate the effect of personal blinkers
– to raise awareness of the importance of language use in the recording of observations

Materials: One copy of the task sheet (*Photocopiable resource 5* on page 157) per participant

Timing: 30–45 minutes

Classroom organisation: Individual to small group to whole group

Procedure:

1. Participants carry out Task 1 on the sheet individually.
2. In small groups, participants share the outcomes of Task 1 and discuss the questions in Task 2.
3. Whole-group round-up of findings.

Variations: Authentic notes from other contexts, including the participants' own, could be used to create a similar activities. It will be important, though, that the observers have a genuine purpose for the observation, which is probably not to do with supporting the professional development of the teacher observed, and that for one of the observers the context will be an unfamiliar one.

Comments:

Some of the differences usually mentioned between the two accounts are:

– Observer A describes the children and the room, Observer B doesn't.
– Observer A includes the account of children going to the water fountain, Observer B doesn't.
– Observer B includes (15–18) a transcription of the words from the board (?) into English script, Observer A doesn't.
– Observer B mentions the step (19) 'teacher checks whether they know words', Observer A doesn't.

This will often lead to the (accurate) conclusion that Observer B was more familiar with the context, and interested specifically in the pedagogy, possibly with a literacy focus. Observer A, on the other hand, was new to the context and interested more in making sense of the cultural context of the classroom.

There are several places where interpretations and judgements can be seen. Observer A describes some children as 'grubby and scruffy' – a judgement, and in line 2, interprets the differences in cleanliness as showing 'visible difference in socio-economic backgrounds'. In the same line Observer A uses the word 'but' – an indication of a preconceived idea of what the visible manifestations of 'poor' might mean in this context. In line 9, Observer A describes the group as chanting, while Observer B records this as repeating chorally (13–14). In a sense, as with all language use, these are both indications of interpretations, with 'chanting' being perhaps slightly more loaded. Observer B, although more factual in the account, also interprets the children's behaviour at one point as being 'more interested' (21). On the other hand, Observer A, in lines 6–7, seems aware of an urge to interpret, and attempts to resist immediate interpretation.

Participant reaction:

'At first, it was difficult to see that this was the same lesson being described.'
'This activity really showed how important it is what is in the observer's mind.'

Acknowledgements:

We are grateful to Jayne Moon (Observer B), School of Education, University of Leeds, for permission to use her observation notes, and to David Hayes, Project Manager, Primary English Language Project, Colombo, for inviting Angi (Observer A) and Jayne on the consultancy where these notes were taken.

4.8 Focused observation

This is the second example of a video-based observation practice activity (see also 4.6). It demonstrates a variety of different types of observation schedule, from those requiring ticks indicating items observed, to those requiring tallies indicating the number of occasions, or length of time a specific item was observed, to guided comments or more open recording of events. In addition to allowing practice of focused observation and discussions of its relevance and use, this activity also serves the purpose of presenting locally available published material.

Aims:
– to practise and consider focused observation
– to inform on locally available sources and types of observation schedules

Suggested position in course: After introductory work on Observation, and after e.g. *Rabbits and snakes*

Materials: Copies of 4 or 5 published observation schedules from different sources (e.g. Wajnryb 1992; Richards and Nunan 1990; *The Teacher Trainer* (T. Woodward (Ed.) Canterbury: Pilgrims Publications), etc.). The schedules will be of different types (tallies, graphs, diagrams, tables, scripts, etc.), but focusing largely on the same aspect of teaching. (Or see *Variations* below.)

Timing: Length of video observation + 30 minutes

Classroom organisation: Small groups to individual to same small groups to cross-groups to whole group

Procedure:
1. Small groups, each group with a different kind of observation schedule, prepare themselves for the observation by discussing the merits and drawbacks of their particular schedule, and checking they understand what they are required to do, etc.
2. Participants watch the video, recording observations according to the schedule they have.
3. Participants in the same small groups as 1 above, compare their observations and their predictions as to the merits and drawbacks of the schedule with regard to its actual use.
4. Groups are re-formed so that each group is composed of participants who used different observation schedules. They compare the results of their observations, discussing the reasons for similarities and differences. They go on to share the merits of their particular schedules for the purpose of the observation.
5. Whole-group round-up of insights from the experience.

Variations: The activity could be done using the same type of schedule for a variety of aspects of teaching. If there is no immediate access to such publications described under *Materials* above, the set of example schedules in *Appendix 1* could be used.

Comments:
This activity can reveal the difficulty of focusing per se. It also raises issues to

do with the ease or difficulty of using particular observation schedule types, as well as their effectiveness or otherwise for observing and recording the aspect of teaching chosen. This will highlight the need for the appropriate choice of type of observation schedule for a particular purpose, and possibly the need to devise one's own for specific tasks.

Most groups agree that focused schedules can be useful if/when a mentee has asked for observations on a particular aspect of their teaching, or for the mentee to use when observing other skilled teachers in order to notice a particular aspect of their work.

Participant reaction:
'It's really hard to observe and fill in the sheet at the same time.'
'I found myself wanting to make notes on other things too.'
'I hadn't realised there were so many different kinds of observation sheets.'

4.9 Helping the mentees see

This activity is designed to help mentors understand the role of demonstration at the beginning of their work with student-teachers, that is, at the beginning of the coaching process (see Chapter 1: 1.4.1 *Notions of reflection: modelling*). This role involves helping student-teachers see clearly not simply at the level of activities and techniques, but more deeply into the teacher's intent, into the principles underlying those activities and techniques. For example, student-teachers need to be able to see when, and possibly how, the teacher/mentor tried to get the children's attention, arouse their interest, get them to focus on the bit of language to be learnt or to make explicit existing constructs and so on. For mentors in training this means two things: building up the confidence to demonstrate these principles when being observed, and developing a range of context-specific observation schedules that will guide mentees into seeing the rationale underlying the techniques and activities.

The course leader will need to think carefully about how they begin this activity, about how *they* get attention, arouse the interest of the particular group of participants they are working with and so on. As these particular skills will be closely observed at the beginning of the activity, the leader needs to be confident about modelling a clear demonstration.

Aims:
– to raise awareness of the need for careful preparation for demonstration teaching to exemplify principles rather than simply behaviour
– to practise some micro-teaching for this purpose
– to explore the design features of observation sheets for this purpose
– to develop some observation sheets and follow-up task sheets for this purpose

Suggested position in course: After observation training and when the group knows and trusts each other

Suggested position in session: There needs to be a break between Stages 2 and 3 to allow for photocopying of the prepared observation schedules. This could be done during a session break, but equally Stage 3 could be done the following session

Materials: Copies of the Getting Attention/Rousing Interest Observation Schedule (*Photocopiable resource 6* on page 158) for each participant; copies for each participant of each of the observation schedules made in Stage 2 (see below)

Timing: Stage 1: 30 minutes; Stage 2: 45 minutes; Stage 3: 5 minutes micro-teaching + 10 minutes discussion per group

Classroom organisation: Whole group to pairs or small groups to whole group

Procedure:

Stage 1

1. Before the beginning of this activity, the course leader secretly gives three or four participants the Getting Attention/Rousing Interest Observation Schedule, inviting them to sit to one side and observe the beginning of the session, rather than participate.
2. The rest of the participants brainstorm ways of expressing stages of learning. These are written on the board. (See *Comments* below for one such list.)
3. These are then refined, ordered and agreed as being fundamental to any language teaching and learning situation.
4. At this point, the Getting Attention/Rousing Interest Observation Schedules are given to each participant and the observers are asked to comment on their observations of the course leader.
5. A whole group discussion may ensue on other ways the course leader could have got attention and roused interest.

Stage 2

1. Participants, in small groups, either choose or are allocated one of the principles from the brainstormed list in Stage 1 to be demonstrated in a piece of micro-teaching.
2. Each participant describes the different techniques they use to do this, and decides on the clearest way to demonstrate the principle to the whole group through micro-teaching.
3. Before demonstrating, however, each group develops an observation schedule to help the mentees notice both what happens and why it happens when the particular principle is being demonstrated. The original observation schedule could be used as a model.

Stage 3

1. A member of each group in turn has five minutes to micro-teach their demonstration of their particular principle, with the other participants trying out the prepared observation schedule.
2. After each demonstration, there is a short discussion about the clarity of the demonstration and the effectiveness of the observation schedule.
3. Observation schedules are refined and copied into a pack for the whole group.

Comments:

On one occasion, we led into this activity with a chat about the blues concert we had been to the night before in order to get attention and went on to consider what were the stages of learning the players had gone through in order to get to that level of expertise. Having roused their interest, we then went on to look at the similarities and differences between that and language learning in the school context.

The brainstorming phase in Stage 1 will almost inevitably lead to a debate on what constitutes universal features of the learning/teaching process, regardless of any aspects of context, such as the teacher's personal beliefs, those of the culture, class-size, age of students, language being learnt, etc. Typical of the lists that the participants on our courses have produced is the following:

- *managing learning*
- *getting attention*
- *getting at existing constructs*
- *arousing interest*
- *getting pupils to focus on what is to be learnt*
- *getting understanding*

- *checking understanding*
- *providing relevant sub-skill practice*
- *providing relevant whole-skill practice*
- *providing opportunities for feedback*
- *providing opportunities to measure/ appreciate progress*
- *providing visions of the goals*

Some of these elements will be seen only in part of a lesson, while others can be seen throughout. The observation schedules will have to take this into consideration, even though the micro-teaching demonstration by a particular group will be of a single instance only. We have often found that published observation schedules on such things as classroom management, the treatment of errors, etc., if used too early in student-teacher learning, may encourage the student to remain at the level of technique and activity. The schedules developed in this activity are not only useful because they are about seeing principles in action, but will also be context specific (see Figure 2 *The Teacher Iceberg*).

Participant reaction:

'That was great, I don't feel so scared about being observed now.'
'I'm glad we've got the observation sheets, they'll be a great help.'

4.10 Being observed

This activity is aimed, as it were, at the bottom of the participants' *Mentor Icebergs* (Figure 3), and encourages participants to recall their own experiences of being observed in order to help raise awareness of all the affective factors involved. This, in turn, will not only raise issues of appropriate mentor behaviour before, during and after observations, but also begin to create a 'need to know' in participants in readiness for interpersonal skill development work (see next chapter). In addition, participants need to make their models – learnt through experience – of the behaviour of observers explicit in order to challenge those constructs.

Aims:
- to consider the importance of affective considerations in being observed
- to begin to consider appropriate mentor behaviour before, during and after observations
- to enable participants to make explicit the models of the behaviour of observers learnt through experience

Suggested position in course: During work on observation, before the beginning of the interpersonal skills strand. Possibly after 3.5 *Going back to your mentor*

Materials: One copy of the 'Being observed' sheet (*Photocopiable resource 7* on page 158) per participant

Timing: 30–45 minutes

Classroom organisation: Individual to small group to whole group

Procedure:
1. Participants work individually on Task 1 on the 'Being observed' sheet.
2. In small groups, participants work on Task 2 on the 'Being observed' sheet, sharing their memories and working on a summary of implications for their work as mentors to share with the whole group.
3. Whole-group round-up discussion.

Variations: The activity could be preceded by a visualisation which takes participants back, say, to the last time they were observed

Comments:

In the round-up, discussion groups invariably mention negative words when referring to their feelings. (See *Participant reaction* below.) This leads to discussion on the importance of establishing a relationship with the mentee and making sure they understand the purpose of a mentor's observation as well as to general considerations of how mentors might behave before, during and after observations, especially the first ones, to minimise the risk of negative feelings in mentees.

Participant reaction:

'It was striking how all the groups used words like "scared", "nervous", "anxious" and so on.'

'It is going to be hard getting mentees not to see us as a threat.'

'This activity made me think about a lot of things, what I should do before an observation, how I should behave during the observation – controlling my facial expression and so on.'

'One thing I know – I won't be much help if I behave like my observer did!'

Acknowledgements: This is an adaptation of an activity devised by Sue Mace, British Council Regional Advisor, Cluj-Napoca, Romania.

5 Challenging appropriately

Introduction

Whether a mentor is assigned or chosen by the mentee, the very fact of their existence will make a difference to the mentee's professional development. Their existence will, in Freeman's words (1992) intervene in what might have been the mentee's natural, or 'mentorless' path. These interventions can make a difference to the pace, depth or breadth of learning, as well as to a complex mass of psychological factors which affect that learning in both its process and outcomes.

As we said in Chapter 1 (1.4.2 *Helpful relationships*) we have chosen to use Freeman's term 'intervention', rather than, say 'influence' (Tomlinson 1995) or even 'mediation' (Williams and Burden 1997), as it underlines the concept that everything a mentor does, says, or even, arguably, is, will make a difference of one sort or another to the development of the student-teacher. These interventions will either enhance, impede or send off-course the mentee's development. It is, therefore, essential that the mentor is as conscious as possible of the potential impact of everything they choose to say and do. The fact that they need to choose what they say and do means that they need to have enough options to choose from, as well as the skills to select and implement their choices. In other words, with any one mentee the mentor will need to be able to select appropriately from a range of possible acts of intervention and use these with great sensitivity. In addition to knowing theoretically about techniques and being able to select and use them appropriately, mentors need the interpersonal and counselling skills which help them to make instantaneous appropriate selections.

This chapter contains activities designed to encourage participants to consider the aims, objectives and possible dangers of their role, as well as work on the development of the interpersonal skills needed for counselling and challenging appropriately. Spontaneous, appropriate selection and implementation of choices can be further practised in the whole skill mentor role-plays of Chapter 6.

Activities

5.1 Butterflies

This is a beautiful and powerful metaphorical activity for showing that however well-meaning and energetic a mentor is, inappropriate intervention may do more harm than good.

Aims:
- to raise awareness of the dangers of inappropriate intervention
- to emphasise the need to put the mentees' needs and stage of development first

Suggested position in course: Fairly early, in the introduction to work on intervention to raise awareness, or towards the end of the course, as a summary

Materials: A copy of the task sheet (*Photocopiable resource 8* on page 159)

Timing: 1 hour

Classroom organisation: Half-half, to pairs, to individual, to small groups, to whole group

Procedure:
1. One half of the group imagines they are caterpillars reluctant to emerge as butterflies. They collect ideas for why life as a caterpillar is preferable. The other half of the group imagines they are butterflies, and collect ideas for why life as a butterfly is much better than it was as a caterpillar.
2. In pairs of one 'butterfly' and one 'caterpillar', each 'butterfly' tries to help the 'caterpillar' believe that it is worth becoming a butterfly.
3. Step 2 is repeated in different pairs, at least once (see *Comments* below).
4. Whole-group round-up on the reasons (personality, style, arguments) it was or was not easy to feel better or help someone feel better.
5. Each participant receives and completes the task sheet above.
6. In small groups participants compare decorated butterflies and discuss implications.
7. Whole-group round-up, as appropriate.

Variations: The role-play phase could be done on a separate occasion. Participants might prefer to draw their own butterflies.

Comments:
Repeating Step 2 is important because although the only change is in the people (as the situation, objectives and possibly even arguments will be the same), the interactions themselves will inevitably be different, producing different processes, feelings and outcomes. This highlights the crucial importance of interpersonal skills.

   Although caterpillars seem to need different things to make them feel better about the coming changes, many have reported feeling better if butterflies displayed empathy by saying that they themselves were once caterpillars and by explaining the stages they went through to become a butterfly.

   The second butterfly on the task sheet, often contains such words as: 'patience', 'chance to try again and again', 'peace', 'trust', 'honesty', 'respect' and so on. These are often mirror images of those in the first butterfly.

Participant reaction:
'Beautiful – moving and thought-provoking.'
'I wonder how many wings I've spoiled in my over-enthusiasm.'
'Pre-mentor state = caterpillar, mentor = butterfly. I desperately want to become a butterfly.'

Acknowledgement: We first learnt the half-half role-play idea from David Jolly, at The South Devon College for Arts and Technology, Torquay. The use of the *Zorba the Greek* text is an idea taken from Brandes, D. and P. Ginnis (1989). *The Student-Centred School*. Oxford: Blackwell.

5.2 We don't listen when . . .

Everyone is familiar with the situation when someone who is talking to you suddenly asks you a question, and you realise you haven't a clue what they were talking about! Your ears have heard the words but you weren't *listening to the person*, to what they were *meaning*. We turn off for all sorts of reasons, indeed we have had to train ourselves to be selective in what we listen to as our ears never stop hearing. Many people are not very good listeners, and all counselling training includes active or attentive listening practice. This is the first of a series of activities we use to work on improving listening skills. These skills are invaluable for mentors who will need to, as it were, *listen behind the words* of the mentee to gauge how the mentee is feeling and viewing things – both affective and cognitive states – in order to make decisions for their own next 'act of intervention'.

Aims:
– to raise awareness of 'normal' listening patterns
– to introduce the notion of active, supportive listening

Materials: Blackboard

Timing: About 20 minutes, depending on discussion generated

Classroom organisation: Pairs or small groups to whole group

Procedure:
1. Participants tell each other about an occasion when they were talking to somebody and suddenly realised they had no idea what the other person had just said. They discuss what happened, and why they weren't listening.
2. Whole-group discussion of reasons for not listening, collected on a board or poster, as

     We don't listen when . . .

3. Whole-group discussion on risks in mentoring of 'not listening'.

Variations: Brandes and Ginnis in *A Guide to Student-Centred Learning* (Basil Blackwell 1986) have a variation where the course leader tells a story, and then asks the participants for thoughts that distracted them while listening.

Comments:
The comments collected at Step 2 generally include: when I'm thinking about what I'm going to say next; when I'm day-dreaming; when the relationship with the speaker is not particularly important; when I remember a similar incident; when I disagree with what the other is saying; when I'm bored, tired, hungry, etc.; when I begin making value judgements; when I start thinking about the other person's appearance or character and so on.

Participants generally agree that the major risk to mentoring of 'not listening' is that it can lead to a breakdown in understanding and a lack of empathy. This can result in either no development for the mentee, or worse, 'dangerous' mentoring.

Participant reaction:

'I felt we did some very important things today when we looked at our listening habits.'

'Active listening is very difficult for me, as I know I am a "talker". So it is good to know we will focus on it as a skill we can learn.'

5.3 We listen when . . .

This activity will probably follow straight on from 5.2 *We don't listen when* . . . as it deals with another aspect of the counselling skill of active listening. Having discovered what can stop us listening, this activity explores factors that help us listen well. Identifying these factors allows mentors to consider consciously how to create the conditions for effective, active listening.

Aims:
– to raise awareness of the features and conditions of genuine, supportive listening

Materials: Board or flip chart; music appropriate for visualisation

Timing: 20 minutes

Assumptions: The group, including leader, is happy with visualisation work

Classroom organisation: Individual to pair work to whole group

Procedure:
1. Course leader talks participants through an initial visualisation procedure (see, for example, 3.5 *Going back to your mentor)* continuing as follows: 'Imagine you are with a close friend or family member who is talking to you about something very important to them . . . Who is the person? . . . Where are you, indoors or outside? . . . Do you feel warm or cold? . . . What can you hear? . . . Can you smell anything? . . . Look carefully at the other person . . . Are they standing or sitting? . . . Look at their face . . . What expression can you see? . . . What are they saying? . . . Listen for a while . . . Now, see yourself through their eyes . . . Where are you in relation to them? . . . What position are you in? . . . What gestures are you using? . . . What is the expression on your face? . . . Do you say anything? . . . How are you listening? . . . Now, come back inside yourself . . . What are you feeling? . . . What is going on in your head as you listen to the other? . . . Move away from the scene . . . Have one last look at the two of you . . . Then let the image gradually fade away . . . And when you are ready, open your eyes and come back into this room.'
2. In pairs, participants disclose as much of the visualised scene as they wish, discussing the features and conditions for genuine supportive listening.

3. Whole-group round-up, collecting the features on the board under, for example,

> *We listen when . . .*

4. Whole-group discussion of implications for mentoring.

Comments:
The features for genuine supportive listening can be both external and internal. External aspects will include eye-contact and general body language, as well as certain kinds of spoken language, such as paraphrasing, encouraging, etc. Internal aspects will include ignoring all the inner thoughts and voices, maintaining a non-judgemental attitude, feeling and displaying empathy, etc. In mentoring terms, this can lead to considering the relationship, working on the ability to empathise, being aware of and using body language as well as supportive spoken language.

Participant reaction:
'I loved the visualisation, it was so clear and such a wonderful experience.'
'I could feel all the same feelings of warmth I had then, but I wonder if I can be so attentive with someone who isn't so close to me.'

5.4 'That's exactly *what I mean!*'

Paraphrasing by a listener involves them in reflecting back to the speaker the listener's understanding of what they have heard, and expressing that understanding in their own words rather than those originally used by the speaker. It is helpful to speakers as it can help them to clarify their thoughts as well as indicating the attention of the listener. It also helps listeners to focus carefully on what is being said, thus blocking out any distractions. Whatever the level of English of the participants, it will be useful to remind them of the linguistic exponents available for paraphrasing (see *Procedure*, Step 2 below for examples).

Aims:
– to practise attentive listening, paraphrasing and summarising

Suggested position in course: Near the beginning of the course, early in active listening practice, before complex role-play activities

Suggested position in session: After initial awareness-raising activities (see, e.g. 5.2 *We don't listen when . . .*, and 5.3 *We listen when . . .*)

Materials: Board or flip chart

Timing: 20 minutes

Classroom organisation: Whole group to individuals to pairwork to whole group

Procedure:
1. Course leader elicits a definition of paraphrasing from the group.
2. The group brainstorms the language of paraphrasing, e.g. 'In other words

. . .', 'So you mean . . . ?', 'What you mean is . . .', 'So . . .', etc., and these are collected on the board.

3. The course leader asks participants to paraphrase a fairly complex sentence, or text, such as, 'I've always thought it might be interesting to look into the question of whether other nationalities use the same body language as we do, because I have a feeling that some of the basic misunderstandings between foreigners come from misinterpreting each other's body language.' Participants try to paraphrase the sentence. If they are not *exactly* correct, the course leader says something like, 'Well not quite, what I meant was . . .', then paraphrases the original sentence, and asks them to try paraphrasing the new one, until the course leader can honestly say 'That's *exactly* what I mean.' The course leader may want to continue the demonstration with further comments on the same topic, with the participants paraphrasing each new thought, or may prefer to go straight into pair work practice.

4. Participants prepare a complex statement of belief or opinion on anything discussed so far on the course.

5. Participants, in pairs, say their prepared sentences for their partner to paraphrase as demonstrated in Step 2.

6. Whole-group discussion on strategies for achieving understanding.

Variations: Step 4 could be given in advance as preparation

Comments:

If team teaching, the demonstration can be done between course leaders, which will undoubtedly have the added advantage of showing how difficult listening/paraphrasing is for everyone.

The discussion in Step 6 often brings out the need to 'read' body language and tone of voice as well as consider the mentee's choice of words or metaphors in attempting to understand the meaning the mentee intends. The discussion often also highlights the need for fairly extensive dialogue where meaning is clarified for both participants – negotiation of meaning. Without this, the mentor may bring their own constructs to the fore and assume they have understood when in fact they have misunderstood. Even if the mentor is reading meaning *from* rather than *into* something the mentee says, it will need to be established whether this meaning was consciously intended by the mentee, or is the surfacing of some new insights that the mentee is as yet unaware of, which need the mentor's skills to make fully explicit.

5.5 Once I had a class . . .

This is an activity which helps to focus on the importance of body language in communication. Participants are often unaware that in face-to-face communication as much as 80% of the messages are sent through situation and body language. The match of the non-verbal with the verbal messages, that is congruence, is vital for effective communication. In addition, by adopting 'active listening' postures consciously, mentors not only help the speaker but actually help themselves to listen better. It is rather like what happens to you when you choose to smile: it makes you feel better.

The activity, as it appears here, will not be appropriate in all cultures, as different cultures have different norms. The examples given here are essentially, and somewhat stereotypically, based on appropriate European behaviour.

Aims:
- to raise awareness of the importance of the listener's body language for both the speaker and the listener
- to provide another opportunity to explore teaching/learning constructs through talk (story)
- to build trust through self-disclosure

Suggested position in course: Early on in counselling skills work, but after 5.3 *We listen when . . .*

Materials: One set of Listener's Body Language Cards, and one Task Sheet per group (*Photocopiable resource 9* and *10* on pages 160–161)
(NB In groups with only 5 listeners, omit any card except Card 2 which describes 'good listening' body language.)

Timing: 20–30 minutes

Classroom organisation: Groups of 5 or 6 'listeners' + one 'story-teller' per group, to whole group

Procedure:
1. Volunteer story-tellers leave the room to think of the details of their 5-minute stories about some teaching-related anecdote. They will also consider how they will engage the interest of their audience. Remaining participants divide into groups of 5 or 6 and receive and study their 'Listener's Body Language Card'.
2. Story-tellers return, one for each group of listeners, and tell their story with the listeners acting according to their cards.
3. At the end of the story, the groups receive the Task Sheet and discuss their reactions to the experience.
4. Whole-group round-up of implications for mentoring.

Variations: Listeners' Cards may need to be redesigned for the context.

Comments:
Participants often find that the normal human tendency towards congruence makes it very difficult for them to remain in the posture dictated by their card if they are genuinely interested in the story-teller as an individual, in their relationship with them, as well as in the details of the actual anecdote itself. In the discussion on the relevance in mentoring, we have used insights from Neurolinguistic Programming to explore the possibility of consciously deciding to use body language, often mirroring the mentee's, to create a supportive atmosphere. Links are also often made to the outcomes of the '*We listen when . . .*' activity (5.3), where the feelings create the body language, rather than the body language creating the rapport, which is explored in this activity.

Participant reaction:

'Congruence is an important concept and we need to think more about non-verbal communication.'

'Eye-contact, body language, gestures – we always use them, but I've never thought about them in such a deep methodological way before.'

5.6 Getting a clear picture

As a mentoring technique, having an authentic communicative reason to describe in detail the events of the lesson, because the other was not present, can be a powerful factor in helping mentees to articulate their practice. Articulation or talking about teaching is an important learning tool, as only when the implicit has become explicit can it be directly challenged and interteaching hypotheses develop (see Chapter 1: 1.3.4 *Interteaching*). As we have seen, this is especially true when the talk is well listened to, as more of the implicit can be brought out.

For course participants, this activity can similarly help them discover and develop their own constructs of teaching/learning, and through the sharing of personal information help develop and maintain relationships. In addition it allows the practice of supportive listening skills, and empathising/visualising as well as informational reporting.

Aims:
- to practise supportive listening; to practise techniques for getting a clear picture of events which happened in your absence
- to practise giving clear descriptions, without interpretations or evaluations
- to provide an opportunity for 'talking teaching'
- to maintain group cohesion (continue work on intermember relations) through exchange of participants' personal experience
- to demonstrate a technique for use in mentoring

Suggested position in course: After initial work on observation and counselling skills, but before *Self-observation* assignment (8.1)

Materials: None

Timing: 45 minutes

Assumptions: Participants have a sufficient level of trust to allow them to 'open their classroom doors' to another. This activity is, however, 'safer' than, for example, peer-observation, as participants are free to choose what they reveal

Classroom organisation: Self-selected pairs

Procedure:
1. In turn, partners recall and describe a recent lesson they have taught. They may choose to use 'I-statements' or other means to give a clear factual, non-interpretative and non-evaluative, description of the lesson. They will say, for example, '. . . and several children were yawning and fidgeting', rather than '. . . they were bored' (interpretative), or 'it was too difficult for them' (evaluative). As a supportive listener, the other partner uses questions, (How

many children were fidgeting? Which ones? What were the others doing?) or paraphrasing ('So you're saying the three boys who usually sit together at the back didn't seem very involved to you, so what were they actually doing?') and so on, until they are sure they have a clear picture.

2. Partners, in turn, talk about how easy it was to *describe* the lesson clearly and objectively, and how useful the listener's actions were in that process.
3. Again, in turn, the partners review the processes they used in *listening to get a clear picture* (as opposed to listening to decide what form of intervention to make, or to evaluate).
4. Whole-group round-up of 'What we have learnt'.

Variations: At a later stage in the course this same activity can be extended to include work on interventions. (See e.g. 8.1 *Self-observation*.)

Comments:

During mentor courses this is a particularly popular activity as mentors are working on their own lessons and contrasting them with descriptions of others'. The process of articulating what happened in the lesson often leads to insights which excite them and give them confidence. 'What we have learnt' tends to produce comments on the value of attentive listening and the importance of being explicit. Participants also comment on how *not* observing the teaching of a mentee makes the mentee have to review the lesson much more thoroughly than if the mentor had seen it. Thus it encourages the kind of reviewing process that the student-teacher will have to do when teaching on their own after completing their training.

Participant reaction:

'Much as I appreciated this activity, I'm not sure how it would fit into normal mentoring.'

'I felt almost as if I had been at my partner's lesson . . . It is more difficult to reconstruct the lesson when we were not personally present, but because of lack of information, we are forced to ask about or point at such things we would overlook in the case of observed lessons.'

'This activity makes the teacher think back and explain procedures that they may otherwise routinely do. In other words, the main advantage is that it can enhance the self-reflection of the teacher.'

Acknowledgements: We first learnt the idea of 'absent observation' from Mario Rinvolucri in a workshop in Istanbul.

5.7 It's not what you say, it's the way that you say it

This activity connects body language (see 5.5 *Once I had a class . . .*) and language. If context and body language account for 80% of the messages sent in face-to-face communication, many of the remaining messages, too, are sent not so much through the actual words used as through the 'key', that is, stress, intonation, pitch, tone of voice, etc.

This activity may appear deceptively easy, but it in fact requires not only a great deal of conscious concentration initially, but a high level of linguistic awareness. Instant improvisation needs practice which not all participants have had. However, an awareness of all messages being sent as well as their possible impact on the mentee is part of a mentor's interpersonal skill.

Aims:
- to raise awareness of the different messages that may be sent through the same words
- to prepare for the improvisation needed in role-play work

Suggested position in course: During counselling skills work, before mentoring role-plays

Suggested position in session: Before 5.8 *Question time* below, possibly as a warmer

Materials: One question per participant; four or five participants should receive the same question. Example questions are shown in *Photocopiable resource 11* on page 161.

Timing: 20 minutes

Classroom organisation: Individual to melee to small groups to whole class

Procedure:
1. Participants receive one question each, and spend a minute or so mentally trying out different stress, intonation and tone variations for asking the question. They choose one way of asking the question, imagining in detail a situation in which it would be appropriate (relationship, feelings, purpose, physical context, etc.) as well as imagining a possible response.
2. Participants mingle, asking each other their questions and improvising an instant reply to others' questions. This will mean responding to the way the question is asked as well as the question itself.
3. Participants with the same question form small groups to discuss the different responses and the reasons for these.
4. Whole-group discussion of the outcomes.

Variations: Working on 'key' rather than questions, the same activity could be done with 'I-statements'.
  Alternatively, there could be a mixture of questions and 'I-statements'.

Comments:
Participants often report that, as the activity progresses, they fine-tune the way they deliver the question as a result of previous, unexpected responses. Discussion at the end of the activity will include realisations that, for example: 'do' questions can seem more aggressive, as they imply permanent habit, than 'did' questions; 'why' questions may be more overtly challenging and judgemental than 'what' questions, etc. However, groups reach the conclusion that all of these are relative, depending on the context, relationship and manner.
  In our context we have found that non-native participants are even more form-focused than native-speakers might be, and understandably have more difficulties with the pragmatics of the English phonological system. We have had long debates on courses about how far non-native mentors and mentees can be expected/'should' internalise native-speaker-like behaviour, and whether,

in fact, it might not increase the chances of pragmatic failure if this is given too much emphasis on mentor courses, as mentees may not share the same understanding and skill. On the other hand, this difference may be compensated for by the more dominant contextual cultural messages present. In addition, this pragmatic competence, which is, arguably, a feature of communicative competence that language teachers need, may be developed in the mentee through the mentoring dialogue.

Participant reaction:

'English intonation is quite difficult for us anyway, so although I understand what we were trying to do, I'm not sure I shall be able to get my intonation right. Perhaps we should use our mother tongue in mentor–mentee discussions?'

5.8 Question time

One of the major linguistic tools of counsellors and teachers or mentors is questions. However, unlike, for example, paraphrasing or 'I-statements', it is virtually impossible to provide any hard and fast guidelines for when to use which kind of question. Counselling literature often advises against the use of 'why' questions, for instance, yet viewed from the educational, challenge perspective they may be perfectly appropriate at certain times, with certain mentees, in certain tones of voice and so on.

Participants on mentor courses, however, often seek formulae to follow, and this is another activity which serves the purpose of demonstrating that this is largely impossible.

Aims:
– to consider the use of questions in effective interventions

Suggested position in course: After initial counselling skills work, at the beginning of interventions

Materials: 5-minute extract of (local) teaching video of a lesson

Timing: 40 minutes

Classroom organisation: whole group to pairs to whole group

Procedure:
1. Participants watch a 5-minute extract of a video on teaching and make 'I-statement' observation notes.
2. Participants choose two different points from their observation notes (for example, something the teacher did, and something a pupil did). For each point participants write a series of questions, at least one of each of the following types: *Yes/No, What, Why, When, Where, How, How much, How many.*
3. In pairs, partners take turns in imagining that they are the 'teacher'. The other partner asks each of their questions, and the 'teacher' reacts each time as they imagine the real teacher would, if this was the *only* question asked about that particular observation point.

4. Pairs discuss the impact (feelings, outcomes, etc.) of the different kinds of question on the 'teacher', as well as any similarities and differences between the two 'teachers'' reactions to the same type of question.
5. Whole-group discussion of the outcomes.

Variations: This kind of work on questions could be done as a follow-up to 5.6 *Getting a Clear Picture*, working from participants' own experience. This would require a high level of trust (see *Comments*), but may be more appropriate for those who find it hard to get into a different role at this stage (see Chapter 6 *Role-plays*).

Comments:
We find that work on appropriate questions for different forms and purposes of intervention always concludes with only one generalisable principle: that the use of particular question types depends almost entirely on the relationship between the mentor and mentee and how the questions are asked. In other words, mentors need to be as certain as they can be of the impact their questions will have on their mentee, rather than relying on a possible series of set categories and forms of questions. In addition, it emerges that mentees will, initially at least, tend to search for the implied criticism behind the question, whatever the form. (See *Participant reaction* below.) Having said that, we find it a valuable activity just because of these realisations. Questions are essential for encouraging, clarifying and for challenging but their choice will depend on the relationship and context and not on any prescribed methodology.

Participant reaction:
'It was interesting to try and work out what my partner really wanted with each question – was it criticism, or praise or was it a real open question?
I can see now how a mentee might react to even innocent questions.'

5.9 Considering questions

As the activity above shows, the effective use of questions depends on a number of different factors, which this activity is designed to explore from a different angle.

Aims:
– to explore some factors affecting the use of questions in a counselling situation

Suggested position in course: During work on counselling skills, before mentor role-plays

Materials: One task sheet (*Photocopiable resource 12* on page 162) per group (for Stage 1); video or audio recording of a mentor/mentee discussion and one card per group from *Photocopiable resource 13* on page 163 (for Stage 2)

Timing: 40 minutes

Classroom organisation: Four groups (or eight, if there are a lot of participants)

Procedure:

Stage 1

1. All participants receive a task sheet, and work in small groups to match the factor to the correct definition, discussing the implications as they do so.
2. The whole group checks the answers (1 C; 2 B; 3 D; 4 E; 5 A), and raises any general points.

Stage 2

1. Each of the four groups is now given a different question factor card. (There will only be four, as question factor 4 cannot be assessed in this activity.)
2. All participants either watch a video or listen to an audio recording of a post-lesson discussion between a mentor and a mentee. They note down examples of the use of their particular question factor.
3. Participants share their examples within their groups, checking their perceptions of the use of the questions they have noted, and discussing the effect that they had.
4. Participants now cross-group, so that members of each new group can present examples and discuss all four of the question factors.
5. A whole-group round-up to address lingering problems of identification or queries resulting from the discussions.

Variations: Stage 1 can be used on its own as a follow up to 4.9 above. The recording could be of a mentoring role-play (see Chapter 6). There may be no need for the whole-group round-up (Step 5 above).

Comments:

Although the first part of the activity is extremely easy to do, it can be rewarding to succeed easily, and more importantly useful discussion usually arises in connection with the five factors. The identification of the different questions on a video or tapescript also leads to discussion. The outcomes will be similar to those of 4.8 and 4.9, with the addition of a deeper awareness of the specific factors described on the cards.

Participant reaction:

'I hope I will be able to use these in practice.'
'I'm looking forward to working with these in role-plays.'

Acknowledgement: We have been unable to trace the origin of the question factor text given to us as a handout at a workshop. We would be grateful if anyone could inform us of the source. This activity was developed with the collaboration of Geoff Gibson, Kossuth Lajos University, Debrecen, Hungary.

5.10 Excavating the iceberg

One of the problems we have faced when observing mentors at work and also mentor role-plays (see Chapter 6 *Role-plays*), is that very often the discussions remain at the level of lesson planning and the only learning that occurs is at the superficial level of new activities or teaching tips. Effective challenging must delve into the mentee's knowledge, understandings and beliefs about teaching and learning if there are to be fundamental changes in their constructs.

Although mentor–mentee discussions are often mentee led, the mentor will have been making notes during the lesson observation, presumably for a particular reason. One of the hardest parts of a mentor's job is to present these pieces of evidence, regardless of whether they are evidence of something the mentor approves or disapproves of, in order to challenge the mentee's thinking at deeper and deeper levels.

Traditionally supervisors have concentrated on things they felt were 'wrong', and this activity can help mentors to break away from that tradition. In addition, mentors need to be able to help mentees to understand how they have achieved their successes, if they are to be able to repeat them. This focused role play format gives participants the opportunity to prepare the challenge in pairs, then try it out, with one of them acting as mentor and the other observing the effect and outcome. They also have the additional perspective of an observer who was not part of the planning. (For focused observation of this skill, see 6.8 '*Excavating*'.)

This is a complex activity with three stages.

Aims:
– to practise noting down objective evidence during lesson observation
– to explore constructs at all levels presented in the Teacher Iceberg metaphor (Chapter 1 Figure 2)
– to practise the mentoring skill of challenging mentees' constructs for learning

Materials: Videoed lesson or extract; one copy of the 'lesson plan' per participant; sufficient copies of the individual cards (*Photocopiable resource 14* on page 164) so that each group of 3–5 participants has one set; one copy of the Teacher Iceberg (Chapter 1, Figure 2) per participant

Timing: Length of video + approximately 1 hour

Classroom organisation: Stage 1: whole group, pairs; Stage 2: small groups of 3–5; Stage 3: whole group to pairs to fours to whole group

Procedure:
Stage 1
1. Participants familiarise themselves with the videoed lesson plan.
2. They watch the video and make notes (either general, or according to a specific focus) using an objective 'I-statement' technique (see 4.6 *I heard, I saw, I noticed . . .*). The course leader also makes notes in the same way.
3. In pairs, participants look through their notes and decide if they are really objective, or if they contain interpretations and/or judgements. If they are not objective, they work on turning them into pieces of pure evidence. The course leader may want to work with them.

Stage 2
1. The participants are now re-grouped into small groups of 3–5.
2. The course leader copies the outline of the Teacher Iceberg on the board, eliciting as they draw ideas about what it might be, adding the sea line and the words SCHOOL CULTURE, EDUCATIONAL SYSTEM, SOCIETY and CULTURE in the appropriate places (see Chapter 1 Figure 2).
3. One member of each group copies the drawing on to a sheet of A4 paper.

4. The course leader explains that this is a metaphor for a teacher, and gives each group a set of the shuffled cards above to place in their iceberg.
5. The course leader takes suggestions for the positioning of the words, and writes them into the drawing on the board. A general discussion of the significance of the metaphor leads to the addition of the arrows as participants become aware of the two-way influences (see Chapter 1: 1.3.2 *The dynamic interplay of practice and theory*).

Stage 3

1. Each participant receives a copy of the Teacher Iceberg (Chapter 1 Figure 2). The course leader explains that it can also be used as a framework or guide to help mentors to work with mentees at various levels of their learning.
2. The course leader invites participants to share some of their 'I-statements' (these do not necessarily have to begin with 'I', but must be objective pieces of evidence), and writes them up.
3. Participants are then asked how they could be used to challenge the mentee to 'excavate' the lower levels of the iceberg. The course leader may want to demonstrate this by starting with one of their own observation notes, role-playing, with the help of a participant as 'teacher', how a mentor could use this idea. (See a possible example in Figure 8 below.)

Excavating a Teacher's Iceberg

(Part of a post-lesson discussion between a student-teacher and her mentor)
Mentor: I saw the students doing an information gap pair work activity (*'holding up the mirror'*)
Teacher: Yes, I wanted them to get some practice – to ask for information – questions. (*planning*)
Mentor: What made you decide your pupils need this? Did you consider other ways for them to get practice? (*selection/knowledge*)
Teacher: I could have done drills and things, I suppose, but they need practice in communicating. (*selection/knowledge/conceptualisation of language learning*)
Mentor: So, what aspect of communication did you want them to practise? (*knowledge/ conceptualisation*)
Teacher: Well, you know, if you ask a question it's because you need to know the answer, and it's unpredictable, what will happen (*conceptualisation*)
Mentor: Mm, and is that in the curriculum – the need for your pupils to communicate, to use the language? I mean, what are they learning the language for? (*knowledge/ conceptualisation*)
Teacher: Umm, I'm not sure actually, I should probably look at it! (*planning learning*)
Mentor: OK. So, tell me more about why *you* think they are learning the language? (*knowledge, beliefs*)
Teacher: Well, I know why I wanted to learn it! I believe . . . (*feelings, beliefs, attitudes and values*)

Figure 8 An example of *Excavating the iceberg*

4. In their original pairs (Stage 1), participants now return to their observation notes and decide on either two or four points (depending on

time available) they want to raise with their mentee. Half can be 'positive' challenges, things the mentor approves of, and half 'negative', events the mentor is less happy about.

5. Each pair considers the kind of questions they would need to ask, or ways of probing they might need to use, after presenting these initial pieces of evidence ('I-statements') to challenge the mentee to examine more deeply their underlying constructs.

6. Each pair now joins up with another pair. In turn, one partner of each pair takes the role of the 'mentor' and presents evidence to the 'student-teacher' (one partner from the other pair). The 'student-teacher' will try to react in role, and a dialogue will ensue with the 'mentor' asking questions to help the 'student-teacher' to excavate the deepest levels of their own teaching iceberg.

7. The other two participants act as 'observers' – one an 'insider' who knows the planned procedure, the other an 'outsider'. They take notes.

8. At the end of five minutes, the role-players and the observers will share their reactions and notes, discussing ways in which they might improve their performance, and what they have learnt from the experience.

9. The procedure continues with different 'mentors' and 'student-teachers' in each group of four each time until all the points have been role-played and discussed.

10. A whole-group discussion might follow on any issues that the participants wish to raise.

Comments:

One of the great advantages of using this technique with mentees is that it is a genuine challenge for them, and seems to side step the issue of judgement and criticism. They become engaged in trying to find the origins of their actions, and they seldom become defensive because they recognise their behaviour as stemming from constructs that they may not have even been aware of. It enables them to be more objective about their actions and to see them as manifestations of beliefs they may no longer choose to hold. By exposing those beliefs they can confront them, and reformulate them to fit their new understandings of teaching.

The value of having both an 'insider' and 'outsider' observer is evident from the animated discussions that follow these role-plays, and the different perspectives that each brings to the observations. Another very interesting outcome has been that on more than one occasion, the same challenge has come from both pairs, but one pair considered it 'negative' and the other 'positive'! It is in the resulting discussion that many of the participants' own understandings and beliefs are challenged.

Some of the participants' comments arising from such discussions have been:
- *We're working from the seen to the unseen and back.*
- *We're digging together.*
- *We* guided *– they* made sense.
- *It took practice to get it right.*
- *It matters what words are used.*

Participant reaction:

'It was good to be able to practise challenging like this. Sharing our observation notes helped me to see when I was really giving objective evidence, and when I was already interpreting.'

'The iceberg metaphor has suddenly made all you have been trying to show us so clear. I am going to show it to my trainees, so they will understand what I am trying to do.'

'I enjoyed observing my partner being the mentor as I could "see" what was going on in her mind, because we had discussed it before. I could also think what I would have done when the mentee reacted differently from what we had expected.'

'I enjoyed your methods of digging, and how you made us search for things that we have already known but never come up with before. You showed us a new learning and teaching perspective on the level of learning mentoring.'

5.11 'I' to 'Why?'

Notes and scripts made during lesson observations can form the bases for useful mentee tasks which are designed to challenge and extend their thinking. They have the advantage of being the kind of task assigned by the mentor instead or as a result of a post-lesson discussion, for the mentee to consider and complete at home. As such they can add to the mentor's repertoire of techniques for intervention. This and the previous activity 5.10 *Excavating the iceberg* are examples of such tasks. Used on mentor courses, these activities challenge and extend the mentors' own thinking.

Aims:
– to demonstrate a technique for use in mentoring
– to raise awareness of the need to be explicit about the rationale for actions, as a first step to development
– to help participants make explicit some of their own rationale

Suggested position in course: After work on observation and 'I-statements'

Materials: Part or all of the description (objective 'I-statement' recording of events) of the participant's own lesson, from 5.6 *Getting a clear picture*, 8.1 *Self-observation* or 8.2 *Peer-observation*

Timing: 40 minutes

Classroom organisation: Pairs to whole group

Procedure:
1. In self-selected pairs, participants take turns to work from the notes on their partner's lesson, turning observed facts into why-questions and asking them. For example, 'I saw John come into the room and bang his books down on the desk', changes to 'Why did John bang his books down on the desk?', or 'I heard you say "All right everyone, quiet down"' changes to 'Why did you say "All right everyone, quiet down"?'

2. Partners reply, exploring in their answers possible reasons. For example, for the first question above a participant might answer: 'Oh, I don't know really . . . Oh, yes, I do, Christopher told me John had just heard the results of his chemistry test and he'd done rather badly. Come to think of it, that's probably why I couldn't get anything out of him this lesson.' For the second example question, the response might initially be more direct: 'Because they were being noisy . . . Mmm . . . they went on being noisy actually . . . so, perhaps . . .'
3. Whole-group discussion of outcomes, and implications.

Variations: Participants could do this as a written task at home, working from a partner's notes from peer-observation. This would be followed by an in-session discussion of outcomes and implications with the same partner.

The iceberg metaphor and the different levels could serve as a structure for this activity, with answers to the why-questions going to deeper and deeper levels.

Comments:
Participants usually both value the insights into their own teaching this activity offers, as well as recognise its potential as an additional mentoring tool for helping mentees to articulate interpretations and explanations of classroom events.

Participant reaction:
'Practising and getting used to the idea of getting mentees to turn mentor's I-statements into why-questions and try to answer them . . . struck me as a very interesting and good idea.'

Acknowledgement: This is a slight adaptation of a technique we learnt from Roger Hunt, International House, Budapest.

5.12 Opposite scenarios

While the two previous tasks (5.10 and 5.11) looked at why things actually happened in the classroom, this task challenges the mentee to consider what other options there could have been. Creative, lateral thinking is encouraged by asking participants to consider opposites. The activity is an opportunity for fun and laughter as images are created which challenge existing schemata of appropriate classroom behaviour.

Aims:
– to demonstrate a technique for use in mentoring; to raise awareness of a need to help mentees expand their range of options
– to consider (and expand) possible options for different teaching situations

Materials: Part or all of the description (objective 'I-statement' recording of events) of the participant's own lesson, from *5.6 Getting a clear picture*, 8.1 *Self-observation* or 8.2 *Peer-observation*

Timing: 40 minutes

Classroom organisation: Pairs to whole group

Procedure:

1. In self-selected pairs, participants take turns to work from the notes of one of their lessons. Together they change the parts of the script relating to the teacher's actions into an opposite scenario and, at each stage, consider how far the new scenario contains possible options. Using the same example as in the previous activity 'I heard you say "All right everyone, quiet down"' might become:

   'You *wrote* on the board "All right everyone, quiet down".' (Possible discussion outcomes: 'They might not have noticed'/'I often do this, so someone would have noticed and quietened the others'/'I don't know, it's a good idea, I'll try it'); or

   '*John* said "All right everyone, quiet down"' (Possible discussion outcomes: 'Mmm, yes, that's a good idea, I could have a noise monitor.'/'No, that would never happen, John's the noisiest of all of them, although come to think of it . . .'/'Oh they're much too young for that kind of responsibility . . . I think'); or

   'You said "All right everyone, *carry on being noisy*".' (Possible discussion outcomes: 'Oh no, I could never say that, it sounds much too sarcastic' or 'Yes, sometimes I worry too much about noise-levels, noisiness can mean involvement and interest . . .' etc.)

2. Whole-group discussion of implications of the activity.

Variations: This could be a (written) task completed at home, with, for example a pyramid in-session discussion follow-up

Comments:

Sometimes it is difficult to find *the* opposite for a piece of behaviour, but this very difficulty allows participants to explore and discuss a range of different options. Some of these 'opposites' may appear absurd ('I stood on my hands and drew a picture with my toes') but the very absurdity allows for creative lateral thinking, and discussion often reveals viable new options (in this case, for example concerning attention-getting, board use, etc.). The fun element of this activity can be a source of light relief during 'heavier' work on interventions.

Participant reaction:

'We laughed a lot, but learnt a lot too.'

Acknowledgement: We got the idea of opposites from Fanselow, J. (1990). 'Let's see': contrasting conversations about teaching. In J. Richards, and D. Nunan (Eds.) *Second Language Teacher Education*, Cambridge: Cambridge University Press.

5.13 Transcript tasks

Standing back from a mentor's work and attempting to analyse some of the micro-skills involved can be a valuable awareness-raising activity. This can be usefully achieved with the help of written transcripts of discussions between mentors and mentees (mentorials) or role-plays of them, although video or audio recordings add the dimension of the manner in which something is said. These may be pre- or post-lesson discussions with the focus on reviewing or planning, and may or may not have involved the mentor in prior lesson observation. The tasks given here include two on the mentor's use of language (Task 2 – questions and Task 4 – I-statements), one on the functions of what the mentor says, what they are trying to do in terms of challenge and support (Task 1), and one on the discourse structure of the mentoring conversation (Task 3).

Aims:
– to analyse mentor discussions for types of intervention, use of language, and structure

Materials: A copy of the same transcript for all participants (from a recorded role-play discussion, or an actual mentoring discussion); a copy of one of the tasks in *Photocopiable resource 15* on page 165) per participant, so that one set is distributed per group of 4 participants; in a group of 12 participants, for example, 3 people receive Task 1, three Task 2, etc.

Timing: 45 minutes

Classroom organisation: Pairs (or threes) to fours to whole group

Procedure:
1. Participants in pairs (or threes) work on the same task for 15 minutes.
2. Participants cross-group to form groups of four, so that they can share the outcomes of each of the tasks.
3. Whole-group summary on reasons for effectiveness or otherwise of the interventions.

Variations: Other tasks could be devised, such as looking at mentor contributions in terms of whether they are descriptive, interpretative or evaluative styles of intervention, etc.

The tasks could be carried out with role-play groups working on a recording of their role-play with or without a transcript; the whole group could work on the same task.

Follow up work could be done by watching the original video of the mentorial from which the transcript was made to see the differences body language and 'key' make.

Comments:
We have found this activity especially useful as a follow up for recorded role-plays. Often the observer (see Chapter 6 *Role-plays*) misses certain points, or is still uncertain about aspects of intervention, so listening back to the tape and concentrating on certain elements can be immensely valuable. It is certainly time-consuming, but we feel it is time well spent.

Participant reaction:
'Tape-recording our role-plays and talking them through sentence by sentence proved to be very useful, especially when we worked on the tasks.'

5.14 Styles of intervention

Some of the first publications on mentoring in ELT introduced the notion of *styles* of intervention (see Styles cards below). Isolating particular styles in this way is helpful for considering options in mentoring, but, as with many paradigms, in real life mentoring rarely fits so neatly into these categories and usually demonstrates a mixture of styles. In parallel with teaching, most mentoring contexts seem to demand a principled eclecticism, rather than strict adherence to any one particular style.

Aims:
- to consider the mentoring process in terms of mentor style
- to exemplify the usefulness of professional literature in learning mentoring/ teaching
- to provide an opportunity for participants to consider their own experience with their own mentors

Materials: One copy of the relevant Intervention Style Card (*Photocopiable resource 16* on pages 166–167) per style group; one large sheet of poster paper per group + coloured felt pens

Timing: Depending on size of group, 1–1½ hours

Classroom organisation: 4 or 8 small groups (one or two for each style), to melee, to whole group to pairs to whole group

Procedure:
1. Each small group is given the name of only one of the four styles of intervention above. Groups consider and make notes on what the name, as a style of mentoring, implies in terms of the processes, techniques and language the mentor would use in this style.
2. Each group then receives the appropriate Intervention Style Card and works on the task given.
3. Groups prepare a poster to represent their style, based on their readings and discussions.
4. Posters are displayed and presented. Participants meanwhile try to relate the different styles to their own experiences of past or present mentors.
5. In pairs, participants explain their choices of 'style' labels for their mentors.
6. Whole-group round-up discussion.

Variations: A possible extension of this activity, if videos of mentoring are available, is a 'Spot the Style' activity, where participants watch very different kinds of mentors at work and try to 'label' them with a style-name. This can cause quite heated discussions and lead to useful insights. Participants initially automatically judge some styles as 'good' and others as 'bad' or less desirable. The need for mentors to make conscious appropriate choices is highlighted again.

The frameworks for mentorials (Appendix 2) could be introduced at the end of this activity or before or during role-play practice of the whole complex mentoring skill (Chapter 6).

Comments:

Discussion often highlights the need for flexibility of style depending on the general stage of development of the particular mentee, with the mentor adapting the style to the various stages of the coaching process. Typically the progression can be seen more as a continuum from Directive to Alternatives, to Cooperative to Non-directive. Particular mentor–mentee discussions, on the other hand, we see as reversing this order, and the mentor will only adapt his or her style towards the more directive end of the continuum as or if the mentee has not been able to go through some or all of the phases of a critical analysis, to interpret or evaluate or plan, on their own.

Participant reaction:

'I don't think I'm a directive character, but I do find it very difficult not to be a directive mentor.'

'Learning about styles of intervention has persuaded me that there are ways of supervision that can help the teacher to find her own individual solutions, and I can vary my techniques according to the teacher's needs and level of consciousness.'

'It is a great relief to me that there are several styles and you are not supposed to follow one track which would be most limiting. I have decided to ask for feedback from my mentees on the value of my mentoring and I will record some post-lesson discussions to make it a learning experience for myself.'

5.15 Beginner teacher development

Researchers in the field of teachers' lives and teacher-learning are beginning to identify predictable stages that novice teachers go through on their developmental path towards expertise (see task sheet below).

In pre-service education a major goal to which mentoring contributes significantly must be to try to get mentees as far as possible through the stages of beginner teacher development. This is not only to ensure certain minimum standards but also to avoid the risk of losing expensively-trained potential teachers. This is a real risk if the critical stages ('informed pessimism' or 'reality shock') are not successfully navigated while the student-teacher is in the comparatively protected environment of an initial training programme. This responsibility is even greater and requires greater skill, sensitivity and strategic planning on the mentor's part if time for school-based mentoring is limited, when the temptation might be to push or to turn up the heat (but see *5.1 Butterflies*).

Aims:
– to consider the stages of beginner teacher growth
– to consider these stages in relation to participants' own professional development
– to consider mentoring activity appropriate for these stages

Materials: One copy of Beginner Teacher Development sheet per participant (*Photocopiable resource 17* on page 168)

Timing: 45 minutes

Classroom organisation: Pairs, to whole group

Procedure:

1. Participants in pairs imagine they have their diary from their first year of teaching in front of them. They turn the pages, telling their partners about the ups and downs of the first year or so.
2. Participants each receive a copy of the Beginner Teacher Development sheet, and complete the task in the same pairs.
3. Whole-group discussion of implications for mentoring.

Comments:

Discussion generally centres round how and how far mentors can help/ encourage/push mentees through these stages. Participants will frequently refer back to both 5.1 *Butterflies* and 5.10 *Excavating the iceberg*.

Participant reaction:

'I've never thought about this before, but I can remember the stages I went through. It's good to know everybody has similar patterns.'

'It's made me realise that we need to "judge" our students by the stages they are at.'

'I can see now even more why a long TP is a good idea. On a short one, students never really get further than worrying about themselves as teachers, and don't even think about their pupils and *their* learning.'

'I hope I'll be able to help my student teachers reach the stage of informed optimism.'

5.16 Difficult mentoring moments

Whether the mentees and mentors are carefully chosen for each other or not, and regardless of how well they have built up their relationship, there are likely to be difficult moments. These uncomfortable times often happen when there seems to be a conflict between the mentor's need to be both a Supporter and an Educator (see Figure 1). In other words, these are times when attempting to achieve a goal that the mentor sees as very important risks upsetting the trusting relationship (see *Comments* below for examples of such sticky moments). The same may be true for the mentee.

This activity gives the participants a chance to air their fears, or real problems if they are already practising mentors, and role-play their situations to practise confronting and resolving conflict (see Chapter 6 for more details on role-plays).

Aims:

– to discuss typical mentor–mentee conflicts
– to practise conflict resolution skills
– to increase empathy with the mentee

Suggested position in course: After work on counselling skills

Timing: 1 to 1½ hours

Materials: Copies of the Relationships and Goals Sheet and the Role-play Observation Sheet (*Photocopiable resource 18* and *19* on pages 169–170)

Classroom organisation: Individuals, small groups, whole group, role-play groups of 3, whole group

Procedure:

1. Individual participants think of a 'difficult moment'. This may be from their own experience with their mentor, their imagination or a real situation from their mentoring practice.
2. Small groups share their situations and put them into categories.
3. The whole group shares their categories, and the common factor of a tension between the seemingly conflicting needs of maintaining the relationship and achieving a goal are revealed.
4. The Relationships and Goals Sheet is distributed, discussed, and participants invited to identify the kind of behaviour they would naturally tend to use in conflict situations.
5. A format for conflict resolution, for confronting wisely, is then discussed. This will include:
   - The mentor expressing the *effect of the problem on them* (i.e. no accusations)
     [For example, *Mentor:* I'm feeling really puzzled about what to do. It's my job to help you learn teaching, and I know you need to experiment as a student-teacher. The problem is, it is also my responsibility to see that the pupils are learning, and at the moment I don't think they are.]
   - The mentor expressing it as a *joint problem to be solved*
     [cont. *Mentor:* . . . I wonder what we can do about this.]
   - Both mentor and mentee having the opportunity to express their *feelings*
     [cont. *Mentor:* I wonder what your feelings are about this? etc.]
     Both mentor and mentee exploring *reasons* ('excavating the iceberg')
     - Mentor and mentee *negotiating ways for **both** to feel OK*
     - Concrete *action plans*
6. In groups of three ('Mentor', 'Mentee' and Role-play Observer – see Chapter 6 *Role-plays: 6.1 Standard role-play procedure*), the participants have about five minutes to role-play their situations, with the participant whose problem it is taking the role of the 'Mentee' (this is very important, as it helps the mentor to become more empathetic with the mentee). The Role-Play Observer will make notes, using the Role-play Observation Sheet.
7. The 'Mentor', 'Mentee' and Role-play Observer review the role-play, discussing the stages, their feelings, suggestions for alternative approaches and so on.
8. Whole-group discussion of what each group learnt from the experience.
9. Time permitting, the procedure can be repeated with more of the problem situations to give further practice.

Variations: This conflict resolution procedure can be used for looking at other professional interpersonal problems (staff room, line managers, etc.)

Comments:

The type of problems that have arisen in our courses have been to do with:

– when you need to say or do something about personal things, such as appearance, character (shy) and so on
– when mentees want to avoid conflict/be liked by their pupils at all costs (a nice example of this was when a mentor observed to her mentee 'I saw a lot of students cheating during the test' upon which the mentee replied: 'So did I'!)
– when mentees have very strong, rigid, beliefs
– when the mentor's responsibilities for the student-teacher's learning seems to clash with responsibilities for the pupils' learning
– when mentees lack empathy for pupils (teach according to own character/learning style preferences)
– when mentee has language problems (lacks knowledge or proficiency)

Follow-up discussion often raises the following points:
– time and space need to be set aside for this kind of discussion
– the mentor needs to employ skilled active listening and be sure to understand the mentee's position, because the way forward that is found must satisfy *both* parties.
– the mentor needs to genuinely believe that a solution can be *jointly* negotiated, otherwise their behaviour can become 'shark'-like, especially if the mentee is 'teddy-bear' or 'turtle'-like and wants, or believes they should, leave the power with the mentor.

It is worth repeating this activity from time to time during the course, as it helps to reassure both those who have not mentored before and those who have actually experienced the problems.

Participant reaction:

'I really enjoyed the group discussion about "tight" situations. I was happy to see other mentors have similar problems.'

'I've been a teddy-bear, I need more practice being an owl.'

'The role-plays helped me see how to solve problems with my trainees.'

'These role-plays just started to suggest/reveal problem-solving techniques.'

6 Role-plays

Introduction

This chapter contains ideas for one of the most valuable types of activity on mentor courses, that of role-plays and the tasks associated with them. These activities can serve a number of different, but equally valuable, functions to do with the development of mentor skills. They provide time for whole skill practice (see below), a safe space for experimentation, an opportunity for participants to discover their natural or preferred mentor-style, and a range of situations in which to develop the ability to empathise with the mentee. The use of videos of teaching not only allows scope to practise observation, but also provides an opportunity to extend participants' knowledge about a range of activities, techniques and processes currently used in language teaching, as well as an opportunity to develop the local metalanguage that is used to describe and explain them. In addition, the whole complex role-play activity provides yet another shared experience on which to reflect.

The role-plays have three participants: one taking on the role of a 'Mentor' and another that of a 'Teacher' (this will be the mentee in most cases). The third participant does not take a role, but observes and takes notes as the Role-play Observer. The role-plays are preceded by preparation phases and are followed by reflection phases (for details see 6.1 *Standard role-play procedure*). The whole group will be doing their role-plays simultaneously, in other words they do not watch another group's role-play.

Whole-skill development

Repeated use of role-plays allows the practice and development of observation and intervention skills in the safe environment of the course. Two notions are important here: that of skill and that of what it takes to learn skill (see Chapter 1: 1.2 *Teaching*).

Teaching has been described (Tomlinson 1995) as a 'complex open skill': 'complex' because many things are happening at the same time, and 'open' because there is no one right reaction in any given situation. An expert teacher knows what to do at any one moment in her classroom so that her pupils have the best opportunities for learning. Knowing what to do involves both knowledge and action, which are bound together in almost instantaneous, seemingly effortless responses to constantly fluctuating sets of circumstances. The same, we believe, can be said of mentoring: it involves the ability to notice and interpret the mentee's actions, select from a range of possible reactions, act on that choice, notice again and so on – all almost instantaneously. This mentoring skill, then, is 'complex', in that there are a number of things going on at any one time, and it is 'open', in that there are no stereotypical right reactions.

The goal of learning a skill is to develop expertise which is 'fluent, economical, and takes relatively little effort' (Tomlinson 1995:15). Mentors need to reach a certain level of expertise before they begin to work with mentees. This is not only in order to help their student-teacher's development, but also because in the busy lives these teachers lead, they need to be able to apply their mentoring skills with 'relatively little effort' if mentoring is not to be a burden. In order for mentors to be 'economical' in their work, they need to be both reactive and proactive in their thinking. In other words, mentors and their student-teachers will not only explore what has happened in lessons and make adjustments accordingly, but they will also have a long-term plan for development, a 'curriculum' for the practicum, based on the needs of the mentee and the requirements of the mentoring context. This will help ensure that the most efficient learning takes place in the time given. 'Fluent' suggests the mentor's appropriate, easy, almost intuitive reading of the situation – the lessons observed, the pupils and the mentee herself – leading to suitable selection from a range of available options for action. Both fluency and economy in mentoring, as in teaching, are surely derived from knowledge acquired through 'having been there before', having had sufficient opportunity to practise the mentoring skills in the sheltered environment of the training room (see *Experimentation* below).

In looking at whole skill learning, we can identify a number of relevant features:

Time

Skill development takes time, and the amount of time needed to become fluent, economical and almost effortless will vary from one person to another. For this reason, role-plays for whole skill practice form the backbone of our mentor courses.

Experimentation

Role-plays provide a safe environment in which participants can try out options for different types of interventions and experience the different impacts that these will have on different individuals. This can help them to learn how to choose or implement the different types of intervention more appropriately.

Mentor style awareness

Most participants will find a style of mentoring that seems to suit their personalities best. However, they need to be able to develop and practise a wider range of styles so that they can select the one most appropriate to the needs of their student teacher at any one moment. Role-plays can help participants become aware, in a safe environment, of their own natural mentoring style and give an opportunity to work on perfecting other styles of mentoring so that they feel comfortable using them. This takes practice, otherwise adopting a style may be seen as lacking congruence, and therefore as being insincere. The understandings they gain will help them to select a style, as well as individual acts of intervention, appropriately.

Empathising ability

In taking on a variety of 'Teacher' roles, participants develop their ability to empathise with their future mentees. This in turn, increases their ability to act appropriately, using these insights for what Tomlinson (1995) calls 'effective reading of context'. The post role-play discussions (see 6.1 *Video-based role-plays – standard procedure* below) will provide a further opportunity for discussing how it felt to be the 'Teacher'. This is further enhanced through the post-role-play discussion.

Focus for reflective practice

Role-plays provide a powerful experience for developing reflective practice. The first experience (a 'controlled' cycle) is provided by a video-recording of a student-teacher's lesson, during which the participants make observation notes. They then prepare for their part in the role-play that follows, in which the 'Mentor' and the 'Teacher' act out a post-lesson discussion, using the techniques developed so far on the course. In other words, they are simulating the way in which student-teachers can be helped by the mentor to reflect on their experience and then plan what to do next and how to do it. Meanwhile, they are being observed by a Role-play Observer, who is making notes. After the role-play, all three participants reflect on the whole experience. The Observer will provide evidence of what they observed during the role-play by 'holding up the mirror'. For example, the Observer might say 'I noticed that the "Teacher" looked surprised when you asked her why she had given the instructions in the mother tongue'. In this way, the observer will be leading the 'Mentor' to explore not only the reasons for her choice of I-statement, but also the effect it has on the mentee – in effect the Observer will be mentoring the 'Mentor'. As the trio reflect on the experience, all three participants have the opportunity to develop insights into the mentoring process. Since role-plays are used throughout the course, all participants will have the chance to take all the roles, which will not only give them plenty of practice, but also help to reduce any potential stress that might arise from being in any of the roles.

Materials

Role-play activities require a number of different materials, such as videos and associated materials, role-cards, observation tasks and follow-up discussion tasks. While this chapter contains examples of most of these, course leaders will need to select for themselves the most appropriate videos.

It is far more practical to use videoed rather than live lessons for the first phase of the role-play procedure, even though what can be observed will have already been selected to some extent by the focus of the camera. The use of videoed lessons allows the course leader to make varied and appropriate selections according to certain methodological aspects or to standards and styles of teaching and so on. A variety of videos can provide a range of methodology, through different teachers teaching different kinds of lessons in different settings. This can extend and develop the participants' metalanguage for talking about teaching, leading to a shared discourse which will ideally include the explanations, language and terminology that the mentees have learnt. The methodological focus of the videos can be either familiar or unfamiliar to the participants. If it is unfamiliar, it can be an opportunity to learn some new methodology, its rationale and the language to describe it. If it is familiar, the language the participants use to describe it could nevertheless vary in which case it is likely that the rationale or explanation will also be different. As an example of this, what one teacher might call a 'pre-reading activity', another might call 'the beginning of top-down discourse processing'. With different language, and therefore almost inevitably different explanations, the two teachers' interpretations and judgements will be almost incomprehensible to each other. It is crucial, therefore, that the mentor and mentee develop a shared understanding of the language they are using, and this will be something they may need to work on.

Commercially produced videos of teaching can usefully provide new methodological input. In addition, because they are likely to be from unfamiliar contexts, participants can practise observing the unfamiliar and searching for rational explanation. Locally-made videos, on the other hand, are often seen as more immediately relevant. The challenge here is a different one, as the participants may find it more difficult to 'notice the familiar' (see Chapter 4 *Seeing clearly*), and more importantly find it harder to question the assumptions and explanations of what they have observed.

Using videos of the local context may mean that mentor course leaders have to be involved in their production. We have found that it is useful to try to put together a video pack, which includes:

– video of a lesson;
– lesson plan for the lesson videoed;

– materials used in lesson: text-book or relevant extract, and/or supplementary materials;
– lesson plans for preceding and following lessons;
– scheme of work in which videoed lesson appears;
– examples of pupils' work and/or feedback on the lesson(s);
– audio or video recording of pre- and/or post-lesson discussion with mentor;
– relevant extracts from mentee's and/or mentor's journal.

However, if videos of teaching in the local context are already available, but do not have any of the accompanying materials mentioned, this need not be a problem. Lesson plans, for example, can be created from the video, the course books used on the video will be locally available, and other supporting material can be invented, which may, indeed, be more appropriate to the needs of the participants.

In addition to the standard role-play procedure, this chapter contains a variety of role-cards and observation and discussion tasks that can be used to 'complement' the standard procedure.

Procedure and role-cards

6.1 Video-based mentoring role-plays – a standard procedure

The main tools on our mentor courses for practising mentoring skills and techniques are mentoring role-plays. In the following role-play procedure, 'Mentors' get valuable practice in mentoring skills and personal feedback on these from both 'Teacher' and Role-play Observer. Although the 'Teacher' role requires the most 'acting', which some people find difficult, it is nonetheless very important that participants experience what it is like to be on the receiving end of mentoring, and thereby develop the ability to empathise, to consider their interventions from the point of view of possible impact on their mentee. The Role-play Observer who does not participate in the actual role-play, has a genuine mentoring role, albeit of mentoring beginner mentors rather than teachers. They are therefore practising their own mentoring skills in a real situation. Repeated role-plays allow participants to take on all of these different roles.

In addition, work with videoed lessons can also refresh participants' knowledge about teaching methodology or provide new insights.

What follows is a description of a standard procedure for mentoring role-plays, which is almost infinitely variable through, for example, different combinations of the kind of Role-cards, Role-play Observer's tasks, or Teacher's Biography Cards such as those presented in this chapter after this activity description.

Aims:
– to practise the mentoring skills of observation, note-making, counselling, supporting and challenging
– to work on ability to empathise through taking on roles

Materials: Videoed lesson or extract + one copy of the 'lesson plan' (genuine or invented) per participant; standard Role-play Observation Sheet; Standard Post-role-play Discussion Sheet (*Photocopiable resource 20 and 21 on pages 171–172*)
(For alternative/optional cards see the rest of this chapter)

Timing: Length of video + 45 minutes

Classroom organisation: Whole group to three role-play preparation groups (of all 'Mentors', all 'Teachers' or all Observers), to role-play groups of 3 (one of each), to whole group

Procedure: The following is a diagram of the stages of the activity, which we generally present before the first role-play of this type, since the procedure can be confusing.

Stages of the role-play

Stage 1
All Participants
Familiarisation with lesson plan

Stage 2
All Participants
Video-viewing and note-making

Stage 3

Mentors	Teachers	Observers
Role-play preparation	*Role-play peparation*	*Role-play preparation*

Stage 4

T+M	T+M	T+M	T+M	T+M	T+M	T+M
O	O	O	O	O	O	O
Role-play	*Role-play*	*Role-play*	*Role-play*	*Role-play*	*Role-play*	*Role-play*

Stage 5

O	O	O	O	O	O	O
TM	TM	TM	TM	TM	TM	TM
Discussion	*Discussion*	*Discussion*	*Discussion*	*Discussion*	*Discussion*	*Discussion*

Stage 6
All Participants
Whole-group discussion of insights

Figure 9 Stages of the role-play

1. Participants familiarise themselves with the videoed lesson objectives and plan, and lesson observation schedule if used.
2. They watch the video and make notes (either general, or according to specific focus, or role if given at this time).
3. Participants, in three role-play preparation groups study their role-cards and carry out any specific tasks in preparation for the particular role-play.

4. In groups of three, one 'Mentor' and one 'Teacher' role-play a post-lesson discussion, with the Observer sitting slightly to one side, taking notes as instructed on their sheet.
5. The Observer in each group, acting as time-keeper, indicates when the role-play should stop, and chairs the post-role-play discussion according to the post-role-play sheet.
6. Whole group report-back of learning from each role-play group.

Variations: The format for video-based role-plays essentially remains the same, whatever the focus. Variations could include:
– repeating the role-play after the discussion, either in the same or different roles;
– assigning roles before or after the video-watching;
– participants working in role-groups before the video-watching (Step 2), in preparation for the role-play (as well as or instead of preparatory work after video-viewing);
– 'Mentors' informed about the focus of the Observer's task, or not informed about the focus of the Observer's task, or choose the focus of the Observer's task;
– recording the role-play (see *5.13 Transcript tasks*);
– watching a videoed pre-lesson mentoring discussion about the lesson first, doing the role-play as above, then comparing it with a video of the actual post-lesson discussion.

Comments: Over the years, in the light of participants' feedback on the immense value of these experiences, we use more and more role-plays on courses.

Participant reaction:
'Very useful because of the three points of view.'
'I'm beginning to enjoy the role-plays; it's getting easier to *feel* my role.'
'I felt the need to develop myself towards becoming an assertive mentor who articulates her opinion in a straightforward but non-aggressive way. Now I would modify this since I realise that I can be an assertive self-confident mentor but still refrain from expressing my opinion explicitly if the mentee would not benefit from it.'
'Many things we worked on early in the course which seemed such heavy tasks then, e.g. use of body language, active listening techniques, have now become natural just by being put into practice over and over again.'
'When I played the "Teacher" I knew instantly which questions the "Mentor" asked because she was interested, and which merely for the sake of making me talk. When the latter happened, I became very uncooperative, making her job very difficult as well. Because I now know what it is like to be interviewed, I have a better understanding of how to conduct a post-lesson discussion myself.'

Role-cards for specific role-plays

The following three specific role-plays were included because, in our context at least, they are standard types of mentor/mentee discussion or mentorial

6.2 Lesson-planning role-cards

See *Photocopiable resource 22* on pages 172–173. These cards are for use in simulated planning discussions. (See Appendix 2: *Frameworks for mentorials*.)

6.3 Full post-lesson discussion role-cards

See *Photocopiable resource 23* on pages 174–175. These cards are for use in role-plays simulating mentorials which take place after a particular lesson, and when there is enough time for a full discussion (see also Appendix 2).

6.4 Five-minute post-lesson discussion role-cards

See *Photocopiable resource 24* on pages 176–177. These cards are for use in role-plays simulating those occasions after a lesson when there is not enough time for a lengthy discussion.

Focused observation tasks for role-play observers

The following are a selection of tasks for use by the Observer during mentoring role-plays. (They could also be used for observing mentors at work with real mentees.) The tasks are designed to focus on some of the discrete skills involved in mentoring. These may be selected by the course leader according to the syllabus of the course initially, and later by the participants taking the 'Mentor' role as they become more aware of their own individual needs.

As each of the tasks is linked to work on a particular mentoring skill, the relevant practice activities are given as reference.

6.5 Supportive listening

See *Photocopiable resource 25* on page 177. This schedule focuses the role-play observer's attention on evidence of supportive listening.

See 5.2 *We don't listen when . . .*, 5.3 *We listen when . . .* and 5.5 *Once I had a class . . . .*

6.6 Paraphrasing

See *Photocopiable resource 26* on page 178. This schedule focuses the role-play observer's attention specifically on the mentor's use of paraphrasing.

See 5.4 *'That's exactly what I mean!'*

6.7 I-statements

See *Photocopiable resource 27* on page 178. This schedule focuses the role-play observer's attention on the mentor's use of I-statements and requires them to record those statements as objective or interpretative, or evaluative.

See 4.6 *I heard, I saw, I noticed*; 5.6 *Getting a clear picture* and 5.11 *'I' to 'Why?'*

6.8 'Excavating'

See *Photocopiable resource 28* on page 179. This schedule focuses the role-play observer's attention on the challenges the mentor makes and the level of the iceberg at which they are aimed.

See 5.10 *Excavating the iceberg.*

6.9 Questions

See *Photocopiable resource 29* on page 179. This schedule focuses the role-play observer's attention on the kind of questions the mentor uses, and how they are asked.

See 5.7 *It's not what you say, it's the way that you say it*; 5.8 *Question time*, and 5.9 *Considering questions.*

6.10 Question factors

See *Photocopiable resource 30* on page 180. This is another schedule which focuses the role-play observer's attention on questions which asks them also to interpret the intent of the questioner.

See 5.9 *Considering questions.*

Teacher biography cards

The importance of a teacher's biography in terms of its influence on their professional development cannot be overestimated. The use of these cards in mentoring role-plays helps to raise awareness of the need for mentors and mentees to explore this influence. In addition, these cards can help 'Teachers' to get into role, and 'Mentors' to practise with a variety of mentees at different stages of development. See *Photocopiable resource 31* on page 181.

The same card is given to the 'Teacher' and the 'Mentor' at stage 1, 2 or 3 of the Standard Role-play Procedure (see Figure 9 *Stages of the role-play*). Obviously, Teacher biography cards can be adapted to suit the particular mentoring context more explicitly, or 'Teacher's characteristics cards' (extrovert, etc.) can be made to suit the teachers on particular videos.

7 Assessing teaching

Introduction

Most mentoring contexts have some kind of written standard of teaching towards which the teacher development process is geared. Mentoring is context-bound, and is generally a service provided by stake-holders (institutions, education authorities and other funders) so that the required standards will be reached. Work will often need to be done on mentoring courses to take account of these standards, and to begin a process of interpretation and internalisation of the standards. If mentor course participants belong to the same system (of initial teacher education, probation schemes and so on), and especially if the system is award-bearing, this work will also help create a notional shared understanding in order to ensure fairness in the system, standardisation and a certain inter-rater reliability. There are however a number of dangers. Our view of learning sees the responsibility for development ultimately lying with the individual, and the education process as being primarily concerned with ensuring that that individual has both the ability and willingness to undertake that responsibility.

The dangers of outsider evaluation

An important aspect of understanding of professional development is that ultimately it is the (student)-teacher who is the initiator, the decider in all parts of the process. They participate in a teaching/learning event, then describe, interpret and evaluate that event, and go on to draw up action-plans for their own further learning, which may include drawing on others' interpretations of available data, before acting again and so on. The reflective teacher is not reliant on someone else's judgement of their effectiveness in managing learning processes in the classroom. These learning processes cannot be seen and judged on an evaluator's snapshot picture of only one lesson, an 'exam lesson' (which is unfortunately what happens in some initial teacher training systems). When they are lucky enough to have an observer in their classrooms, a reflective teacher is likely to bombard that observer with things to watch out for, informing them about what they are working on at the moment. For the reflective teacher, the observer's offerings of data and interpretations will be far more valuable than any evaluation.

It follows that we believe outsider evaluation is of limited use, as opposed to the outsider's valuable functions as data-gatherer and offerer of another set of interpretations. Judgement is even potentially dangerous if constantly used, as it can deprive the mentee of the opportunities of working towards autonomous professional development. Judgement is, after all, only an expression of the difference between the observer's and the observed's stages on the interteaching continuum (see Chapter 1: 1.3.4 *Interteaching*) and relies heavily on the observer's ability to see clearly (see Chapter 4).

We are not trying to suggest that in the process of learning to be a reflective practitioner, an outsider's judgement is never helpful. If it is to be useful, however, it has to be carefully considered, as with any other form of mentoring intervention, in terms of its potential impact on the mentee's learning processes. It goes without saying that we believe judgements, when they occur, will draw on data from more than one lesson, and preferably from the same course or courses.

The dangers of the tools of assessment

There are dangers lurking not only in the act of judgement itself, but also in the tools used for assessment. Standards are usually embodied in check-lists of teaching competencies or behaviours. Check-list items might include such things as 'Planning: appropriate selection and sequencing of activities for the objectives of the lesson'; or 'Application: gives clear appropriate instructions'; or 'Rapport: pleasant manner conveying approachability'; or even items in categories such as 'Personal' or 'Ability to reflect' which might include things such as 'has a pleasant speaking voice' or 'is capable of self-evaluation' (see e.g. Appendix 3). Often these check-lists will be accompanied by detailed descriptors for each point, so that assessors can judge whether a candidate is 'excellent', 'satisfactory' or 'unsatisfactory', for example, in any given area (see e.g. Appendix 4). However detailed, check-lists are nonetheless only crude lists of the main elements of a hugely complex process, and as such, in our view, cannot possibly represent all aspects of 'good' teaching and professionalism. In other words, a 'good' professional teacher is more than the sum of the ticks on any check-list we have ever come across. Mentor course participants, then, need to become aware of the limitations of check-lists, despite the temptation to view them as comforting all-round yardsticks.

On the other hand, global descriptors (e.g. Appendix 5), referring to such things as subject knowledge, professionalism both in the classroom and school and so on, or profiles of teaching competencies (e.g. HMI Survey, 1987, *Quality in Schools: The Initial Training of Teachers*) can capture some of what is missing from check-lists, but run the danger of increasing the subjectivity of interpretation. They demand even more work on standardising interpretation (see 7.3 *Bench-marking*). However, used in conjunction with check-lists (as check-lists for observation, rather than points for evaluation), they are useful additions to the teacher-evaluator's tool-kit.

These check-lists and descriptors will often endeavour to capture the essence of the notion of 'good' teaching and professionalism for a particular context. Yet that, as we have seen in the interteaching model in Chapter 1: 1.3.4

Interteaching, is not only something which has not been fully described, but is an ever-elusive goal. How, then, can we expect student-teachers to measure up to these often very high standards at the *beginning* of their careers? In our combined experience of more than half a century of teaching, we doubt we would consistently earn an 'excellent' on all the categories of the check-lists we have seen (or even a 'satisfactory' on some). This may be because the item does not belong to our view of 'good' teaching and professionalism, or because it is low on our list of priorities of things needing attention. We do believe, however, we have become increasingly better teachers for more people on more courses. What is needed, then, is a way of measuring a student-teacher's ability and commitment to improving their own management of courses as well as their role in the quality and effectiveness of the learning of the people on those courses, including themselves.

Although it is important to have a vision of the ultimate goal, this is obviously not a reasonable aim, as we have said, for a beginner teacher. Perhaps this is why many evaluators we know intuitively 'make allowances'. A more valid minimum standard, we believe, would include evidence of engagement in and commitment to a process of making sense of teaching and learning, coupled with some notion of at least 'not being dangerous' in the classroom (see e.g. Appendix 5). 'Not being dangerous' is in quotation marks here as it is a notion that one of us first encountered in nursing training. In that context, it referred to the dispensing of drugs, the placing of drips, the treatment of wounds and so on. Crucially, it also included the ability to listen to and observe patients well enough to at least recognise possible medical emergencies and take appropriate action, if not positively intervene in the healing process. For a language teacher, this can be translated into not being dangerous with regard to, say, the teaching of rules, the treatment of errors, blackboard use and so on, as well as careful listening to and observing of pupils in order to at least recognise 'learning emergencies', if not actively promote that learning. In EFL, we have seen the results of dangerous rule teaching with respect to the past perfect, and the usage of the second form of the verb, to name a couple of the teaching equivalents of iatrogenic (doctor-induced) illnesses. We have seen pupils too frightened to open their mouths for fear of ridicule; inaccurate and unhelpful notebooks resulting from inaccurate and unhelpful boardwork, and learners who have given up as a result of teachers missing or not acting upon the signs of their learning emergencies. As this shows, even not being dangerous will require considerable skill.

Returning to the importance of the student-teacher's ability to self-evaluate as a tool for their continuing professional development, clearly it is the mentor's duty to ensure that mentees not only reach the standards required by their particular context, but that they too have internalised a set of standards by which they can self-evaluate in the future, and from which they can develop their own personal set of criteria.

Ideally, then, student-teachers need to share in all stages of the evaluation process, from the selecting and writing of criteria to the final decision-making on their own graded evaluation, measured against the standard embodied in those criteria.

This section contains three activities which encourage an exploration of the problems concerned with the subjectivity of the selection and interpretation of written criteria, as well as of their limitations in general. (See also Chapter 4 *Seeing clearly.*)

Activities

7.1 Beer bottles, carob pods, conkers or stones

This activity considers the subjectivity of the evaluation process which derives from individuals' previous experiences, knowledge, feelings, beliefs and so on.

Aims:
– to provide an illustration for the universal subjectivity of evaluation
– to provide an illustration of the difficulty of describing criteria

Suggested position in course: Towards the end

Suggested position in session: As an introduction to work on evaluation, after an appropriate warmer (e.g. 3.16 *Smelly socks*)

Materials: A display of 6–10 different numbered beer bottles, carob pods, conkers, stones or any other group of objects which share the same name, but have differences in appearance. The choice of object will depend on the context, and works best with one which generates memories and affective associations for participants.

Timing: 45 minutes

Assumptions: The choice of object will neither offend, nor fail to generate associations for participants

Classroom organisation: Individuals to small groups to cross-groups to whole group

Procedure:
1. Participants individually decide on which of the objects they like best and which they like least and why.
2. In small groups, participants share their choices before writing a set of agreed criteria, under 'excellent', 'satisfactory' and 'unsatisfactory'. If shape is a criterion, they will have to find a way of articulating exactly what kind of shape is 'best', less good or no good and so on.
3. Individuals then evaluate each object according to their agreed criteria.
4. In the same small groups participants compare and contrast similarities and differences in evaluations, and try to account for these.
5. Participants are cross-grouped so that each new group has one member from each of the original groups in Step 2. Participants in turn present the results of their evaluations, which object is judged 'best' and so on, and the group tries to guess the criteria on which this judgement was made.
6. In the same small groups, participants now compare and contrast the written sets of criteria accounting for differences.

7. The groups then summarise insights from the whole activity on:
   – Selecting criteria
   – Writing criteria
   – Using criteria
8. In the whole-group round-up, a spokesperson from each group reports on the outcome of Step 7.

Variations: We have found that a variety of little bottles and jars of herbs and spices also serve well for this activity, and may be more easily available for some course leaders

Comments:
Outcomes of this activity centre around the influence of personal and group 'baggage'. This subjectivity emerges right at the beginning in the selection of criteria processes, highlighting the importance of negotiating criteria with all concerned (all stake-holders). Subjectivity is also present in the interpretation of the written criteria (what constitutes 'delicious' or 'a pleasing shape', etc.), underlining the need for bench-marking (see 7. 3), and ideally group negotiated writing of criteria, in order to go as far as possible towards a common understanding.

If evaluators (and evaluated) have not been part of the selection and writing process the need for both repeated bench-marking for evaluators, as well as work with the 'evaluated' to help them internalise agreed understandings is even more vital. A mentor's responsibility, then, is not only to internalise the standards of the context through bench-marking work with other evaluators, but also to help the mentee understand the criteria in the same way. (See 7.2 *Using check-lists* below.)

Participant reaction:
'Beer bottles was a real eye-opener!'
'I loved the activity with the stones and things, it really made us see how we all value things differently.'

7.2 Using check-lists

If check-lists exist for evaluation purposes, mentors and mentees will want to use them periodically for diagnostic purposes. In these cases they will act as multiple-focus observation schedules. As well as fulfilling a valuable diagnostic role, the occasional use of the evaluation check-lists can help mentees develop a shared understanding of the goals of the evaluation process.

If written check-lists do not exist for evaluation in the particular context, it is a good idea for mentor and mentee together to establish a list of possible observation points for their work together – a homemade check-list, which can be added to as the mentee gains new insights.

Aims:
– to raise awareness of the uses and limitations of multiple-focus check-lists

Suggested position in course: Towards the end of the course, after focused observation practice, during evaluation work, after e.g. 7.1 *Beer bottles, carob pods, conkers or stones*

Materials: Videoed lesson of a student-teacher + lesson plan, and ideally place in scheme of work, or longer-term planning and previous lesson plans; copies for each participant of the check-lists mentors will be expected to use in their mentoring contexts

Timing: 1 hour

Classroom organisation: Whole group, to small groups, to crossed pairs, to whole group

Procedure:
1. Participants watch the video. Half the group uses their check-list as an observation schedule, while the other half of the group makes full global observation notes (i.e. no given specific focus).
2. Participants individually evaluate on the basis of their notes, grading the teacher as follows: Excellent, Good, Satisfactory, Poor, Fail (or using the scale appropriate in the context). This evaluation is kept secret until Step 5.
3. In small groups of participants with the same kind of observation notes (i.e. all with check-lists, or all with global notes), participants compare and contrast the *content* of their observations and discuss the reasons for differences.
4. Each check-list observer pairs up with one global observer, and again they compare and contrast the *content* of their observations and discuss the reasons for differences.
5. Whole group: Participants now reveal the grades they each gave; these are collected on the board in two columns, 'Check-list' and 'Global'.
6. Still in whole group (or if very large, first in small groups), participants summarise the implications of the activity for observation and evaluation.

Comments:
It invariably emerges that check-lists are difficult to use as observation instruments and they tend to be filled in from memory which is both selective and seems to store interpretations rather than descriptions or information. During observation, participants find themselves wanting to make notes that they have difficulty finding a home for on the check-list, and therefore scribble them in the margins. This seems to exemplify our comment about teaching being 'more than the sum of the ticks' (see introduction to this section), particularly as these comments tend to be more 'global' in nature. Global note-makers on the other hand, will often have failed to comment on many of the check-list points (especially if they were judged to be 'good' or 'satisfactory'), but may have noted things that those using check-lists missed.

In Step 5, grades in both columns are often equally mixed and lead to realisations that evaluations depend as much on the evaluator's 'baggage' as on the instrument used.

Participant reaction:
'Very useful. Interesting to see the different opinions.'
'It's really important who the observer is and what they are observing with.'

7.3 Bench-marking

Bench-marking is a standardising process which attempts to ensure inter-rater reliability in criterion-based assessment procedures. Before real assessment and grading takes place, the evaluators do a trial or mock marking exercise together, in order to have a common interpretation of the criteria. Bench-marking teaching practice involves watching videos of teaching, and each individual evaluator using the given written criteria to make judgements. These are then discussed by the whole team of evaluators until all can agree on a grade and see why and how it was achieved.

The need for bench-marking as such was discussed above. This activity raises awareness of that need, as well as providing a format for doing it.

Aims:
– to raise awareness of the need for bench-marking
– to demonstrate a procedure for bench-marking

Suggested position in course: During work on evaluation, probably after *Using check-lists*, above

Materials: Videoed lesson; a copy per participant of the written evaluation criteria used in the context (whether a list of points only or accompanied by descriptors, etc.)

Timing: Viewing time + 1 hour

Classroom organisation: Individual to groups of 6–8, to whole group

Procedure:
1. Participants watch the video, and make notes on evidence that might relate to the criteria.
2. Participants individually make their judgements for each of the criteria.
3. In groups of 6–8 participants take each criterion in turn and attempt to reach an agreement on assessment of it. This will involve both clarifying the scope of meaning of individual words in the criterion, as well as discussion of observed evidence with regard to it.
4. Whole-group round-up.

Variations: If participants all come from different contexts, you will probably want to choose the most detailed set of descriptors you can find to use with everybody. If participants come from two or three different contexts, they will need to be grouped accordingly at Step 3.

Comments:
Step 3 can take a lot of time as participants struggle to reach an agreement. This struggle is valuable, as it is through this process that shared understandings are reached. In addition, individual participants may become aware of shortcomings in their observation skills.

Participant reaction:
'It was very difficult to agree.'
'I was surprised by how differently we understood the criteria.'

Acknowledgements: We owe a debt of gratitude to Charles Alderson and the Lancaster University testing team who showed us the value and necessity of bench-marking during work on developing our language exams at CETT.

7.4 Negotiated evaluation – role-play

Many possible role-plays could be devised to help mentors empathise with the experience of being evaluated and evaluating, and consider its impact on the mentee's development. In role-play situations, of necessity, this evaluation can only be done on the basis of one lesson. However, we strongly believe that evaluation of teaching should be of the process, that is, of a series of lessons, or a whole course, rather than a one-off, often artificial 'display' exam lesson, where teaching techniques may be seen but the impact of the teaching on pupils' learning can rarely be gauged.

The following is an example of a role play on evaluation to demonstrate the usefulness of negotiated evaluation.

Aims:
– to consider the possible intervention impact of negotiated evaluation
– to demonstrate a way of using negotiated evaluation

Suggested position in course: During work on evaluation

Materials: Videoed lesson + Post-role-play Discussion Sheet (see Chapter 6) + Role-cards (*Photocopiable resource 32* on pages 182–183)

Timing: Length of viewing + 1 hour

Procedure:
See Chapter 6: 6.1 *Standard role-play procedure*

Comments:
For the 'mentors' this activity is like a test of all the counselling skills practised on the course so far. In order to negotiate, the mentors not only have to be prepared to relinquish the evaluations they made in the preparation stage of the role-play, but quite possibly fight against often strong, culturally-based, models of the 'supervisor as evaluator'. In order to do this, they need to draw consciously on all the counselling skills they have been practising on the course, as well as work in a collaborative style of intervention.

8 Observation tasks

Introduction

The key factor of these tasks is that the participants are engaged in observation of real teaching (unlike the video-based activities of the sessions). Because it is each participant's own teaching which is the focus for observation, these activities will also provide an opportunity to gain insights into how a mentee might feel and react to being observed. It follows that the consequent discussion and offering of data and interpretations are also real, thus providing an opportunity for mentors-in-training to get genuine feedback on their skills. The mentoring sub-skills that are being practised are those of observation and helpful reflective behaviour.

Tasks and activities

8.1 Self-observation

The reason for asking participants to go through this activity is that as mentors they will be helping mentees to develop the observation and processing skills involved in self-observation. The ability to observe oneself and one's classroom is an important part of 'enabling' mentees (Prahbu 1987) to undertake their own continuous professional development. Once clear evidence, in the form of descriptions of classroom events, is amassed through self-observation, mentees need to be able to go through the kind of cognitive processing that leads to considered interpretations, decisions, further action and professional growth (see e.g. 5.10 *Excavating the iceberg*). Initially, this processing of evidence will be facilitated through talk with the mentor. The goal, however, is that the mentees, like their mentors, will be capable of autonomous further development. This activity, therefore, gives mentors practice in modelling what mentees will be expected to do.

A further use of this activity for participants is that it provides another occasion for talking about teaching, both at the level of being able to say *how* they did what they did, and at the level of saying *why* they do/did what they do/did. It can prove extremely difficult for a skilled teacher (who has yet to become a mentor) to describe, for example, exactly *how* they kept a class under control, let alone refer to underlying beliefs about learning to explain *why* they chose (possibly subconsciously) those particular techniques for those learners. This issue of 'talking teaching' is further complicated for those participants who may have followed a different professional development route and who therefore may not have the same professional language as their prospective mentees. It may also be a problem for those who are non-native speaker teachers.

Between-session task

Aims:

– to provide experience in selecting an observation focus and appropriate tool for recording self-observation
– to provide practice in self-observation; to provide, for further discussion, a common experience of self-observation

Suggested position in course: After introductory work on observation, and some work on counselling skills (see Chapter 5)

Materials: Possibly, a range of published observation and self-observation schedules from the literature on classroom/action research, observation, etc. or see Appendix 6

Timing: Depending on task chosen, up to one school lesson

Assumptions: All participants are active teachers, or can arrange to teach a class

Procedure:

1. The assignment and its rationale are given to the participants and discussed.

Assignment specifications:

a) Choose an aspect of your teaching for self-observation. (This may be something you are already working on or want to work on – e.g. learner-training; something you want to try out in your teaching – e.g. drama techniques; something you know you are instinctively successful at, but cannot explain why – e.g. explaining vocabulary, etc.)
b) Choose an appropriate means of recording this observation (written formats, see Materials).
c) Observe and record the lesson or appropriate part(s) of the lesson.
d) Bring the written record of self-observation to the next session.

---

2. Participants carry out the self-observation.

Comments:

We have run into difficulties occasionally because participants have failed to carry out the task by the given deadline. We have learnt that it is important to negotiate realistic deadlines in order to be able to carry out the follow-up activity.

Participant reaction:

'Through self-observation we understand that we should take the responsibility for our own development, and it is a tremendous professional challenge to prepare ourselves for the task.'

'I don't like looking at myself. I know it's important, so I'll have to practise.'

In-session follow-up

Aims:
- to develop the ability to talk about (their own) teaching explicitly
- to develop the skill of processing the evidence in a way that leads to decisions and possibly further action
- to develop the skills of active listening (empathy, questioning to get a clear picture, reserving judgement, etc.)

Suggested position in course: After the assignment above

Materials: Participants' own self-observation record sheets

Timing: 1 hour

Classroom organisation: Pairs to whole group

Procedure:
1. a) One partner is given 20 minutes to talk about their self-observation, first describing what they observed. The other partner listens, tries to visualise the scene and asks any necessary questions to enable them to do so.
   b) The speaker goes on to say what they have so far concluded from their observations and any resulting decisions they may have made. The listener, without imposing their own opinion, attempts to, for example, draw the speaker's attention to evidence that has not been discussed, or suggests ideas for alternative action, if the speaker seems undecided. In other words, the listener will do all they can to help the speaker process the evidence in ways which are personally meaningful and acceptable to the speaker.
   c) Still in pairs, during or after this discussion, the advantages and disadvantages of the selection and format of the self-observation recording tool itself are discussed.
   d) Partners give feedback to each other on their ways of describing, 'talking teaching', listening helpfully, making suggestions, etc.
2. Roles are reversed, and the above is repeated.
3. Whole-group feedback and discussion.

Variations: Should any participant have failed to complete the assignment on time, they can take the role of observer of a pair who agrees to have them, joining in Steps 1d and 2d

Comments:
Ideally, partners for this activity are self-selected, but if not, it will be necessary to ensure that partners trust each other and/or have a similar level of self-assurance, experience and language.

Participant reaction:
'When we were having the discussion after the self-observation, my partner said she would have talked more if I had asked her questions.'
'If the mentor herself goes through the hard and sometimes painful phases of self-observation and self-critique she will be able to understand and guide her mentees much better.'

8.2 Peer-observation

Not only is peer-observation another opportunity to practise observation and the skills involved in facilitating helpful reviewing, but it helps to foster the culture of professional cooperation, which in turn helps to guard against the risk of teacher isolation, a factor which can hinder professional development. In addition, it is a further opportunity for the participants to explore their own constructs and make them explicit.

The following two activities consider the use of the two most common forms of review process in our context: *immediate oral review*, and *delayed written review*.

Delayed oral review is, of course, also possible, and has the advantage of allowing a less emotive discussion of the lesson, as distance in time provides scope for greater objectivity. With good observer's notes, it will be possible for both partners to remember most of the lesson, though some details may be lost. On the other hand, immediate written review, in effect the handing over to the mentee of the observer's observation notes, which could, in theory, also precede or follow a post-lesson discussion is far more difficult to effect skilfully. It requires that the observer has learnt the skill of noticing and recording descriptive evidence *all* the time while observing, rather than recording personal interpretations or judgements. In addition, it requires the observer to have clear rapid written presentation skills. It carries the further drawback that the selected content will inevitably be more to do with the mentor's perspective and internal agenda, than that of the mentee, even when a focus has been agreed.

Peer-observation can be difficult to set up as so often timetables overlap, permissions may be difficult to obtain, etc. However, the learning potential is so great, that it is well worth the effort.

8.2.1. Peer-observation: immediate oral review

In many mentoring situations, timetabling and time constraints mean that immediate, often concise, oral discussion of the lesson is the only option. Having to discuss lessons immediately requires a high level of skill, as the mentor has almost no time consciously to prepare the selection and wording of the observations in the most helpful way for the mentee's development.

Between-session task

Aims:
– to give observation skill practice
– to practise and consider immediate oral review
– to foster the development of a cooperative staffroom culture

Suggested position in course: After self-observation, and after initial work on counselling skills and observation (see Chapters 4 and 5)

Materials: Optional: participant-selected observation sheets

Timing: One lesson + 15 minutes minimum post-lesson discussion for each partner

Procedure:
1. Participants choose a partner for the activity.
2. Partners agree on times and places where they can observe each other teaching. Each should observe the other once.
3. The observed partner decides on the focus and aim of the observation, and selects, if necessary, an appropriate observation schedule for the observer.
4. Partner *A* is observed by partner *B*.
5. Using partner *B*'s notes and *A*'s recollections, both partners review the events of the lesson based on the focus and aim of the observation.
5. Partner *B* is now observed by partner *A*, according to Steps 3 and 4 above.

Variations: If it is impossible for participants to arrange peer-observations within the group, they can arrange to do this with any colleague in their school, in which case, see *Follow-up variations.*

Comments:
As we mentioned for the previous activity, peer-observation can be difficult to set up. However, the learning potential is so great, that it is worth assigning this activity, whether in the form given above, or in its variation.

Participant reaction:
'I used to consider ideas gained from observation as fruitful side-effects of my job as mentor and kept them for my own benefit. Now I think I'll be more personal and share my experience gained from peer-observation, and I'll encourage my colleagues to visit each other's classes for the benefit of all of us.'

In-session follow-up

Aims:
– to consider the advantages and disadvantages of immediate oral review
– to allow participants the space to review the experience, and give each other feedback

Suggested position in course: After home assignment above

Materials: A copy per participant of the Immediate Oral Review – Discussion Sheet (*Photocopiable resource 33* on page 184)

Timing: 40 minutes

Assumptions: All participants have carried out the task with a partner in the group

Classroom organisation: Peer-observation pairs to whole group

Procedure:
1. Observation pairs are given 20 minutes to work through the task sheet.
2. Participants are invited to share the generalisable outcomes of their discussion with the whole group, leading to a whole-group summary of the advantages and disadvantages of immediate oral review.

Variations: If participants have carried out their peer-observation with a non-participant colleague, they can either pair up together or join, with their agreement, a pair who observed each other, and take part in the discussions as appropriate

Comments:

There are certain advantages to having 'spare' participants joining another pair because of insights they can gain through listening to the feedback they give each other. However, this can be sensitive, and not all pairs will want another person present.

One of the advantages of immediate oral review for both parties is that events are still fresh in their minds. Further advantages are that for the observed it can satisfy immediate and understandable curiosity. What is more, the observed can react immediately to each comment, and the observer can use those reactions to gauge what to say next or how to say it. It is also much less time-consuming than other forms of review. Disadvantages include the fact that the observed is still too involved in the lesson to be as objective as may be desirable, and that the observer has little time to select and formulate the precise content of their contribution to the discussion: one cannot 'delete' what has been said. This form of review relies on a high level of proficiency in counselling skills. Analysis of the success of this proficiency by the two participants may be too sensitive an issue in the immediate round-up stage, especially if the group is not closely bonded. As trainers we have tended to err on the side of caution, expanding on it, possibly, only in the setting up of further peer-observation activities, or in the preparation of mentoring role-plays. ('Remember how you felt as a result of what your partner said, or how she said it, and ask yourself if that's an effect you would want to create in your listener. You may want to adjust what or how you say things accordingly'.)

Participant reaction:

'I did not ask my observer what to focus on, I simply assumed I'd receive an overall, general feedback. I've decided that next time I'll spell out what I expect of my observer, and when I'm the observer I will ask about the teacher's expectations and I will also disclose mine.'

8.2.2. Peer-observation: delayed written review

Because of the pressures of school life, it is not always possible for the mentor to meet their mentees immediately after the lesson, or only for a very brief discussion (see 8.2.1). Mentors, therefore, may choose to write up their observation notes for the mentee to read and think over before they have a proper post-lesson discussion.

Between-session task

Aims:
- to practise the skill of observation
- to practise and consider the use of delayed written review
- to foster the development of a cooperative staffroom culture

Suggested position in course: After self-observation, and after work on observation and counselling skills

Materials: Optional: participant-selected observation sheets

Timing: One lesson + time to write up observation notes, for each partner

Procedure:

1. Participants choose a partner for the activity.
2. Partners agree on time and place of observations (each partner to observe the other once).
3. The observed partner decides on the focus and aim of the observation, and selects, if necessary, an appropriate observation schedule for the observer.
4. Partners observe each other, and both observers prepare a written review, which is exchanged and read by the agreed session deadline, but not discussed.

Variations: If it is impossible for participants to arrange peer-observations within the group, they can arrange to do this with any colleague in their school, in which case, see *follow-up variations*

In-session follow-up

Aims:

– to review the experience of writing an observation review
– to review the experience of receiving a delayed written lesson review
– to work on the clarity and effectiveness of written reviews

Suggested position in course: After home assignment above

Materials: A copy of the Delayed Written Review – Task Sheet per participant (*Photocopiable resource 34 on page 185*)

Timing: 1 hour

Assumptions: All participants have carried out the task with a partner in the group

Classroom organisation: Peer-observation pairs to whole group to same pairs

Procedure:

1. Observation pairs are given 20 minutes to work through the task sheet.
2. Participants are invited to share the generalisable outcomes of their discussion with the whole group, leading to a whole-group summary of the advantages and disadvantages of delayed written reviews.
3. Partners work together to rephrase the written reviews in ways that are more acceptable to both in view of all discussions above.

Variations: If participants have carried out their peer-observation with a non-participant colleague, they can either pair up together or join, with their agreement, a pair who observed each other, and take part in the discussions as appropriate.

Comments:

Some of the advantages of this form of lesson review that usually emerge are that for the observer it allows time to think, ensuring, for example, that the content fits the aims of the observation (and for beginner teachers, their stage of development), and that the writing process allows time to find appropriate wording, even removing anything they feel might be inappropriate. For the observed, advantages include: allowing privacy for receiving and digesting the comments, as well as time to 'recover' from the emotions of being observed. Disadvantages raised are often that for the writer it is very hard to gauge at a distance the effect their comments might have, and for the reader/observed the anxiety and frustration of waiting, together with possible frustration at being unable to respond immediately.

The discussions following this activity usually centre around suitable styles for effective written review. We have found it helpful to discuss some of the general features of any kind of writing, such as having a clear sense of audience and purpose at the outset, deciding on a suitable text-type for the purpose, selecting and ordering content, then drafting the text to suit that audience and purpose.

Further discussion may arise when working in English with non-native participants because of language and discourse differences.

Participant reaction:
'I found it terribly difficult not to just write my opinions.'
'It was frustrating to read all this evidence. I wanted to know what he thought.'
'Writing up my observations was hard work because I wanted it to be useful as well as truthful.'
'I was glad to be able to read the comments on my own – it was less embarrassing.'

8.3 Drawing conclusions

This is another more guided follow-up task for use after peer-observation. It has two separate tasks: *Observer and observed* and *Messages to mentors*. The second activity draws on the outcome of the first. Since the messages will need to be typed up for the final discussion, the whole activity will probably span two sessions. The activity is an example of a structured, guided discussion, allowing participants to share their experiences with someone else who has been through the peer-observation but was not their 'peer'. It will also give participants practice in active listening, and lead to some generalised 'hints' for mentoring, which will be discussed by the whole group.

Aims: To review the peer-observation process in a structured way; to gain insights into another's perceptions and experience of peer-observation; to practise the skills of active listening; to draw out some guidelines for mentoring

Suggested position in course: After 8.2 *Peer-observation*

Materials: A copy for each participant of the two task sheets (*Photocopiable resource 35* on page 186) (*Messages to mentors* can only be fully prepared after the completion of the first part of the task). 2–3 scraps of paper per pair

Timing: 30 minutes then 15–20 minutes in later session

Classroom organisation: Task 1: pairs, but not the same as the peer-observation pairs; Task 2: individuals, small groups to whole group

Procedure:

Task 1: Observer and observed

1. The participants are given the Observer and Observed Task Sheet, and 2–3 small pieces of paper.
2. They take it in turns to go through the questions in Task 1, with the listener practising skills of active listening (paraphrasing, clarifying questions, etc.).
3. They then consider the implications of the experience for mentoring, and write two or three 'messages' for future mentors.
4. The written messages are handed in.

Task 2: Messages to mentors

1. When all the messages have been written up, each participant gets a copy (see example of Messages to mentors Task Sheet below), and completes the task.
2. In small groups, participants share their opinions.
3. Finally a spokesperson for each group reports to the whole group for a general discussion.

Comments:

The reason that we ask the participants to write each message on a separate piece of paper is so that we can easily group them before typing them up. We always include every message, even if several are very similar, because as one participant remarked in her feedback 'I always wait to see if my comments are included'. In addition, the particular phrasing of each message may make all the difference to how the message is received.

We have found this activity generates a great deal of discussion and reveals much about the participants' present constructs of mentoring. It can therefore serve as a diagnostic activity to see where more work is needed and where understanding seems to have been reached. The following is a short selection of messages our groups have 'sent' which reveal a variety of stages of development in their thinking about mentoring.

1. Use open ended questions
2. Give advice only not commands
3. The lesson cannot be taught again, so talk about those points which can be changed in the future
4. Give information about the pupils and the habits of the classroom
5. Don't be afraid of noisy lessons – language can't be taught in silence
6. Using course books doesn't mean you are bound to them
7. Try to be a fly on the wall – invisible
8. Concentrate on one main activity each lesson which was decided before the lesson. It's impossible to pay attention to everything
9. Don't express your negative feeling during the lessons (e.g. gestures, etc.)
10. Be careful with your body language and facial expressions
11. Mentees need to get honest feedback on performance
12. Share ideas and give advice if necessary
13. Mentors need to lead the feedback discussion with great empathy

14. It's worth building up a collaborative style of mentoring
15. Don't be dominant as a mentor – let the mentee be an equal partner
16. Aim for partnership – to analyse the lesson and plan for the future
17. Try to accept your mentee's concept even if it is different from yours
18. A good mentor gives freedom to trainees to try out their own lesson
19. Encouraging student-teachers to reflect on their lessons is very important
20. A very important task of the mentor is to improve student teacher's self-evaluation

Participant reaction:

'Statements about peer-observation didn't mean the same for everybody as it turned out when we were discussing them.'

'We are in the process of learning about mentoring, but we do not seem to tolerate differences of opinion.'

'In my opinion Messages to mentors was very effective for me. It's good to exchange ideas and experiences.'

'Messages to mentors opened the door again to new thoughts.'

Acknowledgement: This activity was developed with the collaboration of Geoff Gibson, Kossuth Lajos University, Debrecen, Hungary.

9 Reading tasks

Introduction

Integrating existing outsider theories (public Theory, with a capital *T*, see Chapter 1: 1.3.2 *The dynamic interplay of practice and theory*) into participants' personal understandings of mentoring is a major thread of mentor courses. We attempt to achieve this through specific reading tasks with in-session follow-up work, as well as through more general, participant-selected background reading.

For reasons of copyright and length, we are including only one example of the kind of reading task we give throughout the course. We create and set similar tasks and follow-up activities for each of the major course content areas: learning and teaching, observation, reviewing lessons, counselling skills, styles of intervention, as well as models and phases of professional learning.

We have found that suitable texts for reading tasks need to be short, whether they are complete articles or extracts from books (this means a maximum of approximately 4,000 words, depending on the density and/or unfamiliarity of the concepts). Introductions to books or chapters often have suitable sections with condensed summaries of principal concepts.

The main objective of the tasks is to draw the reader's attention to the ideas and concepts in the text that are relevant to the course by encouraging an active interaction with the text. This can be achieved in two ways. The first is by positioning the task in the appropriate place *within* the text (a cutting, pasting and photocopying job – as long as copyright laws are not being infringed), or by setting the task after a certain section of the text has been read, and before participants read on. The second is by creating a task which encourages the participants to concentrate on the particular concept or idea, typically in the light of their own beliefs, past experience or other theories or texts encountered on the course.

Sample reading task

The sample task included here is taken from Ur, P. (1996). *A Course in Language Teaching: Practice and theory.* Cambridge University Press: pp. 5–8.

Between-session task – models of professional learning

We have chosen to base our example on a text which is not only appropriate as preparation for the *Professional learning cycle* assignment (see Chapter 10), but also describes principles underlying our own training approach.

Aims:
- to provide participants with input on the nature of professional learning
- to provide participants with tasks to help them process what they are reading in ways which are personally significant for them

Suggested position in course: Before *Professional learning cycle* assignment (see Chapter 10), or as appropriate

Materials: One copy of text and task sheet (*Photocopiable resource 36* on pages 187–191)

Procedure:
Participants receive the assignment and agree on a deadline for completion of the task.

Comments:
Near the beginning of courses, we have found that some participants are reluctant to fill in their task sheets. Participants have subsequently hinted that they were afraid to be seen as 'ignorant' or 'wrong'. Increasing trust, as well as the experience that every contribution is valued, and there are no 'rights' and 'wrongs', usually means that by the second or third reading-based task, sheets are duly completed by all.

Participant reaction:
'Sometimes too theoretical for me, maybe it takes me a little bit longer to connect these things with practice.'
'I read the articles and do the tasks with growing enthusiasm . . . They serve as a means of giving theoretical input, helping us remain open-minded, providing us with the eagerness and desire to gain more and more information, and with all this raising our consciousness, self-awareness, and confidence.'

Acknowledgement: We are grateful to Penny Ur and Cambridge University Press for permission to use this text.

In-session follow-up

Aims:
- to encourage participants to compare and contrast their own thinking with that of others
- to exemplify the importance of sharing ideas through 'talking teaching and mentoring'

Suggested position in course: After home assignment above

Materials: Participants' own completed task sheets

Timing: 20 minutes

Assumptions: Everyone has completed the task (see *Comments*)

Classroom organisation: Small groups

Procedure:

1. Small groups share their responses to the tasks, and agree on a group ending for the stem 'The biggest insight for us was . . .'.
2. Whole-group round-up.

Variations:

Some texts, with sectioned content (on Styles of Intervention, for example), could be dealt with at this stage by small groups focusing on one section and then presenting the outcomes of their discussions to the group, jig-saw fashion

Comments:

The particular text we have chosen for this example is dense in concepts, and needed, we felt, rather more 'processing tasks' than we would normally design for this length of text.

Participant reactions:

'I never thought discussing homework with my mates could be interesting. IT WAS!'

'The article was a bit difficult to understand, but it's clearer after the discussion.'

'It is useful to have group discussions about the articles we read at home because new ideas can come up from the others.'

'We seem to be very reluctant to share our ideas sometimes, particularly if the texts are long, difficult and theoretical, but they still form a good basis for more practical activities.'

10 Writing tasks

Introduction

Writing is one of the most demanding tasks in that it requires us to articulate our thoughts in a way that will be comprehensible to another person. Unlike a conversation partner, the reader, who may or may not be known to the writer, cannot ask for clarification or check understanding and so on; in other words they cannot negotiate the meaning. The process of attempting to articulate messages is often a learning process in itself as new connections are made and previously implicit understandings are put into words. The act of writing also encourages the process of reviewing, as inevitably the message, or what is written, will be a synthesis of the thoughts acquired from the learning so far, and will require standing back from those experiences in order to crystallise their essence. It is for these reasons – the clarity of articulation, the learning and the reviewing – that written tasks are valuable.

This chapter includes the two types of writing task we set on our mentor courses.

Tasks and activities

10.1 Professional learning cycle

A professional learning cycle provides a model for continuous professional growth. The ultimate goal of mentoring is to ensure that mentees have the skills, knowledge and desire to continue their own development.

This assignment is another example of a task set so that mentors become fully aware of and experienced in the processes they will be guiding their mentees through (see also discussion under 8.1 *Self-observation*). It is a multi-phased task, which includes the following stages:

1. Task-based reading and follow-up (see Chapter 9, both as an example and as an appropriate text for this phase of *this* task), *or* leader-led input phase on professional learning cycles.
2. Between-session task 1.
3. Between-session task 2.
4. Follow-up.

Between-session task 1 (with in-session preparation)

Preparing and implementing the learning cycle

Aims:
- to provide mentors with experience of going through a formalised professional learning cycle, for their own development and so that they can better support their mentees' professional learning
- to provide further opportunity to formulate their thoughts about teaching in writing
- to demonstrate that professional learning can be in the hands of the practising teacher

Suggested position in course: Assigned somewhere near the middle, to be returned towards the end. After task-based readings on professional learning cycles (see Chapter 9), and linked to outcomes from self-observation and/or peer-observation outcomes

Materials: Self-selected readings, observation schedules, etc., according to focus of investigations

Timing: This is a process which covers several weeks, with at least two in-session phases on separate occasions. For preparation Stage 1: 45 minutes, and Stage 2: 30 minutes

Assumptions: Participants have read given texts on professional learning cycles, and completed the related tasks (e.g. see Chapter 9), and have begun to think about an area for their own investigation

Classroom organisation: Stage 1: small groups, cross-groups, whole group; Stage 2: individual; Stage 3: small groups or pairs; Stage 4: individual

Procedure:
Stage 1
1. Participants are divided into small groups, one (or more) for each phase of the learning cycle (e.g., grouped according to the Ur model in Chapter 9, with one or more groups concentrating on 'Experience', 'Reflective observation', 'Abstract conceptualisation' and finally 'Active experimentation'; or grouped according to the 'Experience', 'Reflect', 'Learn' and 'Plan' model, etc.). These groups discuss possible appropriate actions for the assigned phase, that is, what the phase might mean in practice. For someone looking at the use of group work, the 'experience' phase, for example, might include experiencing using group work in their teaching, as well as experiencing being part of learning groups during the mentor course. The 'reflective observation' phase could include self-observation, peer-observation, pupils' observation (feedback), keeping a reflective journal on being part of learning groups, etc.
2. Participants are cross-grouped into new groups, containing at least one representative from each of the previous 'phase' groups. Participants exchange information from the previous discussions, so that everyone has a range of options of concrete 'things to do' for each phase of the cycle.

3. Either in the same groups, or perhaps in pairs, the participants then discuss how this relates to their own plans for employing the cycle.
4. Whole-group discussion to clear up any further issues arising from the small group work.

Stage 2

Participants carry out the first phase of the between-session task which is to choose the focus/topic for their investigative learning cycle. Their topic may derive from their own experiences (possibly something that emerged during self- or peer-observation tasks), or from observing others, reading or anything that they are interested in. They then *plan*, in writing, their actions for starting the cycle, with some ideas for further phases.

Stage 3

At the next session, participants form small groups or pairs and share their plans, inviting comments and new ideas, and revising the plans accordingly.

Stage 4

1. Participants now complete and write up the cycle according to, for example, the specifications in *Photocopiable resource 37* on page 192.
2. Course leader(s) read assignments and prepare a separate written response sheet in the form of three or four questions: two or three for clarification of content or meaning (of the 'How many teachers did you ask?' or 'Was this in the same class you described before?' or 'What do you understand by "error" here?' variety), and one which may challenge the writer's thinking more directly (such as 'Do you think another teacher might interpret these data differently?' or 'Can you think of any other ways of doing this?', or 'If you could do this again, what changes would you make?').

Variations: The assignments could first go to peers who would respond in the same way. In some contexts such detailed assignment specifications may be inappropriate. Other forms of response could be used.

Comments:

One of the most difficult phases for most participants in this assignment is the choice of topic. It needs to be one of enough personal significance to warrant the investment of time and energy, yet needs to be narrow enough for participants reasonably to expect some achievement within the scope of this assignment. In our context, popular areas for investigation include: the issue of teacher talking-time versus student talking-time; the handling of spoken errors; the use of the mother tongue, etc

Between-session task 2

Using questions as a written response provides further practice in their appropriate use and possible effects begun in Chapter 5.

Aims:
– to practise the use of 'genuine' questions, for clarification or 'challenge'
– to consider and categorise question types

Suggested position in course: After previous home assignment

Materials: Participants' cycle reports, leader's feedback questions

Timing: 5 minutes in class

Assumptions: All participants have completed their cycle reports

Classroom organisation: Pre-determined pairs (probably determined according to personalities, but possibly also level of experience and/or awareness, similarity of topic and so on)

Procedure:

1. Reports and feedback questions are returned to each participant at the next session. They have a few minutes to glance through them.
2. Partners exchange cycle reports (but not the leader's feedback questions). Participants are given the task of reading their partner's report at home, and writing responses in the form of three or four questions, similar to the ones they have themselves received (clarification and 'challenge').

In-session follow-up

Aims:
- to get useful reader response
- to practise giving and receiving feedback in a real, non-simulated situation
- to consider the use of 'genuine' questions, for clarification or 'challenge'
- to talk about the shared experience

Suggested position in course: Following the home assignment above, and activities like e.g. 5.10 *Excavating the iceberg* and 5.7 *It's not what you say, it's the way you say it*, 5.8 *Question time*, 5.9 *Considering questions*

Materials: The participants' Professional learning cycle reports + leader's and participants' questions; one copy of the task sheet (*Photocopiable resource 38* on page 193) per participant

Timing: 1 hour to 90 minutes

Assumptions: All participants have completed Between-session task 2

Classroom organisation: Pre-determined pairs as above

Procedure:

1. Participants form pairs with the partner whose report they have read, and have 30 minutes to complete the task sheet. In turn, they ask each other the questions they have written. In answering, each elaborates and makes any relevant connections with the questions they have received from the course leader.
2. Whole-group round-up on questions as a form of feedback.
3. Participants are randomly re-paired (something lively and physical, see Chapter 2: *Course procedures* 2.3), and, possibly also after a session break or relaxation break, participants consider the whole process of reading about, implementing and writing up their professional learning cycles. They summarise major outcomes under a 'What we've learnt' heading.
4. Whole-group discussion – of outcomes of 3 above and corresponding implications for mentoring of whole process/activity.

Comments:
Many of our course participants have never done anything like this before and therefore need considerable guidance, which is why the activity has so many stages. Because the participants have usually by this time had some practice in counselling, and have also got the course leader's questions, they tend to write questions which help the writer of the report to identify lack of clarity in either thinking or writing.

Participant reaction:
'Discussing the cycle from the point of view of our own experience made it quite practical and manageable. It will be a challenge to put it into practice.'
'It seemed difficult at first but when I actually got down to it, I became very excited and learnt a great deal in terms of reflective teaching . . . I can recommend it to my colleagues/mentees not merely as a theory but as a very effective tool indeed in both personal and professional development.'
'As a mentor I would recommend this method for teachers who think their problem is too big, too intangible for them to cope with, since it enables them to specify "the monster" and face the challenge.'
'Completing the cycle taught me a lot about myself and made me understand that an expert is not a person who has no problems in his or her field, who knows all the answers, but a person who can facilitate a positive change by reflecting on the problem and analysing it in a way that leads to workable tasks he or she can test in practice.'

Acknowledgements: This activity was devised in collaboration with Péter Rádai, CETT, Budapest.

10.2 Development reports

We assign these development reports as a means for participants to review and make explicit their learning from the course process. The procedure described below generates the precise specifications for the form of the main body of the report, and we also require a final section in which participants evaluate their progress on the course against their own criteria (see *Procedure* below). This again models what mentees will be expected to do in terms of self-evaluation.

Development reports are also a way for course leaders to gauge the extent to which the course objectives are being met, both for the group as a whole, and for individuals. The tutorials following these reports provide even more information for leaders as well as the opportunity for individual counselling.

Aims:
- to provide an opportunity for participants to review and evaluate their progress on the course
- to provide another opportunity for making constructs explicit
- to provide another source of evidence for leaders on course and individual progress

Suggested position in course: Two or three times spaced out over the course

Timing: 15 minutes in-session preparation time, before the first report

Classroom organisation: Whole group to individual

Procedure:

1. Participants brainstorm possible contents of the development report. Ideas are collected on a board or poster and individuals then use those ideas to write what they have learnt, why, and any applications of that learning to either their teaching or mentoring, if already practising.

2. Participants then brainstorm criteria for evaluating that learning. These, too, are collected and discussed. Participants make clear in their reports what criteria they are using and why, before using them to evaluate their own progress. These may be linked to areas of course content and draw on course journals for evidence of increasing understanding (e.g. about observation, mentoring styles, etc.). The criteria will also include evidence of their personal whole mentoring skill development often centring on mentor role-play experiences as well as sub-skill development, which may draw on evidence from experiences outside the course, such as work with pupils or colleagues in schools, or even family discussions (e.g. active listening).

3. A hand-in deadline is agreed.

4. Participants write and hand in reports by the agreed deadline. Leader(s) read and make notes for the ensuing tutorial. (Written responses could also be given.)

Comments:

We find that the first report tends to focus on how participants have used course activities in their own EFL classrooms. Gradually, the emphasis changes to applications of their learning for their future mentoring work. Practising mentors will always relate how their learning has affected their mentoring work, and the shift for them is in increasingly critical appraisal of their past mentoring practice, to appreciation of their new approaches.

Participant reaction:

'I like the title "Development report" because it implies that you _have_ developed.'
'I was worried about how to write the report, and what I'd put in it, but when I started I realised I had a lot to write, and what's more I _could_ write about it!'
'How can I self-evaluate, when I don't know what I don't know?'

In-session follow-up

Aims:
– to provide an opportunity for individual tutorials on course progress
– to model one-to-one counselling skills

Suggested position in course: After each Development report

Suggested position in session: Either outside session time, or in-session, during 'teacherless tasks' or self-access work

Materials: Development reports and leader's notes/responses

Timing: 15–20 minutes per participant

Assumptions: Participants have handed in reports

Procedure:
One-to-one tutorial, beginning with participant's agenda.

Comments:
Although this is a time-consuming activity we find it very valuable, not only because it is a way of working on teaching/learning relationships but it also gives an opportunity for personal review discussion.

If giving tutorials during 'teacherless tasks', the other participants can practise paraphrasing and summarising skills for 'tutorial returnees' to get back into the task.

Participant reaction:
'I'd be glad to send you development reports in the future, to get responses back.'
'It was really good to talk about my problems with a more experienced "mentor". I'd like to have more opportunities.'

Conclusion

In this concluding section we will first describe a couple of activities we often use to disband the group at the end of a course. We will then go on to talk briefly about ways of evaluating mentor courses and leaders, as well as mentors themselves, before discussing methods and processes for continuing the development of mentoring skills.

Group disbanding activities

We like to use a variety of group ending activities that would be suitable for any course. The first of these is given in the same format as all the activities in the book, while the other is simply described.

1. Art collection

As on any course the final disbanding phase of group life will need as much attention as the ice-breaking and group-forming phase. Because of the very personal nature of this kind of work, we have found it even more important on mentor courses. This is an example of the kind of activity which gives members a chance to share their stories of the course, and to review the experience not only in terms of learning, but also in terms of phases and feelings.

Aims:
– to review the course – concepts, stages, feelings, relationship
– to disband the group

Suggested position in course: In the last session

Suggested position in session: Final or penultimate activity

Materials: A3 paper per participant, Blu-tack/pins/sellotape, coloured felt-tip pens or crayons, music (3–4 minute, atmospheric piece)

Timing: 30 minutes (depending on size of group)

Classroom organisation: Individual to small group

Procedure:
1. Participants stand in a circle around the room facing a blank piece of paper on walls or tables. They have coloured pens/crayons.
2. As the music starts, each participant starts 'drawing' on the paper in front of

them. These drawings can be representational or simply abstract interpretations of the music.

3. After about thirty seconds the music is paused, and all participants move round clockwise to the second or third 'picture'.

4. The music starts again, and participants continue to draw on the piece of paper now facing them. They may continue drawing the picture already started, or continue their own thoughts.

5. Steps 3 and 4 are repeated until the music ends.

6. Participants walk around admiring the art collection, and select one piece of art each, and sit down with two or three other people, depending on size of group.

7. The small groups arrange their pictures in a sequence that illustrates the 'story' of the course.

8. Two members from each group go on a round of visiting. The remaining members will narrate their story to each set of visitors, who will question the interpretation of the various squiggles or elements of the drawings.

9. When the 'visitors' return to their own group, the 'story-tellers' then go on a round of visits, with the old 'visitors' now narrating the stories.

Variations: If the group is very large, 'visits' can be restricted to three or four groups only

Comments:

We use 'Bridge over troubled water' by Simon and Garfunkel, as this is both atmospheric, long enough and has clear metaphors. We have a wonderful art collection from past courses, and the pictures tend to reveal a great deal about how the course evolved, and which parts were especially significant for the group. It is additional feedback for us as course leaders.

Participant reaction:

As this is done on the last occasion, we do not collect feedback in the usual way, so we have no written comments. It is, however, a moving experience for most participants.

Acknowledgement: We first came across a version of this at South Devon College, Torquay, learnt, we believe from Anne Pechou.

2. *Big fleas have little fleas upon their backs to bite 'em* and little *fleas have lesser fleas and so ad infinitum*

This is a typical affective disbanding exercise we have come across at workshops. A piece of A4 paper is attached to the back of every group member, leader included. Everyone writes one positive comment about that person on each person's back, regarding their contribution to the writer's experience of the course. The activity produces long lines or circles of people each writing on the back of the person in front. Because it is slightly comic to watch everyone bending down to make writing easier and shuffling forward to catch a passing back, some of the emotional tension is released through laughter. At the end of this, everyone removes their sheet of paper and has it as a permanent, esteem-boosting record of their contribution to the work of the group. Comments vary from external compliments like 'I like your smile' to remarks about learning, 'your comments helped me to understand things better', or relationships, 'giggling with you always brightened my week', to thanks or memories of specific incidents, 'I'm glad I did *Blind adventure* with you'. In reading these through, people are often moved to tears of mourning, yet are left feeling valued and positive. As one participant wrote to us later:

'I loved the final activity. It made me think of my colleagues and value and appreciate them as they really are. And at the end of the task I too ended up feeling happy, valued and appreciated.'

Last sessions will also need to include space for mentors to agree on formal or informal networking, discuss strategies for maintaining the development of their mentoring skills and so on. We also ask our participants to fill in a standard course feedback form that we developed for the first course we ran.

Evaluating mentor courses

The most useful tools for evaluating the course (and indeed the leaders) are products of the activities and process of the course itself: session feedback slips, development reports, tutorial discussions, mentoring tapescripts and so on. All of this provides evidence from different perspectives and different times, which can act as formative or summative evaluation. Course leaders may also have taken the opportunity to video themselves at work or invited observers into sessions. In addition, one of the major advantages of team-teaching the course is the constant peer-observation and review that this involves. Conventional 'End of course feedback' forms can also add useful information, although we have found they seldom give us the depth of feedback provided by the other methods mentioned in this paragraph. Evaluating the long-term impact of courses is perhaps more important than immediate post-course summative evaluation, whatever data is used (Lamb 1995). We have carried out a formal survey (Bodóczky and Malderez 1997) of the impact of mentor courses on the mentors' own teaching and on the staff of the school. This revealed useful data for strategic planning at the level of the whole mentor programme, as well as direct feedback on elements of courses, and of the effect of mentoring on the mentors themselves.

Evaluating mentors

We have discussed the question of student-teacher evaluation at length in Chapter 7 *Assessing teaching*. Student-mentor evaluation has the same basic minimum standard of not releasing mentors from courses who could be potentially 'dangerous' to their mentees. On our pre-service mentor courses ongoing assessment is carried out through a 'profile', made up of observations of participants' contributions during sessions, their work in role-plays and other related activities, various assignments (see Chapter 10 *Writing tasks*), and individual tutorials. On courses where the participants are already practising mentors, it is possible to observe them in their schools working with mentees. The development of observation criteria could be done on the course. The mentor observation check-list in Appendix 10 was compiled by a group of primary school mentors and is used as a framework during and after the observation.

Further feedback on the effectiveness of the mentors' work comes from questionnaires the mentors give their mentees during and at the end of their practicum. The results of these questionnaires are also made available to us (for examples of such questionnaires devised by the mentors themselves, see Appendices 7, 8 and 9). The mentors' need to devise and administer these questionnaires, and other more formative types of feedback, has been attributed directly to having experienced during the mentor course the value to practitioners (whether trainers, mentors or teachers) of such feedback. It is another example of the necessity of modelling reflective practitioner behaviour and *dialogue* in teaching and learning rather than one-way transmission (see Chapter 1: 1.2 *Teaching*). These student-teacher questionnaires provide data for mentors that will help them in their continuing development as well as giving us insights both into aspects of the course itself that might need changing and into issues that can be explored in ongoing professional mentor meetings.

Continuing mentor development

It would be professionally irresponsible simply to trace the impact of courses without following it up with opportunities to help mentors in their continuing development. If mentors have become reflective practitioners, they will need and actively seek opportunities to talk about mentoring with fellow professionals. The course may have set up a network of mentor support, and there may be more than one mentor working in any one school, but this may not, however, give them the range of perspectives that would help them to move forward.

Opportunities for professional debate in our context include a national mentor journal (*School Experience*), national and international mentor conferences as well as other local and national mentor events, most of which were initially sponsored by the British Council. Regular twice a semester mentor meetings at the Centre for English Teacher Training, Budapest, allow not only the mentors to attend to their own personal mentor development agendas through discussions with their peers, but also allow the course leaders to address issues that have arisen from the feedback on courses and mentors (see above). These meetings are also attended by college-based tutors working with student-teachers during their teaching practice, thus strengthening the links between schools and the training institutions and providing valuable input to each other on various aspects of their respective roles.

Whole-programme concerns can be addressed in certain joint sub-committees. In our context, for instance, there was a sub-committee of mentors and tutors responsible for revision of the teaching practice evaluation criteria (see Appendix 5). Decisions were made in sub-committee then put before whole staff and whole mentor meetings for amendment before the final publication of the criteria. This joint decision-making helps to strengthen further the links between schools and training institute.

Conclusion

Perhaps the ultimate source of professional development is trying to write it all up. This project, the writing of this book, which began some six years ago after we had run our second mentor course, has seen changes in our professional/ personal development as we have taught new courses, in new places and with new people. Our own understandings of the processes of learning, teaching and learning teaching have developed, and the effort to try to articulate this has led us to yet newer understandings. On a personal level, one of our greatest senses of achievement has been seeing our own CETT graduates, who had been mentored during their practicum by mentors we had trained, coming back after several years of teaching to take the Mentor Training and Development Course to become mentors themselves.

Photocopiable resources

NB In some places, for reasons of space, we have only included the text and an indication of the layout for a task sheet. We would normally copy this at the top of a blank A4 sheet, extending the columns or other layout features as appropriate.

Photocopiable resource 1 (page 36)

DIRECTIVE	ALTERNATIVE	COOPERATIVE	NON-DIRECTIVE
FOCUS ON OWN BEHAVIOUR	FOCUS ON PUPILS' BEHAVIOUR	FOCUS ON PUPILS' LEARNING	
DO	REVIEW	LEARN	APPLY
NAME	APPLY	RECONCEIVE	
EXPERIENCE	REFLECT	LEARN	PLAN

© Cambridge University Press 1999

Photocopiable resource 2 (page 70)

Transparency 1 The teacher's perspective

Transparency 2 The observer's perspective

Transparency 3 'Baggage'

© Cambridge University Press 1999

Photocopiable resource 3 (page 72)

TASK

There are 8 rabbits hidden in this picture. You have 30 seconds to find them all.

© Cambridge University Press 1999

Photocopiable resource 4 (page 72)

TASK

There are 8 snakes hidden in this picture. You have 30 seconds to find them all.

© Cambridge University Press 1999

Photocopiable resource 5 (page 78)

Different observers task sheet

1. The two sets of observation notes below were written by different observers about the same segment of a lesson observation in a Sri Lankan classroom. As you read, note the similarities and differences in the accounts of what happened.

OBSERVER A

Year 1. Sinhala lesson. Reading.

1   35 + children. White uniforms + ties – immaculate for some, grubby and scruffy for others -
2   visible difference in socio-economic backgrounds – but all wearing shoes. Wooden,
3   blue-painted tables and chairs – small size – 4 or 5 children per table. Pictures on walls, and
4   children's own craft-work on display. Words on board with long 'a' sound. T points at syllables
5   with long stick, and sounds out, syllable by syllable, each word, before saying the whole word.
6   Group standing close to board. T asks children to cross arms at one point – (why – control
7   fidgeting? What did she notice?), and goes to physically draw in 'stragglers' at the back.
8   T explicitly talks about the long 'a' sound and the letter (s?) it is associated with. Child takes
9   over the pointing and group chants, as teacher watches. Boy arrives, kneels at T's feet (kisses
10 them?) before going to water fountain to drink. (Year 4 pupil who had had this teacher in year
11 1.) Girl arrives, and again kneels and bows at T's feet before going to drink. T pats children and
12 steers them towards fountain.

OBSERVER B

Sinhala – year 1.

13 T written words with same sounds. T breaks down words into sounds and children repeat
14 chorally. T sounds out words.
15 cabe   lei   deipela
16 capulya   leina   deidunna
17 caundray   leinsuva   deiwalaya
18 serra
19 T checks whether they know the words. Children all stand around T near board. T points,
20 children repeat. Child comes to board, points to word + children repeat. Children crowd
21 closer – more interested.

*2. **Questions for discussion.** In groups, discuss the questions below.*

a) What are the differences, and how and why do think they happened – was it the same event after all?

b) What can you tell about the two observers as people (professional interests, purpose of observation, familiarity with Sri Lankan classrooms, etc. etc.)?

c) What interpretations, preconceived ideas or judgements can you find in the two accounts?

Photocopiable resource 6 (page 82)

GETTING ATTENTION/ROUSING INTEREST OBSERVATION SCHEDULE

As you observe the lesson, fill in the chart below:

What the teacher did to get attention or rouse interest	Why the teacher did it (GA or RI)	What the students did	What your own teachers did to achieve these aims

© Cambridge University Press 1999

Photocopiable resource 7 (page 84)

Being observed

1. *Think back to occasions when you were observed teaching. Individually, make notes on answers to the following:*

How many times have you been observed?
How often?
How long ago was the last time?
Who observed you?
Why?
How did you feel?
What happened before the observation? How did you feel about that?
What happened as a result? How did you feel about that?
What did your observer do during the lesson? How did you feel about that?

2. *In groups share your answers, then decide on an ending to the following to tell the whole group:*

'The two most interesting things we realised as a result of this discussion are . . .'

© Cambridge University Press 1999

Photocopiable resource 8 (page 86)

Butterflies Task Sheet

Read the text below:

I remembered one morning when I discovered a cocoon in the bark of a tree, just as the butterfly was making a hole in its case and preparing to come out. I waited a while, but it was too long appearing and I was impatient. I bent over it and breathed on it to warm it. I warmed it as quickly as I could and the miracle began to happen before my eyes, faster than life. The case opened, the butterfly started slowly crawling out and I shall never forget my horror when I saw how its wings were folded back and crumpled; the wretched butterfly tried with its whole trembling body to unfold them. Bending over it, I tried to help it with my breath. In vain. It needed to be hatched out patiently and the unfolding of the wings should be a gradual process in the sun. Now it was too late. My breath had forced the butterfly to appear, all crumpled, before its time. It struggled desperately and, a few seconds later, died in the palm of my hand.

That little body is, I do believe, the greatest weight I have on my conscience.

(Kazantzakis, N. (1952) *Zorba the Greek*. London: Faber and Faber: 138)

Now decorate the butterfly below, with words and/or colours to represent the conditions that will help you develop into the mentor butterfly you would like to become.

My Butterfly

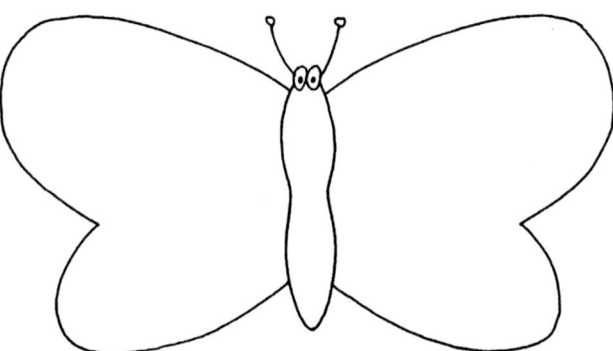

Decorate the butterfly below in a similar way for your mentees so that they can become the best teachers they can be.

My Mentee's Butterfly

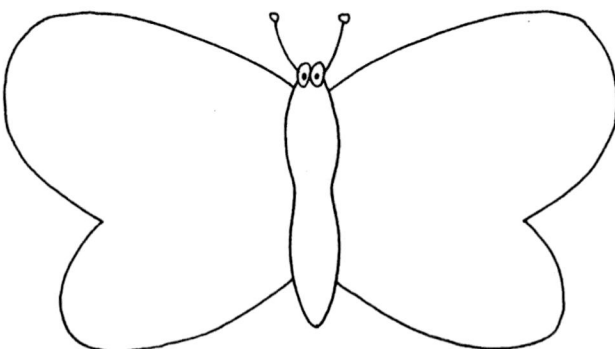

Photocopiable resource 9 (page 91)

CARD 1

Listen to the speaker with
    eyes: in contact
    head/face: still/no smiles
    arms and legs: crossed comfortably
    body: leaning back/defiant slouch

CARD 2

Listen to the speaker with
    eyes: in contact
    head/face: nodding/smiling
    arms and legs: uncrossed/easy or as speaker's
    body: leaning slightly forward

CARD 3

Listen to the speaker with
    eyes: NO contact
    head/face: still/no smiles
    arms and legs: uncrossed/easy
    body: leaning slightly forward

CARD 4

Listen to the speaker with
    eyes: in contact
    head/face: nods/tight smiles
    arms and legs: both crossed
    body: sitting well back in chair

CARD 5

Listen to the speaker with
    eyes: fleeting contact
    head/face: nods/no smiles
    arms and legs: hands crossed on lap, legs crossed
    body: leaning slightly back

CARD 6

Listen to the speaker with
    eyes: looking at speaker, moving, NO direct eye contact
    head/face: in one hand/smiles
    arms and legs: crossed legs, elbow of the arm holding the
       head on one knee
    body: slouched

Photocopiable resource 10 (page 91)

Once I had a class . . . : Body Language Discussion Task Sheet

1. Story-teller: say how you felt telling the story and how easy it was to engage the interest of your listeners.
2. Story-teller: give feedback to each of the listeners in turn, on what you noticed, and how it affected you.
3. Listeners: in turn, reveal the content of your cards to the speaker, and talk about how it felt to try to listen according to those instructions.
4. Discuss the implications of this for mentoring work. Be prepared to share this with the whole group.

© Cambridge University Press 1999

Photocopiable resource 11 (page 94)

DO YOU ALWAYS WRITE THE TRANSLATION OF NEW VOCABULARY ON THE BOARD?

WHEN DO YOU CORRECT GRAMMAR MISTAKES?

WHY DID THE PUPILS LISTEN AND READ AT THE SAME TIME?

WHERE WERE YOU DURING THE PAIR WORK?

HOW DID YOU INTRODUCE THAT ACTIVITY?

WHAT WERE THE PUPILS DOING WHILE YOU WERE WRITING ON THE BOARD?

HOW MANY ACTIVITIES WERE THERE IN THE LESSON?

© Cambridge University Press 1999

Photocopiable resource 12 (page 96)

Question factors

TASK: *Match each factor with the correct definition below. Write the correct letter in the box beside each factor, and discuss the implications with your group.*

The outcome of questioning appears to be dependent upon at least five factors:
1. ☐ The manner in which questions are asked
2. ☐ The timing of questions within the interaction
3. ☐ Whether questions are open-ended or closed off
4. ☐ Whether questions appear early or late in the relationship
5. ☐ Who requires the answer to the question

A. Before asking a question, the counsellor should ask him or herself the reason for the question. If its purpose is to satisfy the questioner, then there is no room for it in the therapeutic situation. If it is for the client's benefit, to enable him/her to clarify an idea, or to explore further, it is probably helpful.

B. If a question is asked about something that was said five minutes ago, it may be experienced as irrelevant to the client, who may have moved on to something else. It would also indicate a stepping away from his or her internal frame of reference. If a question concerns something that has just been said, it may be intrusive.

C. If questions are asked in an off-hand way, they may be experienced as nosy, judgemental or leading. If asked in an abrupt way, they may be considered interrogational or threatening.

D. If the question is closed, that is it requires a 'yes' or 'no' answer, it may block the flow of communication. An open-ended question encourages further exploration: however, there is a danger of asking 'leading questions'.

E. In a relationship based on trust, questions can be taken at face value. Because it takes time to develop such trust, questions asked later in a relationship may fare better than when asked early on.

Photocopiable resource 13 (page 96)

Factor cards

> The outcome of questioning appears to be dependent on at least 4 factors. One of them is:
> THE MANNER IN WHICH THE QUESTIONS ARE ASKED.
>
> *Watch the video or listen to the audio recording, and write down some of the questions, noting the tone of voice, pace, intonation pattern, accompanying body language (if on video) and anything else that describes HOW the question was asked. Note down also the effect the question had.*

> The outcome of questioning appears to be dependent on at least 4 factors. One of them is:
> THE TIMING OF THE QUESTIONS WITHIN THE INTERACTION.
>
> *Watch the video or listen to the audio recording, and note when and why the questioning starts, when and why it becomes more intense, when and why it tails off, if it does – in other words anything relating to the timing of the questions within the interaction.*

> The outcome of questioning appears to be dependent on at least 4 factors. One of them is:
> WHETHER THE QUESTIONS ARE OPEN-ENDED OR CLOSED OFF.
>
> *Watch the video or listen to the audio recording, and note down examples of both these types of question, and what effect they had.*

> The outcome of questioning appears to be dependent on at least 4 factors. One of them is:
> WHO REQUIRES THE ANSWERS.
>
> *Watch the video or listen to the audio recording. Note down some of the questions the mentor asks, and try to decide who required the answer. Did the mentor have a 'hidden' reason for asking the question, in other words was it asked to 'help' the mentee better understand a particular point, or because the mentor wanted to understand something better?*

© Cambridge University Press 1999

Photocopiable resource 14 (page 98)

LANGUAGE PROFICIENCY AND KNOWLEDGE

PROFESSIONAL BEHAVIOUR

REVIEWING

LEARNING

SELECTING

PLANNING

KNOWLEDGE ABOUT: PUPILS, LANGUAGE FORM AND USE, ACTIVITIES, PROCESSES, SKILLS

CONCEPTUALISATIONS OF: EDUCATION, TEACHING, LEARNING, PROFESSIONALISM, LANGUAGE-LEARNING, LANGUAGE, LANGUAGE POLICY

FEELINGS, BELIEFS, ATTITUDES, VALUES

© Cambridge University Press 1999

Photocopiable resource 15 (page 104)

TASK 1

Look at the transcript, and make two lists. The first list should contain statements the mentor makes which you think are supportive in character, that is, when the relationship or the mentee's feelings seem to be the main concern of the mentor. The second list should contain those interventions from the mentor which seem to have a challenge function, when the mentee's learning seems to be of paramount importance. What, if anything, do you notice? Consider, too, the mentee's reactions to each intervention.

TASK 2

Look at the transcript and consider the question forms the mentor uses. What kind does s/he use most? Why?

TASK 3

Look at the transcript and consider if there is an order or framework in the way the discussion progresses. Can you see distinctive phases? If so, what marks the beginning and end of each phase?

TASK 4

Look at the transcript and identify occasions when the mentor uses I-statements (with or without the *I saw/heard/noticed* stem). Consider why they were used, the mentee's reaction as well as whether they are really non-interpretative and non-evaluative.

Photocopiable resource 16 (page 105)

INTERVENTION STYLE CARD – DIRECTIVE

Consider the following descriptions of this style and compare them with the notes you have just made.

'In the directive form of intervention . . . the teacher-educator comments on the student-teacher's teaching, making concrete proposals for change. The educator establishes the purpose of the intervention, determines the points to be raised with the student-teacher based on the observation, and makes a brief statement on each point to which the student-teacher may or may not respond. Discussion often ensues from the intervention, but the roles are very clear: the teacher-educator "directs" and the student teacher "does". ' (Freeman, D. (1990). Intervening in practice teaching. In J. Richards and D. Nunan (Eds.) *Second Language Teacher Education.* Cambridge: Cambridge University Press: 107)

'In directive supervision the role of the supervisor is to direct and inform the teacher, model teaching behaviours, and evaluate the teacher's mastery of defined behaviours.' (Gebhard, J.G. (1990). Models of supervision: choices. In J. C. Richards and D. Nunan (Eds.) *Second Language Teacher Education.* Cambridge: Cambridge University Press: 156)

INTERVENTION STYLE CARD – NON-DIRECTIVE

Consider the following descriptions of this style and compare them with the notes you have just made.

'The purpose of this intervention . . . is to provide the student-teacher with a forum to clarify perceptions of what he or she is doing in teaching and for the educator to fully understand, although not necessarily to accept or agree with, those perceptions. Further, it allows the student-teacher to identify a course of action based on his or her own perceptions and what the educator offers, and to decide whether or how to act.' (Freeman, D. (1990). Intervening in practice teaching. In J. Richards and D. Nunan (Eds.) *Second Language Teacher Education.* Cambridge: Cambridge University Press: 112)

'The essence of non-directive supervision is captured in the following observation by a teacher-in-preparation: "My supervisor usually attempts to have me come up with my own solutions to teaching problems, but she isn't cold. She's a giving person, and I can tell that she cares. Anyway, my supervisor listens patiently to what I say, and she consistently gives me her understanding of what I have just said."' (Gebhard, J.G. (1990). Models of supervision: choices. In J. C. Richards and D. Nunan (Eds.) *Second Language Teacher Education.* Cambridge: Cambridge University Press: 160)

INTERVENTION STYLE CARD – ALTERNATIVES

Consider the following descriptions of this style and compare them with the notes you have just made.

'The educator chooses a point from the practice teaching and raises it with the student-teacher. The educator then proposes a limited number of alternative ways to handle that point in the lesson. The student-teacher rejects or selects from among the alternatives. Discussion follows about the student-teacher's criteria for the choices he or she has made. The purpose of this intervention is to develop the student-teacher's awareness of the choices involved in deciding what and how to teach, and more importantly, to develop the ability to establish and articulate the criteria that inform those decisions.'
(Freeman, D. (1990). Intervening in practice teaching. In J. Richards and D. Nunan (Eds.) *Second Language Teacher Education.* Cambridge: Cambridge University Press: 109)

'In this model the supervisor's role is to suggest a variety of alternatives to what the teacher has done in the classroom. Having a limited number of choices can reduce teachers' anxiety over deciding what to do next, and yet still gives them the responsibility for decision making . . . The purpose of offering alternatives is to widen the scope of what a teacher will consider doing.'
(Gebhard, J.G. (1990). Models of supervision: choices. In J. C. Richards and D. Nunan (Eds.) *Second Language Teacher Education.* Cambridge: Cambridge University Press: 158)

INTERVENTION STYLE CARD – COLLABORATIVE

Consider the following description of this style and compare it with the notes you have just made.
'Within a collaborative model the supervisor's role is to work with teachers but not direct them. The supervisor actively participates with the teacher in any decisions that are made and attempts to establish a sharing relationship . . . The teacher and supervisor work together in addressing a problem in the teacher's classroom teaching. They pose a hypothesis, experiment, and implement strategies that appear to offer a reasonable solution to the problem under consideration.'
(Gebhard, J.G. (1990). Models of supervision: choices. In J. C. Richards and D. Nunan (Eds.) *Second Language Teacher Education.* Cambridge: Cambridge University Press: 159–160)

Photocopiable resource 17 (page 106)

BEGINNER TEACHER DEVELOPMENT

A. Beginning phases of professional development

Compare and contrast the descriptions of stages in the two quotations below.

'Preservice and first-year teaching appears to constitute a single developmental stage during which novices accomplish three primary tasks: (a) acquire knowledge of pupils; (b) use that knowledge to modify and reconstruct their personal images of self as teacher; and (c) develop standard procedural routines that integrate classroom management and instruction'
(Kagan, D. (1992). Professional growth among pre-service and beginner teachers. In *Review of Educational Research* 6(2): 129)

'Our observations suggest that student-teachers may pass through three ordered stages as they become responsible beginner teachers. The sequence seems valid for each student teacher but the rate of progression varies greatly. Unfortunately many students do not seem to reach the third stage during student-teaching. We have labelled the three stages:
1. concern with self,
2. concern with teaching actions and students' behaviour,
3. concern with learning.'
(P. F. Campbell and G. H. Wheatley (1983). A model for helping student-teachers. In *Mathematics Teacher Jan*: 60)

B. The emotions of change

(Adapted from D. Brandes and P. Ginnis (1989). *The Student-Centred School.* Oxford: Blackwell)
The following graph shows the feelings people go though over time as they adapt to changes. The changes can be about learning something new, adapting to a new society or undertaking any new 'project'.

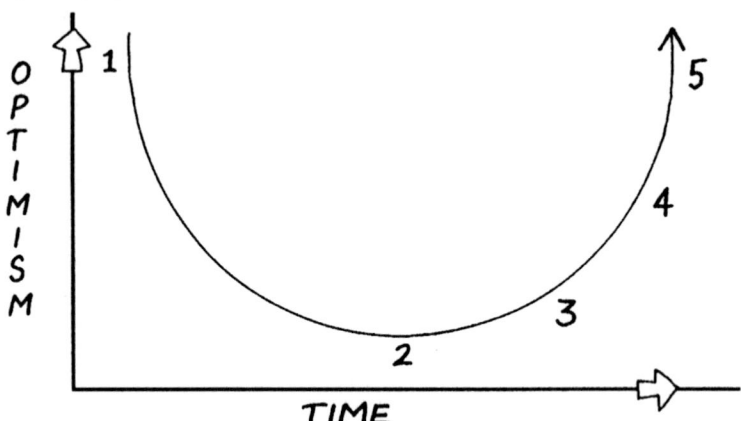

1. Uninformed optimism; 2. Informed pessimism (doubt); 3. Realism (hope); 4. Informed optimism (confidence); 5. Reward (satisfaction)

TASK:
Consider the quotations and the graph above in relation to:
1. Your own stages of growth as a beginner teacher. (Share anecdotes and memories which relate to different phases as you lived them.)
2. The appropriateness of different styles of intervention (directive, non-directive, alternative, collaborative) and different kinds of mentoring behaviour at different phases or stages of beginner teacher development.

Photocopiable resource 18 (page 108)

Relationships and Goals

The diagram below describes various kinds of appropriate behaviour in conflict situations depending on the relative importance of keeping a good relationship on the one hand, and getting what you want on the other.

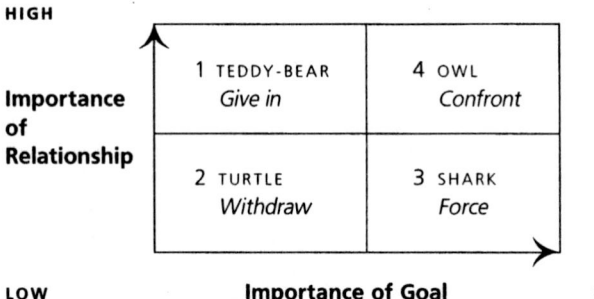

HIGH

Importance of Relationship

| 1 TEDDY-BEAR *Give in* | 4 OWL *Confront* |
| 2 TURTLE *Withdraw* | 3 SHARK *Force* |

LOW   **Importance of Goal**   **HIGH**

Adapted from Johnson, D. W. (1986) (3rd edn) *Reaching Out: Interpersonal effectiveness and self-actualisation.* Englewood Cliffs, New Jersey: Prentice Hall

When the relationship is much more important to you than getting what you want (quadrant 1) it is appropriate to give in to the other and behave like a teddy-bear. In a family situation, when there are differences in opinion about what to do on a free afternoon, for example, you may decide to sacrifice your goal of reading that good book and take the children to the park. Your relationship with your children is more important to you than your goal. A certain amount of teddy-bear-like behaviour may be appropriate at the beginning of the mentor–mentee relationship, when establishing a good relationship may, temporarily, be more important than anything else.

Behaviour as in quadrant 2 is probably never appropriate in mentor–mentee situations, partly because the relationship is always important. Here is an example in real life when it would be appropriate. You are walking home and decide it might be nice to walk through the park, but as you do you are pestered by someone who won't go away. So you change your mind about the walk through the park and return to the road – you withdraw (quadrant 2) – as your goal was not that important to you, and you want no relationship at all with the pesterer.

An example of appropriate shark-like behaviour (quadrant 3) could be when you are bargaining over the price of something in a market. You have and want no real relationship with the vendor, but your goal of getting the best price possible is paramount. This kind of behaviour is unlikely to be appropriate in mentoring situations, unless the goal you are pursuing is urgent and essential and the relationship strong enough to, temporarily, put at risk.

It is the owl-like behaviour of quadrant 4 which is most likely to be needed in mentoring. Here both the relationship and the achievement of your goal are of high importance. If there is conflict in these situations it is appropriate to 'confront', which basically means talk about it openly and negotiate a solution in which both parties are satisfied and the relationship remains intact or is strengthened.

Photocopiable resource 19 (page 108)

Difficult mentoring moments

Role-play Observation Sheet

TASK:

During the role-play: *Observe the 'Mentor' and 'Mentee' and make notes under the headings in the sheet below.*

After the role-play: *Review what happened, getting the 'Mentee's' and 'Mentor's' reactions, using your notes to give evidence of what happened. Decide as a group what you have all learnt from the experience, and be prepared to share this in the whole-group round-up at the end.*

Stages of discussion	Examples of what the 'Mentor' said	'Mentee's' reactions/comments

---

© Cambridge University Press 1999

Photocopiable resource 20 (page 115)

Standard Role-play Observation Sheet

OBSERVER TASKS
N.B. Remember it is mainly the 'Mentor' you are observing.

A. Evidence of supportive listening	**Often**	**Sometimes**	**Never**

(Make notes on the following points)
1. The 'Mentor' uses supportive body language.
Examples:

2. The 'Mentor' encourages the 'Teacher' by 'uh-huh'
etc, and helps them find words
Examples:

3. The 'Mentor' helped the 'Teacher' by
 – paraphrasing (e.g.):
 – clarification questions (e.g.):
 – summarising (e.g.):

B. Types of 'Mentor' communication   **Frequency**
(Mark every time you observe the following points)
1. The 'Mentor' seeks information.
2. The 'Mentor' gives information.
3. The 'Mentor' suggests ideas.
4. The 'Mentor' elicits ideas.
5. The 'Mentor' adds to the 'Teacher's' ideas.
6. The 'Mentor' blocks or objects to the 'Teacher's'
 ideas.
7. The 'Mentor' summarises the discussion.

C. The discussion as a whole
1. What was the proportion of the 'Mentor's' talking time?
 100%   75%   50%   25%   15%

2. What proportion of the 'Mentor's' style was:
 a. Directive (told 'Teacher' what to do)
 b. Alternatives (gave choice of ideas etc.)
 c. Collaborative (worked things out together)
 d. Non-directive (helped 'Teacher' to make own decisions)

Photocopiable resource 21 (page 115)

Standard Post-role-play Discussion Sheet

As Observer you will chair the discussion. Please follow the stages below.

Stage 1:
Ask the 'Mentor' and 'Teacher' how easy or not it was to take on their roles and why.

Stage 2:
Ask the 'Mentor' and 'Student-Teacher' for their feedback on the role-play itself (their feelings in role, interpretations, ideas for improvement, etc.).

Stage 3:
Share the findings from your role-play observation, giving the feedback in as supportive a way as possible.

Stage 4:
Ask the 'Mentor' and 'Teacher' what they have learnt from
a) the role-play itself,
b) the post-role-play discussion.
Tell them what you have learnt by observing.

Stage 5:
Be prepared to summarise this for the whole-group discussion. Think about areas you still need to practise and any questions you would like to raise.

© Cambridge University Press 1999

Photocopiable resource 22 (page 117)

'Teacher' role-card   **Lesson planning**

Materials:
− Lesson plan from recently-viewed video lesson
− Textbook/other relevant material from same video lesson
− Blank lesson plan form

Preparation: (with other 'Teachers')
1. Reflect on elements from the last lesson (video) that you might like to deal with in the next lesson (e.g.: errors, spoken or written; classroom dynamics, etc.)
2. Look at the next part of the textbook, and consider ways in which you might deal with it. Don't make a final decision yet.
3. On the basis of the above, begin to establish broad aims for your next lesson.

Role-play: (with 'Mentor' and Observer)
You are having a lesson planning session with your mentor, whom you like and trust.
1. Talk through your aims.
2. Consider ways (activities, etc.) to achieve those aims.
3. Write the lesson plan with the mentor.

Post-role-play discussion:
The Observer will chair a discussion on the role-play, and give feedback to the 'Mentor'. Be prepared to state what you have learnt from the whole experience.

'Mentor' role-card   **Lesson planning**

Materials:
– Lesson plan from recently-viewed video lesson
– Textbook and/or other relevant material from same video lesson

Preparation: (with the other 'Mentors')
You know that the student-teacher is planning to use the next part in the textbook for at least part of the lesson. Consider as many ways of exploiting this as possible. Explain and demonstrate to each other, in case you want to suggest or elicit these alternatives, when you meet your mentee ('Teacher') for the planning session.

Role play: (with the 'Teacher' and Observer)
You are having a lesson planning session with your mentee, whom you like and trust.
1. Help the 'Teacher' to clarify the aims of the lesson and the reasons for them, before discussing the sequence of activities.
2. Help the 'Teacher' to write the lesson plan.

Post-role-play discussion:
The Observer will chair a discussion on the role-play, giving you feedback. Be prepared to state what you have learnt from the whole experience.

Observer Tasks   **Lesson planning**

Materials:
– Textbook extract
– Post-role-play Discussion Sheet

Preparation: (with other Observers)
Familiarise yourself with the Role-play observation task, below, and with the Post-role-play Discussion Sheet, making sure you know what to do, and why.

Role-play observation task: (with 'Teacher' and 'Mentor')
The 'Teacher' and the 'Mentor' are having a lesson planning session. Sit a little apart (remember, observe only – don't participate!), and make notes according to the following:

– How did the planning process begin?
– Were the aims and objectives for the whole lesson clarified? When?
– How did the 'Teacher' decide on the plan?
– What style of intervention did the 'Mentor' use to achieve this?

Post-role-play discussion:
Chair the post-role-play discussion according to the sheet, making appropriate notes.

Photocopiable resource 23 (page 117)

'Mentor' card   **Full post-lesson discussion**

Materials:
– Lesson plan
– Observation notes

Preparation: (with the other 'Mentors')
1. Discuss and agree on the main points from the observation notes that ideally would need to be addressed in the post-lesson discussion. You may want to discuss how this might be achieved (especially if Teacher Biography cards are being used).
2. Think about any of the frameworks for post-lesson discussions you have read about, and agree on a sequence of stages. The following questions may help you:
   – What is the purpose of this discussion? (think about professional learning cycles)
   – What are the stages your mentee is likely to need to go through to achieve learning objectives?
   – How might the discussion start?
   – Who will begin talking?
   – What about?
   – What is the purpose of this stage?
   – How will the second stage evolve from the first?
   – Who decides on the topic?
   – What is the purpose of this stage?
   – What other stages are there likely to be?
   – What would the purpose of these be?
   – What is the final stage?
   – What is your role here?

Role-play: (with the 'Teacher' and Observer)
Conduct the post-lesson discussion according to your planned sequence of stages. Attempt to cover all stages within the time allotted.

Post-role-play discussion:
Share with your 'Teacher' and Observer the stages you had planned for the discussion, and any problems you experienced with this framework. Consider the sources of these problems.

'Teacher' card **Full post-lesson discussion**

Materials:
– Lesson plan
– Observation notes
– (Optional: Teacher Biography card)

Preparation: (with the other 'Teachers')
1. Looking at your video-viewing notes, think about the reasons why the teacher might have behaved as they did. What underlying beliefs, views of teaching and learning do you think they hold?
2. Select areas that you, as the 'Teacher', would like to discuss with your 'Mentor', and what you would like to gain from the discussion.

Role-play: (with the 'Mentor' and Observer)
Try to achieve your planned objectives for the discussion.

Post-role-play discussion:
The Observer will chair the post-role-play discussion.

Observer task **Full post-lesson discussion**

Materials:
– Lesson plan
– Post-role-play Discussion Sheet

Preparation: (with the other 'Observers')
Familiarise yourself with the role-play observation task, below, and the Post-role-play Discussion Sheet, making sure you know what to do, and why

Role-play observation task: (with 'Teacher' and 'Mentor')
Fill in the chart below.

Post-role-play discussion:
Chair the post-role-play discussion according to the sheet, making appropriate notes.

Main Stages Give each stage a name	**Main Features** Make notes on characteristic features of the 'Mentor's' interventions

Photocopiable resource 24 (page 117)

'Mentor' card   **Five-minute post-lesson discussion**

Materials:
- Observation notes
- (Optional) Teacher Biography Card

Preparation: (with the other 'Mentors')
1. Based on your observations decide on one of the following:
   - two positive aspects of the lesson and two aspects that you feel need work;
   - one or more 'thinking tasks' you would like to set up with the 'Teacher';
   - two or three aspects of the teaching that will need, in your opinion, attention in the planning for the next lesson (content, relationships, balance of activities etc.).
2. Decide on an objective for the five-minute post-lesson discussion as well as a strategy for achieving it, depending on the outcome of Step 1 above (and the Teacher Biography Card, if you have it).

Role play: (with the 'Teacher' and Observer)
Try to conduct the five-minute post-lesson discussion to the satisfaction of both you and the 'Teacher'.

Post-role-play discussion:
The Observer will chair the post-role-play discussion.

'Teacher' card   **Five-minute post-lesson discussion**

Materials:
- Observation notes
- (Optional) Teacher Biography Card

Preparation: (with the other 'Teachers')
Based on your 'experience' (and Teacher's Biography card if you have it), decide what help you would like from your 'Mentor' in the five minutes' discussion time you have. Such as:
- feedback on particular aspect(s) of lesson;
- help with planning for the next lesson.

Role play: (with the 'Mentor' and Observer)
Try to achieve your objective(s) in the five-minute post-lesson discussion.

Post-role-play discussion:
The Observer will chair the post-role-play discussion.

Observer task   **Five-minute post-lesson discussion**

Materials:
- General Role-play Observation Sheet, or one of the Mentor Skills Role-play Observation Sheets
- Post-role-play Discussion Sheet
- Observation notes

Preparation: (with the other Observers)
1. Familiarise yourselves with your Role-play Observation Sheet, and the Post-role-play Discussion Sheet, making sure you know what to do and why.
2. If time, think over what points you would want to raise in the limited time of five minutes.

Role-play task:
Fill in the chosen observation sheet, and act as time-keeper.

Post-role-play discussion:
Chair the discussion according to the sheet.

© Cambridge University Press 1999

Photocopiable resource 25 (page 117)

Observer tasks   **Supportive listening**

Make a tally of every time you notice the following:

The 'Mentor' and 'Teacher'
are in eye-contact.

The 'Mentor' is leaning towards
the 'Teacher'.

The 'Mentor' is smiling.

The 'Mentor' is nodding.

The 'Mentor' is using encouraging
words/sounds like 'ah-ha' etc.

The 'Mentor' is mirroring the
'Teacher's' body language.

The 'Mentor' is asking a question to
'get the picture clear'.

Make notes on anything else the 'Mentor' does that seems:
Supportive:

Non-supportive:

© Cambridge University Press 1999

Photocopiable resource 26 (page 118)

Observer task   **Paraphrasing**

Tick each time you hear the mentor say:

'What I think you mean is . . .'

'What you mean is . . .'

'So you are saying . . .'

'In other words . . .'

'So you mean . . .?'

'So . . .'

(Other):

© Cambridge University Press 1999

Photocopiable resource 27 (page 118)

Observer task   **I-statements**

Listen to the 'Mentor' and make a tally of occurrences of I-statements, as below, noting some examples.
Factual:
I saw . . .
e.g.:
I heard . . .
e.g.:
I noticed . . .
e.g.:

Interpretative:
I saw . . .
e.g.:
I heard . . .
e.g.:
I noticed . . .
e.g.:

Evaluative:
I saw . . .
e.g.:
I heard . . .
e.g.:
I noticed . . .
e.g.:

© Cambridge University Press 1999

Photocopiable resource 28 (page 118)

Observer task	'Excavating'

Make notes in the columns below each time the 'Mentor' challenges the 'Teacher's' thinking. Try to include the 'Mentor's' exact words in the challenge column, as well as the level of the 'Iceberg' at which they are working:

'Mentor's' challenge + level	'Teacher's' response

© Cambridge University Press 1999

Photocopiable resource 29 (page 118)

Observer task		Questions

Note down a maximum of 10 questions the 'Mentor' asks, marking stress and intonation, making notes on tone of voice and accompanying body language.

'Mentor's' questions	Tone of voice	Body language

Post-role-play discussion points:
1. How did the 'Teacher' interpret the questions above and why? (e.g. as genuinely seeking clarification/information, as accusation/evaluation, as thought-provoking/challenge, etc.)
2. Did the 'Teacher' react as the 'Mentor' intended?
3. What might account for any differences between 'Teacher' reaction and 'Mentor' intention in each case?

© Cambridge University Press 1999

Photocopiable resource 30 (page 118)

Observer task			Question factors
Note down a maximum of 10 questions the 'Mentor' asks, noting in the adjacent columns the manner, type and purpose of each question.			

'Mentor's' questions (max. 10) *Try to note down **when** the 'Mentor' asked the question. (exact time)*	Manner Encouraging: **E** Threatening: **T** Neutral: **N**	Type Open: **O** Closed: **C**	Who needs the answer? Mentor: **M** Teacher: **T**

Post-role-play discussion points:
1. *How did the 'Teacher' interpret the questions above and why? (e.g. as genuinely seeking clarification/ information, as accusation/evaluation, as thought-provoking/challenge, etc.)*
2. *Did the 'Teacher' react to the question as the 'Mentor' intended?*

© Cambridge University Press 1999

Photocopiable resource 31 (page 119)

TEACHER A

As a student yourself you had very strict 'traditional' teachers. You are a student-teacher in the second month of school experience. You have taught 24 lessons in the same class so far. Although planning lessons is getting a bit easier, you are beginning to worry that some of the things you do are causing discipline problems. You are frightened of things getting out of control.

TEACHER B

As a student yourself you had wonderful eccentric but effective teachers. Both your parents are teachers. You are a beginner teacher and you still worry that you neither feel nor look like a 'teacher'. You want your mentor to help you know how to be a 'teacher', so that you can stop feeling like you are acting.

TEACHER C

For you your best teacher was one of your trainers. You have just completed your initial teacher training where you learnt a lot of activities and ideas you want to try out and feel you have the skill to do so. (Actually when you think back to your old teachers you think you are probably much better trained than they were.)

TEACHER D

You went to teacher training college because you didn't get into medical school. You have been teaching for some months now and you know you are running out of the ideas you got from your training and you need your mentor to tell you what to do. Recently, you have been having a difficult time with your classes and are wondering if teaching is the right job for you.

TEACHER E

You can't remember particularly bad or good teachers. Your favourite was the maths teacher who had interesting ways of explaining things so that you always understood. You are in the middle of your mentoring period, and although activities seem to work in your classes you are beginning to wonder how much your students are actually learning.

TEACHER F

You were always an average student and are actually quite surprised to find yourself a teacher now. You are nearing the end of the mentoring period, and are already worrying about how you will cope without your mentor. You still feel inadequate and want to get as many ideas from him/her as you can before you part company.

TEACHER G

You were always considered a bright student, had good exam techniques and were top of the class most of the time. Because of this, you always thought you'd make a good teacher. You are nearing the end of the mentoring period, and don't feel your mentor can help you much any more. All your evaluations (negotiated) have been good to excellent and you are feeling pretty confident.

Photocopiable resource 32 (page 127)

'MENTOR' CARD   **NEGOTIATED EVALUATION – ROLE-PLAY**

Materials
- Observation notes
- Evaluation criteria

Preparation (with other 'Mentors')
1. Compare observation notes, and try to agree on evaluations.
2. Taking each criterion in turn, think about the possible stages of the discussion with the 'Teacher' to lead them to a self-evaluation.
3. If you can't find evidence from your observation notes for any particular criterion, imagine previous lessons in which you did make a note of such evidence.

Role-play (with 'Teacher' and Observer)
Discuss each criterion in turn with the 'Teacher', as you decided in Step 2 above.
Try to reach agreement.

Post-role-play discussion
The Observer will chair the discussion.

'TEACHER' CARD   **NEGOTIATED EVALUATION – ROLE-PLAY**

Materials
- Observation notes
- Evaluation criteria

Preparation (with other 'Teachers')
1. Compare observation notes, and try to agree on evaluations.
2. Taking each criterion in turn, think about the discussion with your 'Mentor' and how you will support your self-evaluation.
3. If you can't find evidence in this lesson for any particular criterion, imagine previous lessons in which there was evidence.

Role-play (with 'Mentor' and Observer)
Discuss each criterion in turn with the 'Mentor', as you decided in Step 2 above.
Try to reach agreement.

Post-role-play discussion
The Observer will chair the discussion.

'OBSERVER' TASK   NEGOTIATED EVALUATION – ROLE-PLAY

Materials
– Observation notes
– Evaluation criteria
– Post-role-play Discussion Sheet

Preparation (with other Observers)
1. Familiarise yourselves with the Role-play task below, as well as the Post-role-play Discussion Sheet, and check you understand what you have to do and why.
2. If time, consider the evaluation you would give using the criteria, for silent comparison with role-players during the role-play.

Role-play observation task
Observe the role-play and make notes in the chart below for each criterion as follows:
Criterion: note the name or number of the criterion under discussion
Evidence: note *what* evidence is used, and *who* gave it
Who evaluates: note who, essentially, makes the decision, either 'Mentor', 'Teacher' or both
How: note whether the decision was 'negotiated', 'persuaded' or 'forced', and evidence for your judgement of this.

Criterion	Evidence	Who evaluates	How

Post-role-play discussion
Chair the discussion according to the Post-role-play Discussion Sheet.

Photocopiable resource 33 (page 132)

Immediate Oral Review – Discussion Sheet

Think back to your experiences of immediate oral review after the lesson observations. Discuss each question below and make notes.

1. How did you feel about the immediate oral discussion ?
As observer:

As observed:

2. Who chose the focus of the discussion, and why?
'A' as observed:

'B' as observed:

3. Did the focus of the discussion replace or extend beyond the original aims of the observation?

4. What was the effect of this?
'A' as observed:

'B' as observed:

5. How far did the format of your notes influence the way you discussed the events of the lesson?
'A' as observer:

'B' as observer:

6. What conclusions can you draw about helpful and sensitive review discussions?

7. Summarise what you have learnt about the pros and cons of immediate oral review in the following chart:

ADVANTAGES   DISADVANTAGES

© Cambridge University Press 1999

Photocopiable resource 34 (page 134)

Delayed Written Review – Task Sheet

Think back to your experience of writing a review of an observed lesson. Discuss the questions below and make notes.

1. How useful were your observation notes in helping you formulate the written review?

2. Did you restrict the content to observations on the focus of observation? Why?/Why not?

3. What linguistic form (I-statements, questions, etc.) did most of your comments take? Why?

Now think back to your experience of receiving the delayed written review. Discuss the questions below and make notes.

1. How did it feel to wait for the written review?

2. How did you feel reading the review?

3. What effect did the content of the review have on you?

4. How far was this affected by whether the content was restricted to the aims of the observation or not?

5. What effect did the linguistic form of the comments have on you?

6. Summarise what you have learnt about the pros and cons of delayed written reviews in the following chart:

ADVANTAGES   DISADVANTAGES

Photocopiable resource 35 (page 135)

DRAWING CONCLUSIONS   **TASK SHEET 1**
OBSERVER and OBSERVED
Discuss the following points with your partner:
WHEN YOU WERE OBSERVER:

- Did you find that you were concentrating on anything in particular? Why? How did this affect the conversation afterwards?

- Were there moments when you would have liked to ask something but felt you couldn't?

- If there was anything that you didn't like, how did you bring it up?

- Was there anything that you chose not to bring up, and why?

- How do you think the discussion would have been different if the person observed had been a student-teacher?

WHEN YOU WERE OBSERVED:

- What did it feel like to be observed? Did it affect the way you taught? If so, how?

- When you were talking with the observer who did you feel was leading the discussion, you or the observer?

- Did your observer help you in any way to understand things differently and/or develop alternatives? If so, how, and how did you feel about it?

- Were there any stressful moments during the discussions? If there were, why and what did you do about it? If there weren't, how was this achieved?

MESSAGES TO MENTORS
Decide with your partner on two or three really important 'messages' that you feel would be useful for all mentors, based on this experience. Try to avoid using words like: *should, must, have to,* etc. Write each message on a separate piece of paper.

DRAWING CONCLUSIONS   **TASK SHEET 2**
MESSAGES TO MENTORS
As you read the messages that your group has sent:

- put a tick ✓beside those you definitely agree with.

- put a cross X beside those you definitely do not agree with.

- put question marks ? beside those that make you feel '*it depends . . .*'

(Insert messages here)

Photocopiable resource 36 (page 139)

'Models of teacher learning'

Ur, P. (1996). *A Course in Language Teaching: Practice and theory.* Cambridge University Press: pp. 5–8.

Read the following text and complete the tasks as they appear, making notes in the spaces provided.

Various models of teacher learning have been suggested; the three main ones, as described in Wallace (1993), are as follows:

1. The craft model
The trainee learns from the example of a 'master teacher', whom he/she observes and imitates. Professional action is seen as a craft, rather like shoemaking or carpentry, to be learned most effectively through an apprenticeship system and accumulated experience. This is a traditional method, still used as a substitute for postgraduate teaching courses in some countries.

1. What is your experience of craft learning? Remember at least one instance/example.

2. The applied science model
The trainee studies theoretical courses in applied linguistics and other allied subjects, which are then, through the construction of an appropriate methodology, applied to classroom practice. Many university- and college-based teacher-training courses are based, explicitly or implicitly, on this idea of teacher learning.

2. What aspects of learnt theory have you been able to integrate into your practice? Which areas have you not found of any practical use? Why/Why not?

3. The reflective model
The trainee teaches or observes lessons, or recalls past experience; then reflects, alone or in discussion with others, in order to work out theories about teaching; then tries these out again in practice. Such a cycle aims for continuous improvement and the development of personal theories of action (Schön, 1983). This model is used by teacher development groups and in some recently designed training courses.

3. Which of the three models above did your own initial training follow? Give some evidence.

4. Which of these models have you seen exemplified on this course? What evidence can you cite for your choice?

Which is likely to be most effective? Or, perhaps a better question: how do teachers learn most effectively, and how can this learning be integrated into a formal course of study?

I have several times asked groups of teachers in different countries from what, or whom, they feel they learned their present teaching expertise and knowledge. Various possible sources were suggested, such as colleagues and 'master teachers', the literature, pre- or in-service courses, their own experience as teachers, their students, their own experience as learners; and teachers were asked to rate each of these in importance for professional learning. Every time the majority replied that personal teaching experience was by far the most important. (Try this yourself with teachers you know!)

5. *How have you been learning teaching?*

This answer makes sense on an intuitive, personal level as well. I myself have done my best to read, study, discuss with colleagues, attend courses and conferences in order to improve my professional knowledge. Nevertheless, if asked, I would make the same reply as the teachers in my survey: I have learnt most through (thinking about) my own teaching experience. This does not mean that other sources of knowledge and learning processes do not contribute; but it does mean that they are probably less important.

Thus, I have chosen to base this course primarily on the 'reflective model' as defined at the beginning of this section.

My only reservation is that this model can tend to over-emphasize experience. Courses based on it have sometimes used the (student-) teachers themselves as almost the sole source of knowledge, with a relative neglect of external input – lectures, reading, and so on – which help to make sense of the experiences and can make a very real contribution to understanding. As I see it, the function of teacher reflection is to ensure the processing of any input, regardless of where it comes from, by the individual teacher, so that the knowledge becomes personally significant to him or her. Thus a fully effective reflective model should make room for external as well as personal input.

6. *'As I see it, the function of teacher reflection is to ensure the processing of any input, regardless of where it comes from, by the individual teacher, so that the knowledge becomes personally significant to him or her.'*

– *What theory do you think the author has about the way people learn?*

– *What do we do on this course to help you make 'knowledge personally significant'?*

– *What mentoring activities and processes do you know that also have this goal?*

Perhaps we might call this model 'enriched reflection'! It is described below.

'Enriched reflection'

Kolb's (1984) theory of experiential learning elaborates the idea of 'experience + reflection'. He defines four modes of learning: concrete experience, reflective observation, abstract conceptualization and active experimentation. In order for optimal learning to take place, the knowledge acquired in any one mode needs to be followed by further processing in the next; and so on, in a recursive cycle. Thus, concrete experience ('something happened to me in the classroom'), which involves intuitive of 'gut' feeling, should be followed by reflective observation ('let me step back and look at what took place'), which involves watching and perception; this in its turn is followed by abstract conceptualization ('what principle, or concept, can I formulate which will account for this event?'), involving intellectual thought; then comes active experimentation ('let me try to implement this idea in practice'), involving real-time action which will entail further concrete experience . . . and so on (see Box 0.1).

BOX 0.1: EXPERIENTIAL LEARNING

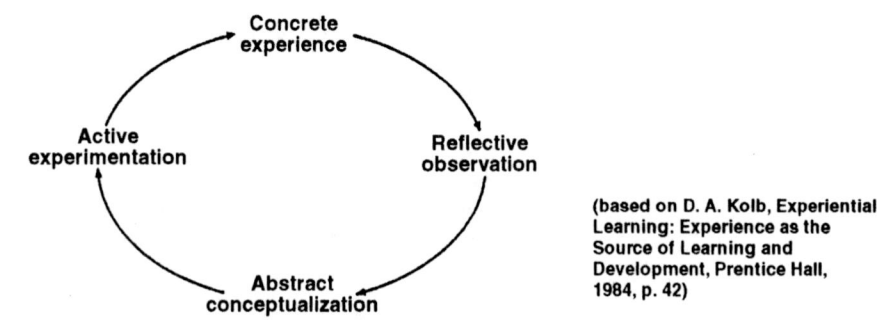

(based on D. A. Kolb, Experiential Learning: Experience as the Source of Learning and Development, Prentice Hall, 1984, p. 42)

---

7. *Relate your experiences of e.g. learning to drive, knit or cook to the different stages of Kolb's cycle (see Box 0.1). How does this compare with your learning to teach?*

This model, however, needs to be enriched by external sources of input. It is unrealistic and a waste of time to expect trainees to 'reinvent the wheel': this is like expecting physics students to discover known laws of physics through their own experiments. There is a lot to be learnt from experienced teachers (as in the craft model), from experts, from research and from reading (as in the applied science model) – provided all this can be integrated into one's own reflection-based theories. So at each stage of Kolb's circle let us add the external sources: experience can be vicarious (i.e. second-hand, such as observation, anecdote, video, transcripts); descriptions of other people's observations can add to our own; theoretical concepts can come from foreign language researchers and thinkers; ideas for or descriptions of experiments from writers or other professionals. And the initial stimulus for a learning cycle of this kind can occur, of course, at any of the eight points, not just at the point of experience (see Box 0.2).

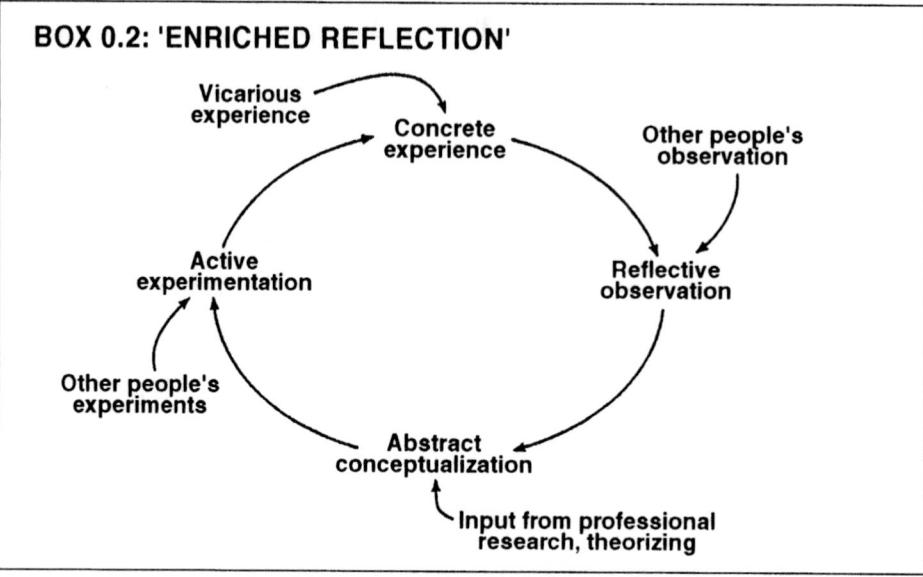

BOX 0.2: 'ENRICHED REFLECTION'

Thus, sources of knowledge may be either personal experience and thought or input from outside; but in either case this knowledge should, in principle, be integrated into the trainees' own reflective cycle in order that effective learning may take place.

To summarize: the most important basis for learning is personal professional practice; knowledge is most useful when it either derives directly from such practice, or, while deriving originally from other sources, is tested and validated through it. Hence the subtitle of this book: *Practice and Theory*, rather than the more conventional *Theory and Practice*.

8. *Think back over your own teaching career. Can you find instances of your own professional learning which began from each of the eight entry points of the 'enriched reflection' cycle (see Box 0.2)?*

Vicarious experience:

Concrete experience:

Other people's observation:

Reflective observation:

Input from professional research, theorising:

Abstract conceptualisation:

Other people's experiments:

Active experimentation:

9. *If you have been unable to fill in any of the above, what might this mean? Does it say anything about the kind of learner you are, the opportunities you have given yourself, your context, the model or what?*

10. *Compare the labels on the 'enriched reflection' cycle model with any other learning cycles you know (e.g. Experience, Review, Learn and Plan)*

The role of the trainer

Such a model of professional learning has, of course, implications for the role of the trainer. In the 'craft model', the trainer is the master teacher, providing an example to be followed. The 'applied science' model also gives the trainer an authoritative role, as the source of theory which the teacher is to interpret in practice. The conventional 'reflective model', in contrast, casts the trainer in the role of 'facilitator' or 'developer', giving little or no information, but encouraging trainees to develop their own body of knowledge.

According to the model suggested here, the function of the trainer is neither just to 'tell' the trainees what they should be doing, nor – just as bad – to refuse to tell them anything in order for them to develop all their knowledge on their own. The functions of the trainer, I believe, are:

– to encourage trainees to articulate what they know and put forward new ideas of their own;
– to provide input him- or herself and to make available further sources of relevant information;
– and, above all, to get trainees to acquire the habit of processing input from either source through using their own experience and critical faculty, so that they eventually feel personal 'ownership' of the resulting knowledge.

11. *Do you agree with these 'functions of the trainer'? If these are <u>aims</u>, what is the methodology, in other words, how can you achieve these aims in your work with a mentee?*

Photocopiable resource 37 (page 143)

Specifications for professional learning cycle assignment

You are asked to carry out all the stages of a professional learning cycle and write them up in the form of a report for fellow course participants. The report should be of approximately 1,000 words. A possible organisation might be:

1. Experience
In this section you will need to explain the experience (of yourself or others) that led to your decision to choose your topic. You will also need to explain details of your context that are unknown to your readers. This is a descriptive section.

2. Reflection
In this section, you will first need to reflect back on the experience, and analyse it, referring to any data you may have (e.g. lesson plans, self- or peer-observation notes, student feedback, etc.). Next, you will need to draw conclusions leading to plans for your learning (see below).

3. Learning
Here you will first need to describe the learning processes you undertook (further reading, observations, consultations – with colleagues or students, etc.), and what new insights you have gained about your topic of investigation through these processes.

4. Planning
Here you will describe the actions you intend to take as a result of the learning above.

5. New experience
This stage is optional, but you may wish to include in your report what happened when you implemented your plans, and any immediate results of that implementation.

Photocopiable resource 38 (page 144)

Professional learning cycle – Discussion task sheet

Consider the questions you have received and given on your reports. Discuss the points below and make notes.

A Receiving
1. In turn, respond to the questions you have received.

2. How did you feel, receiving each set of questions?

3. What have you learnt from the questions about the content and form of your report?

4. What might account for the differences in the two sets of questions you received?

B Giving
1. How easy/difficult was it to construct the questions?

2. Why did you choose the questions you did? What were the underlying principles for your choices?

3. Which questions were not understood in the way you intended?

Are there any obvious relationships between form and purpose of the questions?

References

Alwright, R. (1988). *Observation in the Language Classroom*. Harlow: Longman.

Baudains R. and M. Baudains (1990). *Alternatives*. Harlow: Longman.

Bodóczky, C. and A. Malderez (1992). Co-trainer training. Talk. IATEFL Conference, Lille.

Bodóczky, C. and A. Malderez (1994). Talking shop: pre-service teaching experience and the training of supervisors. *ELT Journal*, 48, 1.

Bodóczky, C. and A. Malderez (1996). Out into schools. In A. Malderez and P. Medgyes (Eds.) *Changing Perspectives in Teacher Education*. Oxford: Heinemann.

Bodóczky, C. and A. Malderez (1997). The INSET impact of a mentoring course. In C. Kennedy (Ed.) *Making a Difference: The Impact of INSET*. Hemel Hempstead: Prentice Hall.

Bolitho, R. and T. Wright (1993). Grids as a reflective training tool on Trainer-Training Courses. *The Teacher Trainer* 7, 2. Canterbury: Pilgrims.

Brandes, D. and P. Ginnis (1989). *The Student-Centred School*. Oxford: Blackwell.

Campbell, P. and G. H. Wheatley (1983). A model for helping student teachers. In *Mathematics Teacher* 76.

Claxton, G. (1989). *Being a Teacher*. London: Cassell Education.

Claxton, G. (1990). *Teaching to Learn*. London: Cassell Education.

Dennison, B. and R. Kirk (1990). *Do, Review, Learn, Apply: A Simple Guide to Experiential Learning*. Oxford: Basil Blackwell Ltd.

Dörnyei, Z. and A. Malderez (1997). Group dynamics and foreign language teaching. *System*, 25, 1: 65–81. University of Linkoping, Sweden.

Edge, J. (1992) *Cooperative Development*. London: Longman.

Fanselow, J. (1990). 'Let's see': contrasting conversations about teaching. In J. C. Richards and D. Nunan (Eds.) *Second Language Teacher Education*. Cambridge: Cambridge University Press.

Freeman, D. (1990). Intervening in practice teaching. In J. C. Richards and D. Nunan (Eds.) *Second Language Teacher Education*. Cambridge: Cambridge University Press.

Freeman, D. (1992). Language teacher education, emerging discourse and change in classroom practice. In J. Flowerdew, M. Brock and S. Hsia (Eds.) *Perspectives on Second Language Teacher Education*. Hong Kong: City Polytechnic of Hong Kong.

Freire, P. (1970). *Pedagogy of the Oppressed*. New York: Herder and Herder.

Fullerton H. and A. Malderez (Eds.) (1998). *Facets of Mentoring in Higher Education 2*. Staff and Educational Development Association.

Gebhard, J. (1990). Models of supervision choices. In J. C. Richards and D. Nunan (Eds.) *Second Language Teacher Education*. Cambridge: Cambridge University Press.

Griffiths, J. and C. Ryan (1994). *Curriculum for the B.Ed TEFL (Three Year Programme)*. Budapest: ELTE CETT.

Hadfield, J. (1992). *Classroom Dynamics*. Oxford: Oxford University Press.

HMI Survey (1987*) Quality in Schools: The Initial Training of Teachers.* London: H.M. Stationary Office.

Johnson, K. (1996). *Language Teaching and Skill Learning.* Oxford: Blackwell.

Kagan, D. (1992). Professional growth among pre-service and beginner teachers. *Review of Educational Research,* 6(2).

Kazantzakis, N. (1952). *Zorba the Greek.* London: Faber and Faber Ltd.

Lamb, M. (1995). The consequences of INSET. *ELT Journal,* 49, 1: 72–80.

Lortie, D. (1975). *School Teacher: a sociological study.* Chicago: University of Chicago Press.

Malderez, A. (1996). Mentoring – learning it and doing it. Paper presented at University of Timisoara, Romania.

Medgyes, P. and A. Malderez (Eds.) (1996). *Changing Perspectives in Teacher Education.* Oxford: Heinemann.

Moskovitz, G. (1976). *Caring and Sharing in the Language Classroom.* Rowley, Mass.: Newbury House.

Prabhu, N. S. (1987). Equipping and enabling. Paper presented at the RELC Conference, Singapore

Ramani, E. (1987). Theorising from the classroom. *ELT Journal,* 41, 1: 3–11.

Richards, J. C. and D. Nunan (Eds.) (1990). *Second Language Teacher Education.* Cambridge: Cambridge University Press.

Rogers C. R. (1983). *Teaching to Learn for the 80s.* Colombus, London: Merrill.

Schön, D. A. (1983). *The Reflective Practitioner: How Professionals Think in Action.* New York: Basic Books.

Schön, D. A. (1987). *Educating the Reflective Practitioner: Toward a New Design for Teaching and Learning in the Professions.* San Francisco: Jossey-Bass Publishers.

Selinker, L. (1972). Interlanguage. *IRAL,* 10, 2: 209–231.

Stevick, E. W. (1980). *Teaching Languages: A Way and Ways.* Rowley, Mass: Newbury House.

Thomas, L. and E. Hari-Augstein (1985). *Self-Organised Learning.* London: Routledge and Kegan Paul.

Tiberius, R. G. (1986). Metaphors underlying the improvement of teaching and learning. In *British Journal of Educational Technology,* 17, 2: 144–156.

Tomlinson, P. (1995). *Understanding Mentoring: Reflective Strategies for School-Based Teacher Preparation.* Buckingham: Open University Press.

Tuckman, B. W. and M. A. C. Jensen (1977). Stages of small-group development revisited. *Group and Organization Studies* 2: 419–427.

Ur, P. (1996). *A Course in Language Teaching: Practice and Theory.* Cambridge: Cambridge University Press.

Vygotsky, L. (1979). *Mind in society: the development of higher psychological processes.* M. Cole, V. John Steiner, S. Scribner, and E. Souberman (Eds.) Cambridge, Mass.: Harvard University Press.

Wajnryb, R. (1992). *Classroom Observation Tasks.* Cambridge: Cambridge University Press.

Williams, M. and R. L. Burden, (1997). *Psychology for Language Teachers: a social constructivist approach.* Cambridge: Cambridge University Press.

Woodward, T. (1991). *Models and Metaphors in Language Teacher Training.* Cambridge: Cambridge University Press.

List of figures

Appendices

Appendix 1

Observation Sheet: Focus on the learners A

Make a list of all the things you would expect students to do in the classroom (some have been given for you). As you observe make a mark (/) each time you observe that behaviour. Note whether you observe that behaviour in one (1), a small group (G) or the whole class (WC) of learners as in the example below.

LEARNER BEHAVIOUR	Observed	Pupil grouping
Activity		
Talk L1	//	G, 1
Talk L2	/	WC

Add any unforeseen categories of behaviour as you observe them. Try to account in your record for everything you see the learners do.

LEARNER BEHAVIOUR	Observed	Pupil grouping
Activity		
Talk L1		
Talk L2		
Write L1		
Write L2		
Read L1		
Read 12		
Listen L1		
Listen L2		

Observation Sheet: Focus on the learners B

DURING THE LESSON

1. Make sure you are seated in a position where you are able to observe when and how the teacher attends to individuals – by names, gesture, stance, facing them or not, eye-contact, verbal prompts, etc.
2. For a portion of the lesson (decide yourself how much of the lesson you wish to devote to the collection of data), keep a record of every time the teacher attends: mark the appropriate box (perhaps with a dot) each time the teacher attends to a particular person.
3. As the teacher's use of names allows you to identify the learners, name each box on your diagram.
4. As far as you are able, try also to make a note (see list below) of the actual attending strategy used by the teacher. Some likely ones are listed. You may like to add others as you observe. It may help to use an abbreviation code. Sometimes strategies overlap or are combined: you may like to indicate this, for example, smile/eye-contact (overlap); name + smile (combined).
5. Note on your diagram, too, whether the students are male or female and any other distinguishing characteristics, such as a difference in age, nationality.
6. You may wish to record some field notes on student response to the teacher's

attending strategies, for example, when the teacher looks at a student to discourage talking, or to encourage a response.

Seating arrangements

Wu F ●	M	F	Matilda ● ● F	M	M	F
M						F
M						F
M						Julio M ● ● ● ●
F					F	
F					F	
M						M ●

Attending strategies

name (N)

nod (↓)

smile (⌣)

eye−contact (⊙)

reprimanding look (⌒)

touch (T)

From Wajnryb, R. (1992). *Classroom Observation Tasks.*
Cambridge: Cambridge University Press: 29.

Observation Sheet: Focus on the learners C

DURING THE LESSON

1. Consider these students' behaviour/role in class and the degree to which they synchronise and co-operate with the teacher. For example, consider a student's:
   - response to the teacher;
   - involvement in tasks;
   - willingness to ask when uncertain;
   - tolerance of other students, etc.
2. There is room in the far right column for any further comments. You may, for example, wish to consider whether the motivation might be described as instrumental, integrative or a blend of these.

Student's name	Motivation	Learning behaviour	Comment

From Wajnryb, R. (1992). *Classroom Observation Tasks.*
Cambridge: Cambridge University Press: 32.

Observation Sheet: Focus on the learners D

DURING THE LESSON

1. Observe the lesson from the point of view of what the learners actually do.
2. Use the chart to help you collect data from the lesson. Note down:
   - what the learners do;
   - what this involves;
   - what you think the teacher's purpose is.

Add any comments in the far right column, for example, whether you would label the activity cognitive, affective, physical.

What learners do	What this involves	Teacher's purpose	Comment
Grouping words according to meaning	*– Referring to dictionary* *– Consulting other students*	*– Teach reference skills* *– Teach two layers of meaning: denotation and connotation*	*Cognitive*

From Wajnryb, R. (1992). *Classroom Observation Tasks.*
Cambridge: Cambridge University Press: 35.

Observation Sheet: Focus on the learners E

For each stage of the lesson find one learner who appears to be off-task. Study that learner and make notes on what they do. Indicate each time you observe a different learner.

Lesson stage	Notes on what the off-task learner does/looks like, etc.

Appendix 2

Mentorial frameworks

A framework for a post-lesson discussion

If at the end of any phase, the mentee has reached his/her own decisions for future action as a result of going through stages of describing, interpreting and evaluating, then the discussion has reached its natural conclusion. In other words, if the mentor behaviour and style of one phase is not enough to help the mentee interpret, evaluate and make decisions for the future – for their teaching or for their own professional learning – then the mentor moves on to the next phase with its corresponding slight change of behaviour and style.

(Reality, of course, is almost always never as clear-cut as the following chart might suggest.)

PHASE	MENTEE ACTION	MENTOR ACTION	MENTOR STYLE
1. 'Talk me through it . . .'	DESCRIBES (and interprets, evaluates, plans)	LISTENS ACTIVELY	NON-DIRECTIVE
2. 'I saw/I heard . . .'	LISTENS INTERPRETS (and evaluates and plans)	DESCRIBES 'Holds up the mirror'	COLLABORATIVE
3. 'Tell me more about . . . How/What else might . . .?'	'FINDS' AND CONSIDERS ALTERNATIVES (plans)	PROBES 'Excavates iceberg'	ALTERNATIVES
4. 'I'd like you to . . . Why don't you . . .'	AGREES!	MAKES DECISIONS, SETS TASKS	DIRECTIVE

A framework for a pre-lesson discussion (talking through a mentee-prepared lesson plan)

Whereas in post-lesson discussions the focus can be on the mentee's professional learning (starting from the evidence about pupil learning or lack of it), in pre-lesson discussions the focus must be on the pupils' intended learning.

The aim is that the mentee articulates planned procedures and their rationale that seem likely to achieve the lesson objectives, and has taken into account and considered how to handle difficulties or problems that might arise. At whatever phase of the discussion this occurs, the discussion has reached its natural conclusion. If, however, one phase of the framework does not elicit this, the mentor will want to move to the next phase with its corresponding slight change of style and behaviour. Again the phases are rarely as distinct as presented here. If the mentor is going to observe the lesson, a fifth stage will be necessary in which the focus of the observation is agreed.

PHASE	MENTEE ACTION	MENTOR ACTION	MENTOR STYLE
1. 'Talk me through it.'	DESCRIBES plan (and explains reasons, discusses alternatives)	LISTENS actively	NON-DIRECTIVE
2. 'Tell me more about how/why . . .'	EXPLAINS reasons for choices in relation to intended pupil learning (and discusses alternatives)	PROBES and encourages links between: – choices and intended pupil learning – choices and previous teaching behaviour of the mentee and its outcomes	COLLABORATIVE
3. 'What if . . .'	DISCUSSES possible alternative courses of action	CHECKS mentee has alternative courses of action ready if necessary, or offers ideas	ALTERNATIVES
4. 'I've a feeling it might be a good idea if you . . .' (planned the boardwork: re-thought your presentation, etc.)	AGREES!	GIVES FURTHER TASKS TO CARRY OUT without which the pupils are unlikely to learn or the teaching is likely to be dangerous	DIRECTIVE

Appendix 3

Teaching practice evaluation form

SCHOOL EXPERIENCE REPORT FORM	

Trainee's Name _____ School _____
CETT Tutor's Name _____ Class _____
COT's Name _____ Date/Time _____

Please indicate whether you consider the trainee's task to have been:
Relatively easy:
Of average demand:
Of above average demand:

Comments

PERSONAL QUALITIES:
Presence/style

Voice quality

Rapport with pupils

PLANNING:
Aims and objectives

Appropriacy of activities

Shape and balance of activities

Preparation of materials/resources

Anticipation of difficulties

IMPLEMENTATION:
Class management

Pace and timing

Use of teaching aids/materials

Clarity of explanation/instruction

Questioning techniques

Accuracy/appropriacy of language

Ability to adapt/extemporise

Pupils' involvement

Awareness/treatment of errors

Achievement of aims/objectives

Pupil evaluation

SELF-EVALUATION:

Appendix 4

Criteria for completing the teaching practice record of performance

(elégtelen = fail; elégséges = fair; közepes = satisfactory; jó = good; jeles = excellent. With the kind permission of the Faculty of Teacher Training, English & American Studies Department, Veszprém, Hungary)

elégtelen	*elégséges*	*közepes*	*jó*	*jeles*
TEACHING SKILLS AND STRATEGIES				
The trainee ... ... shows no evidence of basic planning. ... is almost totally dependent on the mother tongue. ... uses inappropriate teaching strategies. ... uses inappropriate or inadequate resources. ... is not aware of students' needs. ... makes no attempt to adapt materials to the needs of the students. ... is totally dependent on given teaching material.	**The trainee ...** ... shows evidence of basic planning. ... is heavily dependent on teaching materials. ... uses the mother tongue unnecessarily. ... uses inappropriate teaching strategies.	**The trainee ...** ... has some difficulty with execution of schemes of work, e.g. pitch, pace or structure of lessons, but clear evidence of thought in planning. ... uses resources well including audiovisuals and information technology. ... has realistic expectations of students. ... tends to depend too much on the mother tongue when problematic situations arise.	**The trainee ...** ... uses resources (audiovisuals, information technology) well. ... holds students' attention. ... conceives, structures and implements lessons well. ... matches the lessons well to the students' abilities and needs. ... uses a good variety of teaching strategies. ... uses the mother tongue appropriately and selectively. ... has realistic expectations of the students and sets realistic tasks.	**The trainee ...** ... has ability to generate a sense of excitement and enquiry within the subject. ... has a stimulating manner and imagination in devising schemes of work. ... uses appropriate teaching strategies. ... structures her/his lessons well. ... meets needs of students on macro-level (good all-round communication in English) and on local practical level of exams. ... keeps the use of mother tongue to absolute minimum. ... selects and produces resources (audiovisuals and information technology, if available) successfully.

(contd)

COMMUNICATION				
The trainee ... ... does not want or is unable to communicate. ... uses inadequate volume, tonal quality or variety of voice all the time.	**The trainee ...** ... is not able to select appropriate language for communication to whole class or individuals. ... uses inadequate volume, tonal quality or variety of voice rather frequently. ...'s presence is weak. ... has little awareness of students' language and literacy levels.	**The trainee ...** ... has difficulties of volume, tone or pitch. ...'s presence is inadequate with most classes. ... generates little enthusiasm. ... has moderate awareness of students' language and literacy levels. ... is not flexible enough in guiding the course of conversation.	**The trainee ...** ...'s classroom presence is good, enhanced by clear use of language, expressed in an agreeable way. ... is completely aware of students' language and literacy levels. ... is flexible enough in guiding the course of conversation.	**The trainee ...** ...'s presence is very good, highly effective in generating enthusiasm. ... produces rich vocal quality with variety in pitch, volume and tone. ... articulates well and in an interesting way. ... holds students' attention with ease.

(contd)

elégtelen	*elégséges*	*közepes*	*jó*	*jeles*
		ASSESSMENT/EVALUATION		
The trainee . . . . . . marks students' work poorly or not at all. . . . does not pay attention to individuals' attainment. . . . cannot judge the pupils' current level of attainment at all. . . . shows no consistent evidence of having expectations. . . . has illogical requirements. . . . is not aware of strengths and weaknesses of own performance. . . . lacks willingness to reflect. . . . is reluctant to consider advice or criticism and does not accept them.	**The trainee . . .** . . . marks students' work inadequately, unsystematically and it affects the classroom atmosphere negatively. . . . has little awareness of students' attainment. . . . has unrealistic expectations. . . . has limited capacity for reflection. . . . is insensitive to own strengths and weaknesses. . . . does not react constructively to evaluation from others.	**The trainee . . .** . . . marks students' work conscientiously, but not consistently and it does not affect the classroom atmosphere negatively. . . . has difficulty in identifying pupils' level of attainment. . . . has some capacity for reflection. . . . is confused about own performance. . . . has some ability to evaluate teaching and learning outcomes. . . . accepts criticism happily but cannot use it for improvement.	**The trainee . . .** . . . has some insight into agreed criteria of marking . . . 's marking of students' work is largely understood and accepted by students. . . . holds realistic expectations. . . . has developing reflectiveness. . . . reacts in a positive way with a willingness to improve. . . . is able to evaluate own performance reasonably well. . . . considers evaluation constructively in what is, on the whole, a positive spirit.	**The trainee . . .** . . . applies pedagogically sound, fair and systematic procedures to evaluate students' work. . . . 's marking of students' work is understood and highly appreciated by the students. . . . is fully aware of pupils' current level of attainment. . . . is able to use assessment of pupils' progress. . . . 's expectations completely meet the students' needs and current level of attainment. . . . is able to reflect deeply and be self-critical. . . . has highly developed self-critical sense. . . . has good ability to suggest lines of improvement. . . . is not afraid of criticism and may indeed seek it out. . . . is fully co-operative and constructive in the evaluation process.

Developed by Bakonyi Borbála, Balázs Árpádné, Dr Bárdos Jenö, Demény Anna, Doviscsákné Jakab Aranka, Fábián Gyöngyi, Forintos Éva, Horváth Mónika, Hubai Judit, Imreh Enikö, Kenesei Andrea, Korányi Judit, Dr Kurtán Zsuzsa, Materné Pressing Anikó, McGuigan Terence, Dr Méray Lászlóné, Némethné Hock Ildikó, Paksy Etelka, Poór Zoltán, Poór Zsuzsánna, Simon Orsolya, Szekeresné Rózsa Etelka. Veszprém, February 1st 1996.

Appendix 5

CETT end-of-year teaching experience grading criteria

(With the kind permission of the Centre for English Teacher Training, Eötvös Lórand University, Budapest, Hungary.)

CETT END-OF-YEAR TEACHING EXPERIENCE GRADING CRITERIA

The following criteria are grouped under five main headings. They describe the teaching competences of a graduating CETT student. Each of these components are equally weighted and should be graded on a 1 (fail) to 5 scale. The resulting average (rounded up or down) will produce the final Teaching Experience grade. A fail (1) in any of these categories means an overall fail. Grades are to be negotiated as at mid-year. The final decision, but *only* in the case of disagreement, rests with the university-based TP support tutor.

CRITERIA	DESCRIPTION	GRADE
Professional commitment	This student teacher has shown consistent commitment and professionalism through attendance, thoughtful preparation, good record-keeping, and cooperation with teaching partner, mentor (COT) and colleagues. They have shown themselves to be responsible members of staff and have taken an active part in school life (staff meetings, school events, etc.).	
Teacherly skills (use Check-list)	They have acquired a classroom presence and demonstrated a range of classroom management skills. The student has shown confidence and competence in short- and medium-term planning. They have acquired some skills in long-term planning (having an overview of the course, recycling the language, and focusing on the 'end product'). The student has shown confidence and competence in implementation and pupil evaluation (i.e. giving feedback and grades).	
Reflection and awareness	They have shown the ability and willingness to reflect on the teaching/learning process. They have developed an awareness of their own strengths and weaknesses, and are making a consistent effort to improve.	
Language	Their language is such that they provide an adequate model for their pupils. They are constantly working to improve their language skills.	
Concern for pupils	They have striven to discover and take into account learner needs and differences. They are sensitive and responsive to the ups and downs of the pupils' learning process. They have shown concern for their pupils' social and personal development.	
	Final Grade:	

Appendix 6

Self-observation schedule

(Adapted from a schedule compiled by the Institute of Education, London University, 1984.)

OBSERVATION SHEET A1
Observation for development of and by self

If possible record your lesson (90 min. cassette). This will help you have a more objective memory.

SEVEN KEY QUESTIONS

1. WHAT WERE THE BEST POINTS OF THE LESSON?

BEST POINTS	REASON

2. WHAT DID STUDENTS ACTUALLY DO? (Write, speak, play, sing, etc.)

WHAT THEY DID	% OF CLASS INVOLVED	WHAT I'D PLANNED FOR THEM TO DO	HOW DID WHAT I DID AFFECT THIS?

3. WHAT DID THEY LEARN?

WHAT THEY LEARNT	EVIDENCE	WHAT I'D PLANNED FOR THEM TO LEARN	REASONS FOR ANY DIFFERENCES

4. HOW WORTHWHILE WERE THE ACTIVITIES?

ACTIVITY	GRADE (1–5)	HOW COULD I IMPROVE OR REPLACE IT?

(contd)

5. WHAT HAVE I LEARNT?

WHAT DID I DISCOVER IN THE LESSON?	WHAT HAVE I DISCOVERED ON REFLECTION?

6. WHAT DO I INTEND TO DO NOW?

   ACTION POINTS:

7. HOW DO I FEEL, HAVING OBSERVED MYSELF

Appendix 7

Role of the COT feedback form

(COT = Co-Trainer – mentor. With the kind permission of the Centre for English Teacher Training, Eötvös Lórand University, Budapest, Hungary, 1993. This form is administered every November, three months into the year long teaching practice.)

The role of the COTs

(Please put a cross in the box below the symbol that most nearly describes your feeling/ opinion.)

How far does your COT:

1 provide you with day-to-day comfort and support?

    ☺ ☐   ☹ ☐   ? ☐ ?

2 provide help with imminent lesson planning?

    ☺ ☐   ☹ ☐   ? ☐ ?

3 provide help with long-term course/lesson planning?

    ☺ ☐   ☹ ☐   ? ☐ ?

4 help you find and choose supplementary material?

    ☺ ☐   ☹ ☐   ? ☐ ?

5 provide useful post-lesson* feedback?
   (Cross boxes and complete as relevant.)

    ☺ ☐   ☹ ☐   ? ☐ ?

6 give you suggestions for what to observe in your partner's teaching?

    ☺ ☐   ☹ ☐   ? ☐ ?

7 help you sort out any problems between you and other people (pupils, partner, staff, . . . etc)?

□   □   □

8 help you devise and keep a plan of action to improve problem areas?

□   □   □

A final comment:
Ask yourself: Am I as tolerant and as open to different viewpoints with my COT as I expect them to be with me?

YES   NO

Comments:

Appendix 8

COT end-of-year evaluation form

(COT = Co-Trainer – mentor. With the kind permission of the Centre for English Teacher Training (CETT), Eötvös Lórand University, Budapest, Hungary, 1993. This form was designed by the CETT COTs for evaluation by their trainees. It is administered at the end of the year long teaching practice.)

COT END OF YEAR EVALUATION

Designed by the COTs for evaluation by their trainees

Dear Student Teacher,

Please take time to complete this questionnaire, as it is of immense value both to the COTs themselves and to CETT.

Please return it to Caroline Bodóczky (CETT room 1/b or room 8 pigeon hole) as soon as possible. The questionnaires will only be given to the COTs after you have finished your work together, so please be open and honest, as it is the most helpful for all. Thank you very much, and good luck for your future teaching.

Please either circle the appropriate response or put an X on the appropriate spot on the clines. Please add 'evidence', examples or justifications in the comments section.

NAME OF COT:

NAME OF SCHOOL:

A. THE SCHOOL

1. Do you think it is a suitable place for Teaching Experience

    Atmosphere: YES _____ NO

    Students: YES _____ NO

    Facilities: YES _____ NO

    COMMENTS

2. Were you considered as a colleague or a student?

    Colleague   Student

    EVIDENCE:

B. THE COT
a Personal relationship

1. Rank your COT (1–5) for each of the following:

COMFORTING: 1   2   3   4   5

SUPPORTIVE: 1   2   3   4   5

HELPFUL: 1   2   3   4   5

COMMENTS:

2. Was your COT ever hurtful?   YES   NO
If yes, how?

b Professional relationship

1. COT's knowledge of English:
(rank according to your perceived 'ideal' for COT work)

    1   2   3   4   5

COMMENTS

2. COT's knowledge of methodology:
(rank according to your perceived 'ideal' for COT work)

    1   2   3   4   5

COMMENTS

3. Was the time you spent with your COT:

too little   too much   enough?

COMMENTS

4. Which was dominant, pre- or post-lesson discussions?

pre-   post-   equal

COMMENTS

5. Was COT 'evaluation' helpful or hurtful?

helpful   hurtful

COMMENTS

6. Did your COT interfere in your lessons

    disturbingly   cooperatively   not at all

    EXAMPLES

7. Ideally, how often do you think a COT should observe lessons?

a. regularly	b. occasionally	c. rarely
(almost every lesson)	(3–4 × a month)	(3 × a semester)

    d. more often at the beginning, less often at the end

8. Did you ask for help from your COT, and did you get it?
   Specify:

9. Please list the areas you got most and least help from your COT.

most help	least help	couldn't help

10. What have you learnt from your COT that you couldn't have learnt at CETT?

11. Were you able to express and carry out your own ideas?
    Give examples:

12. What kind of feedback did you prefer? Give reasons.

13. If you could change one thing about your COT, what would it be?

14. Overall, would you recommend your COT to other trainees?

    not really   yes   highly

Thank you very much for completing this questionnaire.

Appendix 9

Support teacher evaluation form

(Support teacher = mentor. For self-assessment by the mentor, as well as feedback from the trainees. With the kind permission of the Faculty of Teacher Training, English & American Studies Department, Veszprém University, Hungary.)

SUPPORT TEACHER EVALUATION

The main purpose of this form is for the support teacher to evaluate him/herself. However, external evaluation is always useful and so the form could be filled in by trainees and the results compared.

	☺	😐	☹	
Matching trainees with class				
Quantity of support				
Appropriate balance between pre-lesson and post-lesson support				
Appropriate degree of friendliness/strictness with trainees				
Observation skills				
Listening skills				
Setting targets				
Range of alternative ideas				
Openness to trainees' ideas				
Sensitivity to trainees' problems				
Appropriate degree of directness in feedback				

Appendix 10

Lesson visits: check-list for tutors

(This check-list was compiled on the Lower Primary Mentor Course by mentors and course leaders and used on subsequent school visits. With the kind permission of the British Council Lower Primary Project, Budapest, 1997.)

1. PERSONAL QUALITIES
   - atmosphere
   - attitude – positive, cooperative
   - empathy
   - real interest in student's development
   - open-mindedness
   - flexibility
   - sense of humour

2. THE STUDENT TEACHER – MENTOR RELATIONSHIP
   - partnership, cooperation
   - body language, seating position
   - eye-contact
   - nods, smiles, encouragement
   - tone of voice
   - student-teacher's visible responses

3. ASPECTS OF OBSERVATION
   - focus (how/who decided, appropriacy – methods/topic)
   - where mentor sits
   - pupils' reaction to student-teacher and mentor during lesson
   - note-making (recording)

4. POST-LESSON DISCUSSION SKILLS
   - active listening
   - questioning technique
   - proportion of talking time (who talks, when, how much, why)
   - appropriate, relevant, helpful 'mirror' and interventions (too many, too few)
   - support – how much and what kind – challenge
   - encouragement of reflective thinking and self-evaluation
   - action planning and goal setting
   - threatening or non-threatening

5. DIARY
   Mentors should keep a diary (for showing to tutor at visit) of:
   a) their student-teacher's development as a teacher.
   b) their own development as a mentor.

Index

Printed in the United Kingdom
by Lightning Source UK Ltd.
109652UKS00002B/47-48